THE THEORY
OF
READING

THE THEORY OF READING

OF

READING

Edited by
FRANK GLOVERSMITH

THE HARVESTER PRESS • SUSSEX

BARNES & NOBLE BOOKS • NEW JERSEY

First published in Great Britain in 1984 by
THE HARVESTER PRESS LIMITED
Publisher: John Spiers
16 Ship Street, Brighton, Sussex

and in the USA by
BARNES & NOBLE BOOKS
81 Adams Drive, Totowa, New Jersey 07512

© This edition, Frank Gloversmith, 1984

British Library Cataloguing in Publication Data

The Theory of reading.
   1. Hermeneutics
   I. Gloversmith, Frank
   801   PN81

ISBN 0–7108–0068–1
ISBN 0–7108–0079–7 Pbk

Library of Congress Cataloging in Publication Data
Main entry under title:
The Theory of reading.
   Contents: Introduction—Renoving that Bible/
Valentine Cunningham—Author-reader-language/David
Morse—[etc.]
   1. Reader-response criticism—Addresses, essays, lectures.
2. Reading—Addresses, essays, lectures.
I. Gloversmith, Frank.
PN98.R38T48   1984   801′.95   84–280
ISBN 0–389–20467–6

Typeset in 11 point Monophoto Times by Thomson Press (India) Ltd.
New Delhi, and printed in Great Britain by
The Thetford Press Limited, Thetford, Norfolk

Contents

Notes on the Contributors   vii

Introduction by Frank Gloversmith   ix

1   Renoving That Bible: The Absolute Text of
    (Post) Modernism   1
    Valentine Cunningham

2   Author–Reader–Language: Reflections on a
    Critical Closed Circuit   52
    David Morse

3   Representation and the Colonial Text: A Critical
    Exploration of some Forms of Mimeticism   93
    Homi Bhabha

4   Bakhtin, Sociolinguistics and Deconstruction   123
    Allon White

5   Autonomy Theory: Ortega, Roger Fry, Virginia
    Woolf   147
    Frank Gloversmith

6   Contexts of Reading: The Reception of D. H.
    Lawrence's *The Rainbow* and *Women in Love*   199
    Alistair Davies

7   Making and Breaking the Novel Tradition   223
    Stuart Laing

Index   245

Notes on the Contributors

Homi K. Bhabha is a lecturer in English at the University of Sussex. He was educated at the University of Bombay and Christ Church Oxford, where he held a British Council Award and was elected to a Violet Vaughan Morgan Commonwealth Fellowship. His research interests are focused on theoretical, textual and political issues related to the representation of gender, race and class, and their articulation in the discourses of colonialism. He is also interested in the deployment of 'other' cultures, their normalisation and marginalisation, within contemporary 'radical' theories. He is currently working on *Power and Spectacle: Colonial Discourse in The English Novel* to be published by Methuen.

Valentine Cunningham is Fellow and Tutor at Corpus Christi College, Oxford, and University Lecturer in English Literature; he has recently held Visiting Professorships at Amherst College, U.S.A., and at the University of Konstanz, W. Germany. He is author of *Everywhere Spoken Against: Dissent in the Victorian Novel* (Clarendon Press, 1975), and has edited and introduced the *Penguin Book of Spanish Civil War Verse* (1980). He is a regular reviewer for leading journals and newspapers. His study of literature and society in the 1930s is to be published soon.

Alistair Davies studied at Cambridge, his doctoral study being of the work of Percy Wyndham Lewis. His main interests are in Modernism: a comprehensive bibliography of its major works was published recently (Harvester, 1983); and will be followed by a book of critical studies. He has written on Wyndham Lewis and on post-World War II cultural studies. A lecturer at the University of Sussex, he is a visiting lecturer at Cologne University (1982–3).

Frank Gloversmith was a tutor at Queens' College, Cambridge, and has taught widely in America and recently in Germany at the Universities of Munich, Bayreuth and Passau. He has edited Elizabeth Gaskell's *Wives & Daughters* (Penguin), and written on D. H. Lawrence's *The Rainbow* (E. Arnold), besides editing *Class Culture & Social Change: A New View of the 1930s* (Harvester 1980). His present work is on the changes in ideas about narrative in the 20th century.

Stuart Laing studied at Cambridge and at the Centre for Contemporary Cultural Studies at Birmingham University. He has published articles on Walter Greenwood, John Summerfield's *May Day* and Mass Observation and Philip Gibbs and the Newsreel Novel. Forthcoming articles on Literary Production and the post-war Novel will appear in *Society and Literature 1945–70* in the Methuen Contexts series to be published in 1983 and on John Braine's *Room at the Top* in *Popular Literature and Social Change* (Macmillan, 1983). Since 1973 he has been a Lecturer in the School of Cultural and Community Studies at the University of Sussex.

David Morse is a lecturer in English and American Studies at the University of Sussex. His interests include film studies and the history of popular music, on which he has written and broadcast. His main publications are *Romanticism: A Transformational Analyis*, and *Romanticism: A Structural Analysis*, both published by Macmillan, 1982.

Allon White has studied at the University of Birmingham, Cambridge, and the Ecole Pratiques des Hautes Etudes, Paris with the late Roland Barthes; Research Fellow of Trinity Hall, Cambridge (1978–80), he has lectured in Comparative Literature at the University of East Anglia and is now lecturer in English and European Studies at the University of Sussex. His book on early modernist fiction *The Uses of Obscurity* was published in 1981 and two further books *Profane Illumination* and *The Politics and Poetics of Transgression* (with Peter Stallybrass) will appear in 1984.

Introduction

Introducing the postwar publication of his 1916–18 Cambridge University lectures, Sir Arthur Quiller-Couch remembers how, while reading them out, his thoughts often strayed to rural classrooms 'where the hungry sheep look up and are not fed'. *The Art of Reading* (1920) is part of his generous (if massively condescending) effort to give these 'piteous groups of urchins' some eventual access to the Humanist heritage. The 'general redemption' of English, its language and its literature, must come about through the art of reading, 'from a poor child's first lesson in reading up to a tutor's last word to his pupil on the eve of a Tripos.' This mingling of the academic-parochial with the wider social concerns lasts through the series: the resolutions are always in terms of reading – English Masterpieces, Tripos texts, the Classics, and (above all) the Bible.

The Introduction and the dozen lectures give the Professor's own sense of his adversative stance, as the individualist 'Q' – his affectionate nickname – skirmishing with the Establishment. But the central concepts and basic assumptions about what the Art of Reading comprises are stolidly traditional, or rather, moralistic, Victorian, unquestioningly élitist. 'Literature understands man and of what he is capable.... All great Literature is gentle towards that spirit which learns of it' (Lecture II). This makes (great) books into Bibles, and baptizes the classics, fairy tales, and Tripos texts. The neo-mystical hypostatization of Literature is no mere incidental rhetoric, though the urchin sheep might well feel even hungrier. The power that should bring redemption to their remote rural classrooms gets more and more removed, hardly reachable through any skill to be acquired in the school or the Academy.

'Q' himself sees no difficulty: 'comprehension' is his pejorative term for the deliberative process, that intention to analyse and to grasp meaning that shows man's arrogance and intellectual conceit. This hubristic activity – commonly seen in philosophers – is the opposite of learning, which is only by 'apprehension'. This is Wordsworth's 'wise passiveness', so that the reader of a masterpiece must 'incorporate it, incarnate it'. The reader becomes the work, the work incarnates itself in him. 'Q' repeatedly quotes Emerson on this intensity of identification: 'It is remarkable that involuntarily we always read as superior beings.' Intuitive comprehension, involuntary response: where is the space for schoolteacher or Tripos tutor? The exemplary exercise on a Keats Ode (Lecture V) sets up definitions of text, reading, and critical commentary that sharply limit such pedagogic space. Two simple readings give 'a working idea of the Ode and what Keats meant it to be'. This sets up the absolute, fully intended, self-revelatory text, 'incorporated' as a totality, which then controls line-by-line examination of parts and details:

> The first obligation we owe to any classic . . . is to treat it *absolutely*: solely to interpret the meaning which its author intended: we should *trust* any given masterpiece for its operation, on ourselves and on others.

Literal and intellectual understanding is distinctly subordinate to recognition, to an accord of spirit, the reading process being defined paradoxically as 'acquiring an inbred monitor' (Lecture XII). The reader scrupulously interprets the meaning, but this is simultaneously given by the work's intrinsic power, its self-clarifying nature.

Literature is 'a grand patrimony' handed to us by great men (Lecture VI); it is direct personal communication of its composers: 'Donne is Donne, Swift, Swift, Pope, Pope . . . .' The individual writer is the sage speaking to moral taste, to the spirit, and interpreting the Common Mind of Civilization. To understand at all, the reader incarnating this wisdom becomes another such superior being, both the Hamlet in the play and the Shakespeare who created him (Lecture V). In the two years of these lectures, this definition of art as timeless, transcendent, taking up the reader into its ideal realm, never takes into account the historicity of specific writing, and never considers the mode of its 'operation' on the particular reader. The 'practical criticism' – of Traherne, Keats, or of *The Tempest* – is guided by the initial 'apprehension', the work's self-presentation of its meaning. The 'least tractable' elements of *The Tempest* – such as the Masque of Iris – are quoted (Lecture XII), to illustrate that even a child reading it can genuinely apprehend it, 'being intent on *What Is*, the heart and secret' of its beauty. The various difficulties – linguistic, semantic, thematic, conceptual – are postponable, and 'background' – equated with 'the kind of men for whom Chaucer (or Shakespeare) wrote and the kind of men whom he made speak' – such a background fits in long after the originary moment of aesthetic response.

Ezra Pound's no-nonsense, make-it-new extension of his polemical *How to Read* in *ABC of Reading* (1934) would seem to be literary light-years away from Q's upholstered moral rhetoric. Literary history, literary canons, critical conventions and the major West European texts are treated with the engaging insouciance of the cultural iconoclast taking stock, re-arranging an animated Imaginary Museum (Gavin Douglas, Arthur Golding, Crabbe, Landor, Whitman alongside Virgil, Dante, Chaucer, Shakespeare). But: 'A classic is a classic because of a certain eternal and irrepressible freshness' – this could be 'Q' again. The Professor would certainly have approved of juxtaposing the Icelandic Sagas with bits of Flaubert's writing (Chapter 5). Pound's collocation is one illustration of his current aesthetic doctrine about '*phanopoeia*, the throwing of an image on the mind's retina'. Again, response to writing is defined in terms of the intrinsic action of the art-language itself. It is charged communication that:

I. throws the object (fixed or moving) on to the visual imagination.
II. induces emotional correlations by the sound and rhythm of speech
III. induces both the effects by stimulating the associations (intellectual or emotional) that have remained in the receiver's consciousness in relation to the actual words or word groups employed

> (phanopaiea, melopoeia, logopoeia) (Chapter 8)

The aesthetic object projects, throws, and induces: it operates upon a receiver, sifting and stimulating his or her responses. Something similar had been I. A. Richard's historically important account of how poems activate, complicate, and finally harmonize a range of neural impulses in the responsive reader. Yet his peroration in turn recalls both Quiller-Couch and Ezra Pound:

The great pages are the most constant and dependable sources of moments when we know more completely what we are, and why we are so, and thus 'see into the life of things' more deeply.... We (humbly) partake with (our authors) of wisdom.

(How to Read a Page, 1943)

The silent, surely quite astounding elisions in each critic are from details of specific texts to moral universals. None makes any naive claims about general pronouncements or philosophical discourse in artworks: quite the reverse, since Richards calls them 'pseudo-statements', and Pound dismisses them as 'dubious bank-cheques'. The general terminology comes out only in the commentaries themselves. A characteristic shift between textual and moral discourses in the mode of *Scrutiny* (1932–53) is between scrupulous details from the 'words on the page' (the concrete) to concepts of 'sensibility', 'maturity', 'reverence for life' (also treated as concrete, because non-systematic, non-doctrinal). No differences being articulated, there is no recognition of the need to connect critically the specific (textual) analysis and the general (evaluative) commentary. The axiomatic principle is ignored that critical enquiry (of any kind) can only take place at a distance from the object which is the target of interpretation. Once admitted, this principle would undercut the enabling definitions of a text, of the process of reading or responding to one, and therefore bring into question what literary criticism itself consists of as an exercise of the mind and the sensibility. It could no longer be blandly assumed to be precisely contoured and guided by the intrinsic nature of an aesthetic text. No artwork can have the mystical (or magical) double nature of being both itself, discrete, an ontological identity; and also of being the transmitter of knowledge *about* itself, auto-declarative, self-interpreting. Criticism is rightly, inevitably interpretive, but is surely confused when it omits (or refuses) to articulate the principles of its analytic procedures.

The very varied work which was produced in the successive phases of New Criticism, in England and America, can now be clearly, historically placed as vitiated by this closed critical circuit (assessed by David Morse in the second chapter). Insisting on the purity of the analytic procedures, on the complete disengagement of 'Practical Criticism' from any ideology whatsoever, went with disclaimers about the values and beliefs discernible in texts. 'Man' and 'artist' were separate, antipathetic roles: the genius handled ideas with an impersonality and a refinement of sensibility beyond violation by ideologies, commitment, or any particular convictions. (Consider T. S. Eliot's remarks on Shakespeare or Henry James.) So the 'prime and chief function (of literature) is fidelity to its own nature' (Warren and Wellek's dictum, 1948). This, like its riddling counterpart – 'A poem should not mean/But be' – is either a critical ultimatum, wholly prescriptive; or an item of an ascetic, neo-mystical belief about literary texts. As David Morse shows, the modifications and radical strategic changes inside the whole movement signal concern about the irruption into critical discourse, into readers' responses, into the literary discourse itself, of elements resisting incorporation into a contained aesthetic field or separable 'literary' communication. So the verbal icon, free of the touch of any ideas – writer's, critic's, reader's, or the text's own – developed a deep penumbra. This is indicated sometimes as the play of connotation, of wit, paradox, irony, or of ambiguity itself – (at least seven types are classifiable). So the 'intrinsic' continued to expand, to incorporate in ingenious ways what the mode insisted on earlier labelling as extrinsic.

The ontologically discrete nature of the text, well-wrought urn or verbal icon, was subsumed at times within the dominant communication model. The author exiled under the Intention Fallacy pronouncement returned silently as the source of insight or its lapses, moral imagination or its failure, and so on. (Consider F. R. Leavis on Hardy, James, Conrad, Lawrence, Woolf.) There had to be a communicator, since the value of literature, accompanying the rapt, intransitive attention of the audience, was somehow formulable in ethical, moral and spiritual effects. The intransitive 'beingness' was simultaneously a specifically transitive meaning. This scholarly, philosophical, and critical handy-dandy usually turns out to have marked traces of positions which are only partly academic and professional defensiveness. Stuart Laing's discussion of the divisions of serious/popular, traditional/commercial, high art/entertainment shows this element mixing with assumptions about education, class patterns and cultural politics. Alistair Davies' study of the reception of Lawrence's major writing brings out strongly the markedly nationalistic prejudices and chauvinistic antipathies which prompted the contemporary response, and which negatively contour the favourable later accounts by Leavis and *Scrutiny* writers. Homi Bhabha, dealing with colonial texts, has to deconstruct a whole rhetoric of Humanism, moral universality, and individual freedom, as it informs the 'objective' categories of literary style, modes, narrative forms and characterization. This analysis of the problematic of representation and mimesis articulates the necessary imbrication of ideology and art, of politics and literary criticism.

The modern versions of New Criticism, especially those operating loudly and clearly in O/A level classrooms, might credibly demonstrate that reports of its death have been much exaggerated. Certainly, Tripos-tutors young and old, provincial and non-provincial, show surprise, shock and strong distaste for recent forms of criticism that disregard the literariness of literature: sociological studies, Structuralism, Marxist analyses, feminist critiques, Deconstruction strategies applied to texts. Not only Q's urchin-sheep in their Comprehensive folds are bewildered at the rapidity of the – isms and the abstractness of the theoretical discussions. But the contentions at the level of *T.L.S.* reviews and carping correspondence in journals are of no importance in themselves. What is important, surely, for the professors, O-level students, and poetry or novel-readers generally is how the nature and the purposes of reading are theorized; not for the hick-hack of abstruse literary debate, but for consideration of how such concepts affect syllabuses, educational training, the acquisition of reading skills and the politics of culture that permeates all these matters.

The possibility of defining a text is the preoccupation throughout these following chapters: the principles for determining what (if any) contours a text has are coincident with fundamental assumptions about what the reading process is like. Defining a text as an aesthetic monad is to define reading as an ascesis, an intransitive response or intuitive recognition. Conversely, showing that non-literary ideological presuppositions closely condition the critical and general reception of a text, as several contributors here do, demonstrates how misleading are the notions that author-text-reader transactions are in a free, aesthetic process. There are many forms of contextualism, as Alistair Davies remarks; and there are multiple ways of reading, where variations can be related to historical period, to cultural and to class differentiation, to ideological receptivity, and (not least) to the range of expectations, the mixture of codes, in any one piece of writing. A fiction by Alan Sillitoe projects a sense of its model reader, but clearly not the same model reader as a work by James Joyce. There can be no single theory of reading, obviously, in the sense that disparate kinds of verse or prose narrative have to be yoked together as uniform subjects of such a mode of apprehension. New Criticism did perhaps pursue this chimera, as some forms of Structuralism and some versions of Reader-theory in their differing ways also did. My discussion (in chapter five) of Ortega y Gasset's theories, and of Virginia Woolf's criticism and experiments in fiction suggests some of the contradictions and the mystifications intrinsic to such approaches.

In describing the crippling constraints of many forms of autonomy theory, with its unitary and passive sense of what reading comprises, the problem that thrusts itself forward is that of a textual plurality, of multiplying interpretations, of the totally open writing. All the options have been canvassed, from the text of rich but contained ambiguities, to the text of *jouissance*, indeterminate, endlessly re-appropriated, positive because illimitable. Discussing Bakhtin's theories, Allon White outlines the closely related concepts of polyphony, dialogism, and the counterposing of discourses which are elements of a notion of complexity of aesthetic form going well beyond various formalisms, including that opposite, inverted formalism of emptying language of referential power. This last critical strategy, almost incidentally removing the conditions for aesthetic form, open or closed, has some connections with Derridean deconstructionism, and several critics here examine its excesses. But it is ideas such as those of the Bakhtin group that help most to displace notions of the intrinsic/extrinsic in writing and in speech; that help to renew the sense of the innate sociality and historicity of language and its aesthetic representations; and that demonstrate some of the fundamental interrelations between understanding utterances in daily life, and those *formed* instances of real utterances and discourses which are the poems and narratives we read, or the plays we watch.

Over the last three decades or so, the revolutionary thinking of the Post-Structuralists and the Deconstructionists apparently undermined all notions of referential power not only for the literature, but for written and spoken language generally. A calm world-weariness coloured even the more modest reformulations which took account of Derrida's critique of the 'metaphysics of presence'.

Though dissociation is a fact of our post-lapsarian state, it is assumed that we should still try to pass through the signifier to the meaning that is the truth and origin of the sign... (This view's) inadequacy becomes obvious as soon as we reflect upon writing, and especially literature, where an organized surface of signifiers insistently promises meaning but where the notion of a full and determinate meaning that the text 'expresses' is highly problematic.

Poetry, Culler adds, is really a series of signifiers 'whose signified is an empty but circumscribed space'. (Jonathan Culler, *Structuralist Poetics*, 1975.) This is the critical hardening into a binarized opposition – signifier *vs* signified – of what for Saussure had been a tactical, provisional splitting. The notions proliferated imperially: action, person, concept, world – old signifieds barely now to be glimpsed in the discursive networks of textual 'traces'. The signifieds were the ever-ghostlier paradigms whose logocentric masquerade could no longer suppress the joyful dance of endless chains of signifiers. Whether the instance is a poem – *Sailing to Byzantium* for Elder Olson – or a novel – *Lord Jim* for J. Hillis Miller – it serves to make the overarching point: texts are shut into a self-reflexive language system which allows no purchase for the extrinsic, for the authority of author, of ideology, of the historical moment or process. This logocentric critique takes in all human utterance, for 'parole' – speech acts, dialogue – (having had a long, long day of privilege) – are second-order instances of what goes on in 'langue'/*écriture*/

writing, in their local sense of producing texts and in their grander sense of the cultural codes that constrain all social practice and exchange.

Though the fallacies have all been re-categorized for twenty years – as the metaphysical, the logocentric, the psycho-logistic, the historicist – the exile of the signified was never totally enforceable. Among much else, Marxist and feminist criticism and philosophy have checked the colonizing of all knowledge by the increasingly confident groups and schools using notions from Structuralism, Post-Structuralism, and Deconstruction. But, as Valentine Cunningham shows (chapter one), most of the confidence and success depended on a single-minded, ideologically-grounded choosing between a synthetic couplet, the signifier/signified. Saussure's tactics finally produced a bogus, invalid separation.

In any case, the ludic play of language – *Finnegans Wake* must be its ultimate, an historic apogee? – has always been a vital, fundamental contributor to the production of humanly significant utterance: it's clear in Anglo-Saxon recitation of verse, as in Lancelot Andrewes' sermons; it's acknowledged by Dr. Samuel Johnson as by Jorge Luis Borges. The anti-concept of *différance* has focused our sense of how elusive, how labile meaning is, spoken or written. But it is no proof that meaning slides ever away, in accelerating, vertiginous regression. Derrida's own texts are a counter-proof: things can get said, reference is made, language and history speak in and through one another. Johnson's *Preface* to his Dictionary replaces the stone he kicked (to refute Idealism) as part-refutation of the notion that language is self-evacuating. Here, Cunningham's detailed analysis of Joyce's text, recondite, offering itself as a self-generating, self-substantive Logos, shows how that astonishingly imploding writing is able, *ab novo*, to shape metonym, the signified, referentiality. They perpetually return from exile, they are always re-arriving: history saturates the text. Signifiers are ineluctably the shapes formed as the signified moves into that space and motion where we make the meanings we prefer.

FRANK GLOVERSMITH

July 1983
Falmer, Sussex

1 Renoving That Bible:
The Absolute Text of (Post) Modernism

Valentine Cunningham

Depuis l'époque où elles sont devenues l'objet d'une observation suivie, les espèces de plantes et d'animaux n'ont presque pas d'histoire: pour prendre les termes de la scolastique, on les étudie dans leur *esse*, non pas dans leur *fieri*. Il n'est pas de même du langage: le langage ne doit point être comparé à l'espèce, immuable par son essence, mais à l'individu, qui se renouvelle sans cesse.

Ernest Renan, De L'Origine du Langage. Préface, 1864.

L'activité ou la productivité connotées par le *a* de la *différance* renvoient au mouvement génératif dans le jeu des différences. Celles-ci ne sont pas tombées du ciel et elles ne sont pas inscrites une fois pour toutes dans un système clos, dans une structure statique qu'une opération synchronique et taxonomique pourrait épuiser. Les différences sont les effets de transformations et de ce point de vue le thème de la différance est incompatible avec le motif statique, synchronique, taxonomique, anhistorique, etc., du concept du structure.

Jacques Derrida, Positions, 1972.

It appears, however, that this concept/of *écriture*/, as currently employed, has merely transposed the empirical characteristics of an author to a transcendental anonymity. The extremely visible signs of the author's empirical activity are effaced to allow the play, in parallel or opposition, of religious and critical modes of characterization. In granting a primordial status to writing, do we not, in effect, simply reinscribe in transcendental terms the theological affirmation of its sacred origin or a critical belief in its creative nature? To say that writing, in terms of the particular history it made possible, is subjected to forgetfulness and repression, is this not to reintroduce in transcendental terms the religious principle of hidden meanings (which require interpretation) and the critical assumption of implicit significations, silent purposes, and obscure contents (which give rise to commentary)? Finally, is not the conception of writing as absence a transposition into transcendental terms of the religious belief in a fixed and

1

continuous tradition or the aesthetic principle that proclaims the survival of
the work as a kind of enigmatic supplement of the author beyond his own
death?

    ... The disappearance of the author – since Mallarmé, an event of our
time – is held in check by the transcendental.

Michel Foucault, 'What is an Author?', in *Language, Counter-Memory,
    Practice: Selected Essays and Interviews* ed. Donald F. Bouchard, 1977.

The post-structuralist battle-lines could not be drawn up more
clearly. Nor, in many of the critical practices currently making
the running in university literature faculties – and so among
what pass for our most educated readers – could they be drawn
up with, seemingly, more absoluteness. The sharpest of readers
and readings of texts in the academy keep declaring that they're
interested mainly, or only, in the text itself: in the text's
internalised and ever imploding selfhood and life, in the 'how'
of meaning as opposed to the 'what' of meaning. In other
words a rising orthodoxy is opposed to that idea of content, the
world, the signified – and beyond that, the *signatum*-towards
which texts were once supposed to lead and to point. Reference
is a much thinned idea. The old polemics of the once 'new'
criticism of the mid-twentieth-century have now risen again
from the death to which a lot of us had thought they'd been
banished in some discredit: risen refreshed, refurbished, en-
ergised as the ancient Biblical strong man ready to run his race.
Neo-formalism rules.

    It has always been a tricky operation to split signs away from
referents, words on the page (or in the mouth, in the ear, in the
head) from meanings out there in the world, to divide form
absolutely from content. And even the most devoted of
splitters have had to acknowledge in some sort the existence of
the world, of origins, presences, meanings, beyond, behind,
around or within the world – (the prepositions, like the
imaginable relationships, vary). The metaphors in Ferdinand
de Saussure's masterful *Cours de Linguistique Générale* (ed.
Charles Bally, Albert Sechehaye and Albert Rielinger; critically ed. Tullio de Mauro, 1969; translated into French by
Louis-Jean Calvet, Paris 1972: the English translation by
Wade Baskin, New York, 1959, is the one I use).[1] Saussure's
metaphors vividly struggle and grope, as is the way of the best
metaphors, for the truth of the linguistic case. 'Le phénomène

linguistique presente perpetuellement deux faces qui se correspondent et dont l'une ne vaut que par l'autre': the linguistic phenomenon always presents two corresponding aspects, or faces, or sides, like the two sides of a piece of paper or the two sides of a coin (where, quite literally, each side only has currency value when it exists in contiguity with the other, and to split the object is entirely to devalue it). Just so, the two components of the Saussurean sign, the signifier and the signified, are in like fashion intimately joined (*intimement unis*) within the linguistic sign, which is the central entity among a whole set of such entities considered by Saussure and which all exist 'à deux faces'. In the matter of the sign, Saussure appears not only to be thinking of sheets of paper and coins; he may also have had something more in mind. He introduces the sign = signifier/signified diagram thus: 'une entité psychique à deux faces qui peut être représentée par la figure...'. Wade Baskin translates *figure* merely as *drawing*. But *figure* means not just a drawn figure, but also a face: the figure is also a two sided face, recalling Janus, the deity who faced in two directions at once.

At any rate, a sheet of paper, a coin, the head of Janus all offer pictures of a bi-directional inseparability – *intimement* even suggests the physical unity of lovers joyfully making 'the beast with two backs' – whose logic Saussure then proceeds everywhere in his reported lectures to defy by choosing to concentrate his own (and so other linguists') attention on one side only of that sheet of paper or coin, on the life of signifiers: a concentration that's been avidly taking up and extended not only by linguists but also by the hordes of literary theorists and would-be theorists pressing along in the Saussurean wake.

The two temporal states of a language system, the synchronic and the diachronic, he thought of as being present in language rather as in the game of chess synchrony and diachrony manifestly coexist. Chess was a metaphor to which Saussure found it illustratively helpful to keep returning. It is easier to play games with chess metaphors than with paper or coin metaphors. In particular it is easier to keep the state of play in a game of chess separate from the history of chess or from the earlier moves in any game under consideration, than it is to contemplate separating two sides of a sheet of paper or splitting coins in two. So chess came in handier as an illustration of the way the synchronic state of a language, which Saussure said was of the main interest to linguistics, could and should be held separate in one's analysis from the diachronic, or historical state. You can, as Saussure suggested, happily play chess without regard, or at least much regard, to the history of the game. You are also, he alleged, at every move in a particular game of chess, preoccupied only with the latest array of the pieces, the latest state of your and your opponent's moves (and 'to describe this arrangement, it is perfectly useless to recall what had just happened ten seconds previously'). The history of the game of chess in general and of any game of chess in particular is an irrelevance. Or so Saussure professed to believe. He was only partly right. Without the evolved and still evolving history of the game, the developing grammar as it were of chess, the etymology of chess's rules, the code of its ritualized restrictions and possibilities, and the vast lore of the game that has accumulated in hundreds of guides, handbooks and histories, no chess match (at however elementary a level of knowledge and skill) would in fact be possible. The veriest beginner at chess is constrained, programmed, by the game's diachronic. The chess champion is self-consciously much more: he/she is usually, in effect, a historian of the game, a student of its past and of what its past-masters have done. Just so, the claim that only the latest state of play in a chess game interests spectators is extremely dubious. In other words, in fact, the very metaphor that Saussure leant on as an emblem of the useful release of language's synchronic from its diachronic, refuses to let history, diachrony, get discarded as easily as he wished.

But still Saussure and his followers have tried to make the disconnection, and they keep on trying. Some critics, especially those influenced (often partially, selectively influenced) by Jacques Derrida's deft scrutiny of Saussure, express regret that this father of linguistic enterprises should have allowed into his discussions even the tiny allowance for the signified, or for history, that he did. His metaphors leave too much scope for presence, origins, voice, history and so on, these people say, Saussure lamentably privileged *parole* and the signified over *langue* and the signifier in his binary parole/langue, signifier/signified models. Derrida's *De la Grammatologie* (1967)[2] endeavours to reinstate *écriture* over *parole*. Colin MacCabe makes believe that the Saussurean signified needs a good deal more repressing (see his *James Joyce and the Revolution of the Word*, 1978, Ch. 4). One is not then surprised to find such observers trying very hard to wrench other metaphors or allegories that seem to have been rather carefully devised to illustrate the impossibility of divorcing history, present meanings, realized content from writing in despite of writing's equally strongly pronounced declarations of its self-subsistence.

Walter Benjamin's little parable of the stocking has become justly famous. In it, a sock is made to stand for the slippery multivalence of dreams and so of writing. When a sock is rolled up in the laundry basket it appears in doubled form as a 'bag' and also as a 'present', a gift. And so it signifies absence and presence, emptiness and fullness all at once. The 'empty bag, sign of an absence, and at the same time the precious contents of that bag, a presence' is how Hillis Miller glosses the allegory in his *Fiction and Repetition* (1982).[4] The 'fulness' of a rolled-up sock and the 'emptiness' if a rolled-out sock are inseparable the one from the other, they are indissoluble mutations the one of the other. Benjamin's emblem powerfully illustrates the necessary simultaneous conjunction within a sign and so within writing of a fullness and emptiedness of meaning, a coexistence of *pleroma* and *kenosis*. It implies the impossibility of a separate existence for either the fullness or the emptiness. And the opening chapter of Miller's *Fiction and Repetition* 'Two Forms of Repetition', appears to respond to the figure of the sock in its twinned aspects. But even within that chapter it soon becomes clear that Miller's sympathies, schooled by his particular readings of Derrida, are veering sharply away from the aspect of fullness/presence/signified towards that of emptiness/absence/signifier. The same is true of the argumentative procedures of his article 'The Two Allegories' (in *Allegory, Myth, and Symbol*, Harvard English Studies, No. 9, edited by Morton W. Bloomfield, 1981)[5] or his discussion of 'canny' and 'uncanny' criticism in 'Stevens' Rock and Criticism as Cure, II' (in *Georgia Review*, 30 (1976), 330–348).[6]

In fact, within poststructuralist/deconstructionist criticism in general, Hillis Miller's strategy and preference (they have become Hillis Miller's favourite strategy and preference) are pretty uniform. A discussion will start with some preliminary gesture towards the dual aspect of language and writing, a dutiful play of Saussurean or Lévi-Straussian binaries. But this will be followed up with a strong siding with one half of the case, one set of the polarized opposites, and usually the more negative, less content-full, the more textual, against the more positive, content-prone, the historical, present and contextual. Derrida's own practice is wilfully confusing (or playfully mixed). His famous and influential declaration of 1967 in 'La structure, le signe, et le jeu dans le discours des sciences humaines', in *L'Ecriture et la différence*, about the 'two interpretations of interpreting' – the one sort pursuing full human meanings, presences, origins, and the other one pleased with the play of playfulness in a text, with endlessness and joyful ungrounded dissemination – at once declares that these two polarized activities are absolutely irreconcilable and also that it is impossible to choose between them. Much of Derrida's writing, of course, straddles edges, *bords*, limits, margins, the borders between textual being and non-being, presence and absence, inside and outside; texts of his such as 'Tympan' in *Marges de la Philosophie* (1972), *Glas* (1974), 'Living on: Border Lines' in H. Bloom *et al., Deconstruction and Criticism* (1979), seek to inhabit just that confused in-between zone denoted by hymens, tympani and other places of *brisure*, the bridging, opening-closing, doubling, articulated disarticulations, entry-exit slots, gashes and other punctures that confuse any strict either-or quest for, or sense of, meaning or presence, and that defy the hierarchical instincts that would give priority to one set of such terms and make the other set its mere supplement, footnote, addendum.[7] It is possible to argue that Derrida's early work lends itself without much strain to a certain activity of priorizing of terms. There's no doubt that many of his professed admirers, especially in North America, have specialized in his name in specializing acts of firm choosing which are indeed acts of persistent supplementation. 'A critic must choose either the tradition of presence or the tradition of "difference", for their assumptions about language, about literature, about history, and about the mind cannot be made compatible'. Thus Hillis Miller in 1971 (in 'Georges Poulet's "Criticism of Identification"' in *The Quest for Imagination* ed. O. B. Hardison, Cleveland, 1971).[8] And again in 1979: critical methods are reducible' to two distinctly different sorts. One kind . . . I would call "metaphysical". The other kind includes those methods which hypothesize that in literature, for reasons which are intrinsic to language itself, metaphysical presuppositions are, necessarily, both affirmed and subverted' ('On Edge: The Crossways of Contemporary Criticism', *Bulletin of the American Academy of Arts and Sciences*, January 1979).[8] And never, it's suggested, shall these twain, the metaphysical and the deconstructive meet.

It's rare to find an equal-minded discussion anywhere, one giving equal credence and place to both sides of the language coinage. Denis Donoghue's discussion in his *Ferocious Alphabets*[9] of this opposition – he labels its *graphi*-writing/reading and *epi*-writing/reading – (on the one hand writing that invites attention as itself, on the other writing that looks beyond itself to the world) – is a special case of such binary antitheses being given equal consideration (and it's one for which, characteristically, enthusiastic deconstructionists appear to have little sympathy: as Jonathan Culler's unenthused note on Donoghue's book in the bibliography of *On Deconstruction: Theory and Criticism after Structuralism* (1983)[10] reveals). Most post-structuralists believe that what Donoghue labels the *graphi* is the more dominant element and probably the most dominant element in writings that matter; that it is in any case the more important element, and that it produces writing that is not only more difficult and more demanding intellectually, but also intellectually more radical, more serious and worthier at this time of attention from the serious reader. It's often in such discussions not entirely clear whether some historical case is not also being made, *i.e.* a demonstration that once the *epi* was the more foregrounded, but that now in the greater wisdom and maturity of the modernist and postmodernist epoch the *graphi* has come truly into its own. Some critics do evidently want us to see historical cycles and shifts of predominance between these opposite kinds of writing: now – and this can be without any value judgement between their respective merits – the *graphi* is up, now it's the turn of the *epi* for predominance. This is in fact Donoghue's position. It corresponds to David Lodge's historically-minded analysis of metaphoric and metonymic writing in his book *The Modes of Modern Writing: Metaphor, Metonymy, and the Typology of Modern Literature* (1977)[11] – a book which, however, for all its praisable effort to de-absolutize these terms and to show the practical overlaps between the figures of metaphor and metonymy, nonetheless really and continually accepts Roman Jakobson's dichotomous and rigid polarizing of the zones of these two sign-making activities in writing, painting, dream-work, and so on, even down to providing a tabulated listing of two sets of terms clustered about the metaphor-metonym poles (p. 81).

The idea of history, such as creeps in to Donoghue's and Lodge's accounts generally calls for apologetic notes, however, especially within American and English post-structuralist circles. For the idea of history is what is being most vigorously exiled and disinfected in much post-structuralist work, just as it was in Saussure's lectures. A-historical assumptions come naturally to structuralists. Hence the belief, never properly scrutinized, that all writing has always been actually *graphi* in orientation. The more historically minded post-structuralist will raid, say, the nineteenth century novel to prove some such case (it's sometimes observed, indeed, that the most well-known American deconstructors have stuck very close in their work to the canon of English and American literature, so that nineteenth century literature figures high on their agendas). But even when old texts are being discussed it's apparent that the authors rarely have much concern to worry about the historical validities of their re-readings: the liberty of interpreting overrides such worries. And whatever the state of the historical consciousness that happens to be displayed the theoretical bias is so enthusiastically pursued hereabouts that when the *epi* in any period (from Old Testament and Homeric times to Stanley Fish's seventeenth century and Hillis Miller's nineteenth) is not being declared to be non-existent, it's being granted only the scantest indeed of value. And vice versa.

So that if one looks at any list of the rigidly binarized positions – despite Derrida's repeated antagonism towards such 'oppositions' as continuing the hierarchies of metaphysics that 'différance' seeks to rebut – that we are now invited with regularity to work with, one sees the Hillis Miller kind of absolute emphasis on one half only of a dichotomous schedule. After Saussure, who turned linguistics towards *sign* and not *referent*, signifier and not signified, *langue* and not *parole*, *différence* and not *référence*, comes Roland Barthes who perceives writing and reading as processes of *significance* but not *signification*, *disentangling* but not *deciphering*, who prefers *texts* (*scriptible, homogeneous to language, held in language*) to *works* (*lisible, heterogeneous to language, held in the hand*); and Julia Kristeva, who prefers *genotexts* to *phenotexts*; then Frank Kermode who prefers the *hermetic* to the *pleromatic*; and Paul de Man who wants to concentrate on the textual *inside* rather than the contextual *outside*. And so on. It is not a necessary set of choices (and Frank Kermode, for one, has shown with some vigour how the *lisible* and the *scriptible* are concepts hard to keep separate, rather as David Lodge finds that the metonymic and the metaphoric keep invading each others' domains: see Frank Kermode's piece 'Local and Provincial Restrictions' in *Essays on Fiction 1971–82*, 1983)[12]. But it is a proliferating rhetoric (handily available for inspection in the essays and editorial comments of Robert Young's *Untying the Text: A Post-Structuralist Reader*, 1981)[13] whose professed tendency is always even-handedly binary, antithetical, but whose preferences are in practice usually hierarchical, and hierarchical in the same direction: turning away from the idea of writing as a description or a transcription of some given reality (based in what is usually dismissed as a metaphysical or transcendental notion that meaning can be made present, can be personal and objective, can reflect people and things – subjects – can suggest presences or origins outside the writing) and towards the idea of writing only as writing – *écriture* – a mere scription or inscription, a scribing or *scriptum*, a *scriptura* or scripture which presents only a written subject and which will concede in the matter of material presences only the materiality of the word, and that only in an increasingly etiolated form.

The grammatological line of thought in Jacques Derrida's writing – the one popularized in his *De la Grammatologie* (1967) and that's been canonized in North America in despite of

Derrida's busy undoings of structuralism's binaries (Vincent Leitch in his believers' handbook *Deconstructive Criticism: An Advanced Introduction* (1983)[14] notes that this is a 'radical misreading of Derrida', but celebrates it nonetheless for 'tactical purposes' – unspecified – p. 182) – this particular message from Derrida provides most of the recent impetus for the now widely received notion of the implosive plunging of language and of texts into themselves, the postmodernist *mise en abîme* of the word into the word. This most popularized aspect of Derrida's enterprise provides the most radical vision of the move away from *reference* towards *différence*: the idea that meaning is always rather a displacing than a placing, that the fullness or presence of meaning is always postponed, deferred, put back. Famously, Derrida has invented the word *différance* to convey not only the plain Saussurian sense of words existing only diacritically in a differential relationship to other words, but also his own post-Saussurean, dynamised view of *différence* as meaning also an intensity of deferment that Derrida believes Saussure shied away from. In French *différance* and *différence* are completely indistinguishable in sound, so that *différance* has to be seen written and palpably exists in its own unique difference when it is written down (which makes a neat little Q.E.D. for the argument that writtenness must be restored from its place as a supplement to spokenness – which is Derrida's major adaptation of Saussure, who is castigated for privileging utterance over writing). *Différance* perpetually declares that it and language are never quite only about *différence* (difference), not only about *différence* (deferring), but that they are always both at once.

Signifiers, the case runs, exist in difference/deferment and mean by deferment/difference. So words never own a fullness of meaning, they only signify ghostly presences of meanings that they postpone, playing them back onto vistas of precedent words. That is to say that words contain only traces of meaning. The language text the texture or tissue of writing. is only as Derrida puts it, 'a fabric of traces marking the disappearance' of 'transcendental' or 'metaphysical' content – which is thought of variously as the human person, an author behind the text, any kind of originating gesture or antecedent world or maker/weaver/creator/producer/

writer/progenitor/ or divinity or divinity-imitating source.

Such scepticism is conceivable as arising from linguistic cases. A *trace* in French is a track, trail, or scent (for Derrida the footpath, the track through the primeval forest, is man's first effort at writing). *Marcher sur les traces* is to follow in someone's footsteps. Footsteps are *les pas. Emboîter les traces,* to fit oneself into or join oneself onto footsteps, is a phrase synonymous with *marcher sur les traces. Les pas* are not, of course, only footsteps; they are also the *nots*, the *no-things*, non-existences. And *emboîtage* is the action of putting things into boxes, or of putting things between the covers of books: it is a boxing-up or (allusion to the early board covers of books) an act of book-binding. So *un emboîtage des pas*, or at least of the sort of footsteps whose imprints Derrida perceives as the readable element in words and texts, approaches the boxing up of nothings, a putting of nothingnesses between covers. In language, in texts, on this view – a view of how writing is boxed into meanings radically distant from T. S. Eliot's concept of the best poetry as a place where 'meanings are perpetually *eingeschachtelt* [boxed up] into meanings' ('Philip Massinger', in T. S. Eliot's *Selected Essays*) – there is in writing's box a relative nothingness, a set of *traces*, of *pas*: in other words, what writing offers is the absence of presence and the presence of absence. We might say (to adapt Milton's phrase about Ben Jonson) that when Derrida in certain moods, and the typical American Derridean in most moods, takes up Benjamin's 'learned sock' it's displayed so that the sock as depletion and emptiness is made perpetually, and vividly, strongly, present to our gaze, even when we might have supposed that we ought rather to think of the sock in its more desirable aspect as gift is being just as obviously if not on occasion more obviously pressed into our possession.

This intense linguistic emptying that has been argued for so keenly in much recent thinking about literature should strike one as odd, or at the least contentious. It seems only reasonable to endorse Jonathan Culler's equable scepticism about the advanced negativity of Paul de Man's reading of Shelley (*On Deconstruction*, pp. 278–80). In the obvious first place negative readings of writings and of the business of writing should not be allowed to attain the force of the positive readings they profess to be displacing without some form of inquiry into what they think they're up to. But even more one should ask oneself why this whole set of preferences has caught on so. The question is of course an obvious one if you believe, contrary to a large number of the kind of critic we've just been looking at, that all thinking, all utterance is constrained by history, by the movements of ideology, by the actions and dictates of institutions. It is a question that those critics – and they do not on the evidence of his *Positions* alone, actually include Derrida[15] – those critics eager to ignore or postpone the historical consideration and thus keen to ditch ideology as a factor in the production of language and writing could do worse than try out. Even if they won't have truck with it, it demands anyway to be put. Is there not, one is compelled to wonder, in this happy reduction of meaning to faint *traces*, more than a trace of historical pressures, ideological moulding at work?

And as soon as one names history and ideological determinations as possible factors in the postmodernist case, their presence becomes so obvious as to make their attempted exclusion appear merely wiredrawn and bogus. Patently historical, social, and so ideological, constraints insist on encroaching onto the language stage even as they are most busily brushed off it. Even Saussure, briskest discounter of history – there was an *absolute* opposition, he supposed, between 'evolutionary linguistics' (old-fashioned, no longer useful) and the 'static linguistics' that claimed his attention, that is the static, synchronic condition of signs whose state was *arbitrary* and *fortuitous* – even the Saussure who could imagine a language so free and contingent as all that could not keep history in some sort utterly at bay. He suggested (in yet another of his extended metaphors) that the lateral cut across the tree-trunk of language is more usefully informative than a longitudinal one. But his metaphor grants that a longitudinal cut is not revelatory of *nothing*. It 'shows the fibers that constitute the plant'. And even whilst arguing for the utter distinction between the lateral (synchronic) cut and the longitudinal (diachronic) one, he actually admits that 'one perspective depends on the other'. And again, even Saussure can't have language wriggle quite free from the grip of social associations.

Language is 'a social institution'; it 'exists only by virtue of a sort of contract signed by members of a community'. 'Semiology', the new science of sign-systems which Saussure adumbrated,[16] is unashamedly social, involving 'rites, customs, etc.' as well as languages; and 'If we are to discover the true nature of language we must learn what it has in common with all other semiological systems'. To be sure Saussure thinks of *society* only as a synchronic business; the social is not, he hastens to insist, the historical. But still he cannot debar 'the community of speakers' from any discussion of language's existence. And if it doesn't take the fact that his French phrase for this community includes the word mass ('masse parlante') to cue in Marxists at this point, neither does one have to be much of a Marxist to have difficulty with that slick Saussurean assurance that the historical has no place in the social. And Marxists of all stripes have, of course, experienced difficulty at just this point.

What amazes is Saussure's continuing anti-historical bias even in the light of his grudging acceptance of language's social dimensions. His faith in language as a non-determined, free zone, arbitrary and fortuitous, somehow apart from real speakers, real *parole*, real history, real semanticity, and thus resistant to the constraints of ideology, produces a touching, but in the light even of his own lectures an awkward and perhaps even an absurd stance. His followers' faith in the unworldly neutralism of language as such, and of the apparatuses for recording and registering language states – I mean dictionaries and the like – is even more derisorily suspect. Roland Barthes, for example, beefing up his position in his notorious 'The Death of the Author' essay, with his proposition that language itself rather than some human individual is the author, the origin of writings, suggests that even if we were to refer texts back to individual authors it would be to some sort of inner dictionary that we were tracing literary production (and I take it that this was the germinating of his later powerful idea of the 'codes' which seminate texts).[17] But what strikes most about this inner lexicon is the notion that dictionaries, even inner ones, are themselves somehow free from history and ideology. But this is apparently just how Hillis Miller takes up the idea in his presentation (in *Fiction and Repetition*) of Conrad's novel *Lord Jim* as locked into language, a self-reflexive language system that subverts the idea of the external, historical authority of authors and of the ideologically shaping forces that authors bring to bear on texts, by presenting itself as an endlessly interlocking, and finally nowhere authoritative circle merely of segments, bits of narrative. '*Lord Jim* is like a dictionary in which the entry under one word refers the reader to another word which refers him to another and then back to the first word again, in an endless circling.'

Such thoughts about language (and so texts) as comprising an endlessly receding or circular chain of signification that never escapes from language, and so existing rather like a dictionary merely within language, are not all that new. Neither, however, do they tend by necessity in the direction Barthes and Hillis Miller would like to have them go. Take Dictionary Johnson. In his *Preface* to his Dictionary (1755), Dr Johnson shows that he feels fully the real difficulty that arises from language's high degree of self-reference, the way it's endlessly boxed in upon itself. Dictionaries, he says, 'interpret a language by itself'. For their explanation, words need other words. And if there turn out to be no unambiguous words by which to explain ambiguous ones such words are going to remain undisambiguated. Some words have just too many possible senses, and remain even after all the lexicographer's efforts, still swamped in the copiousness of their too many possible – lost in what Johnson calls in a powerful phrase 'the exuberance of signification which many words have obtained'. Further, since 'to explain, requires the use of terms less abstruse than that which is to be explained', there inevitably comes a point in the definition of even – one might almost say especially – the simplest words when no simpler terms can be found to explain them by, so that they have to stand more or less for themselves in a lexicographical *cul-de-sac*. So that in a variety of ways, by this enforced need to keep rummaging into itself for the meaning of its own components, language ends up staring into Derridean black holes or receding tunnels where reference is elusive and sometimes virtually all gone, and the idea that the signified might be fixed, made certain, is severely threatened. Expletives, for example, Johnson observes have 'power and emphasis' in 'living tongues', but are too basic to be definable. Also, he finds, English has a lot of common words that have a 'signification so loose and general' and a 'use to vague and indeterminate', 'that it is hard to trace them through the maze of variation, to catch them on the brink of utter inanity, to circumscribe them by any limitations, or interpret them by any words of distinct and settled meaning'.

But – and this is for the moment the important point – despite these labyrinthine endlessnesses and the daunting nature of the lexicographer's engagement with these perplexities – (*lexicographer*: 'a harmless drudge, that busies himself in tracing the original, and detailing the signification of words') – Johnson never abandoned the task that he kept acknowledging to verge upon impossibilities. He accepts, even relishes, the self-referential, metaphoric, fictive language-game aspects of language (his *elephant*, for example, is an extremely pleasant farrago of hearsay, legend, story, fiction). He speculates playfully and seriously (*doily*: 'A species of woollen stuff, so called, I suppose from the name of the first maker' – an original who cannot, of course, be traced). But he never abandons the concept, problematic as his researches have shown it to be for language, that words only come into their own as *parole* in the mouths of living speakers, or as text on the pages of the kinds of author he quotes to illustrate usages by. And he demonstrates repeatedly and successfully that signification, for all the difficulties in tracking it, never stops craning outwards into the substantive, knowable realities of the world where lexicographers drudge, excise-men impose taxes (*excise*: 'A hateful tax levied upon commodities, and adjudged ... by ... wretches hired by those to whom it is paid' – another and more horrid closed system than even the difficult parts of lexicography); the world where patrons trouble the men of letters they lock into closed circles of ardent efforts chasing exiguous rewards (*patron*: 'Commonly a wretch who supports with insolence, and is paid with flattery'). *Lexicon*, 'a book teaching the signification of words', Johnson illustrates with a quotation from Milton:

Though a linguist should pride himself to have all the tongues that Babel cleft the world into, yet if he had not studied the solid things in them as well as the words and *lexicons*, yet he were nothing so much to be esteemed a learned man as any yeoman competently wise in his mother dialect only.

And, of course, what this acceptance of 'the solid things' in language actively implies and continually registers is the historical working, the human pressure of action, prejudice, belief, assumption (that is, ideology), upon the linguistic stuff in lexicons. Hence the unashamed biasedness of Johnson's definitions of taxmen and patrons. Language, on this view, even language sealed into dictionaries, simply is not bounded by a *cordon sanitaire* such as Barthes and his followers have at times craved, a pleasant green belt or cosmetic corset holding off the shifting, transforming, moulding, touching and otherwise intruding worlds of human activities and thoughts.

In the light of the Johnsonian example one is actually compelled to search for the ideologies behind words, especially for the ideologies behind theories about words. And, in the current case, the large ideological position isn't far to seek, even if as is the common case with ideologies it isn't always as clear to the participants what they are up to as some of their more overt indications might lead us to suppose. The rejection of real speakers, real authors, as origins for utterances and texts is explicitly, in the case of Barthes and Derrida and of many others, part of a strong ultimate rejection of the existence and authority of God as author and origin. Derrida's assault on what he calls logocentrism – the idea of the all-powerful word, full of centred, presented, world-referential, personal meanings and messages – is the cutting edge of his massive and ambitious assault on the Christian (and Greek) eras in which he, more or less rightly, sees logocentrism as being centred.

The simple contention is broadly accurate. An old-fashioned, commonsense linguistics has been sustained into our era by what Derrida sees as metaphysical, transcendental, onto-theological, assumptions, Graeco-Christian assumptions (and ones that in Derrida's view Saussure didn't go far enough in shaking off), notions whose backbone has been, in the Christianized world, the sorts of allegation and belief that pack, say, Bishop Lancelot Andrewes' Christmas Day Sermons (the sermons of Andrewes that so excited T. S. Eliot,[19] the same Andrewes who seems so to perplex Professor Stanley Fish[20]). As Andrewes puts it in his Christmas Day Sermon of 1618 on the advent of Christ as the sign of God: '*loquitur signis*, "signs have their speech", and this is no dumbsign'. The birth of Jesus Christ is the phenomenon to which the Logos and the logic of language implied by such a Logos, point: it is the *natus* contained within the very word *signatus* that supports and offers proof of the possibility of acts of reference and signification: 'All is in the thing signified ... it carr[ies] us to a rich *signatum* and worth the finding. ... We are sent to a crib, not to an empty crib; Christ is in it ...'. 'Ye may make a tally between the sign and the *signatum*.' And the sign is therefore 'well assigned by the Angel'. And in the manger the Word appears in its true colours – 'A sign, nay an ensign, His very colours' – and so also do the word in general, words, language. And the faith in Christ the sign who signifies and who is signified by the cradle, readily becomes a faith in such phenomenological realities as that 'cratch'.

One shouldn't though, be as simple-minded about Christian logocentrism as the now repeated talk about logocentrism usually appears to be. Even in Derrida's pages, but especially in the pages of his numerous followers who repeat that what they think has now been undone by the researches and analyses of current criticism of texts is an old theologically sustained logocentrism, there is virtually no analysis of this logocentrism: its flatly simple outlines are simply taken for granted. What is not commonly perceived among those who talk hostilely of logocentrism is that amidst the welter of signs leading to the world of *signata* that Lancelot Andrewes's theological readings of Scripture support and suppose, the mystical self-reference of the Biblical words and so of the Biblical theory of language (if we may so call it) never disappears from view. The words of Andrewes's Biblical texts have divine ends in the world, but they're also always thought of as their own divine ultimate, for these are words uttered by the Word, i.e. Christ, whose signification is Himself, the Word. They are verbal signs about Christ the Sign. Men like Andrewes never forgot that the logos was also a person, who was born in the cratch that Andrewes always makes so knowable, historical and touchable (and that helped sustain T. S. Eliot's historicized Christian faith, as his 'Journey of the Magi' shows); and that this embodied Sign also *did* signs (*semeion*: miracle, or sign). But, further, the historical meanings – the Word in the history of the first century A.D.

and the Word in people's hearts and minds and lives ever since (Andrewes: 'In this sense also it is a sign to sign us with, a signature to make a mark on us') – gained their peculiar power from the parallel intensity also of the text's (and the word's) self-reference, self-existence, self-upholding, in fact by just such a leaking away into mystery or some such progression towards a voiding of meaning (which is also, of course, an enticing prospect of infinite readability, an infinite hermeneutic), as attracts and excites our post-structuralist epoch.

In that Christmas Day Sermon of 1618, then, Andrewes was also driven, and rather startlingly, to meditate on Christ as an infant in the cratch, the *verbum infans*. The non-speaking word, *in-fans*: 'the Word without a word; the eternal Word not able to speak a word;... a wonder sure'. This was a meditation on the silencing – the absenting within the presenting – of Christ (however short-lived that silence) that startled T. S. Eliot into giving back to that Word its voice again in his poem 'Gerontion' even before he'd allowed that It had been made voiceless: 'The word within [not 'without'] a word, unable to speak a word'. Again, on another literary occasions when the Christ of the Gospels is described in the Gospel as engaging in His unique act of writing (the only one ever recorded) his text remains crucially unrevealed by the Evangelistic hand. Instead of replying directly to the accusers of the 'woman taken in adultery' (*St John,* Chapter 8), 'Jesus stooped down and with his finger wrote on the ground'. This action failing quite to silence the woman's accusers, Christ tells anyone of them 'that is without sin among you, let him first cast a stone at her; 'And again he stooped down, and wrote on the ground.' It's a powerful set of utterances and writings; they drive off the opposition; but we never learn of what the writing consisted. And on yet another Biblical occasion, and even more interestingly, there is the description of Christ Himself as a text, a piece of writing, in *I Peter* 2, 21: 'Christ also suffered for us, leaving us an example, that we should follow his steps'. *Epakolouthein tois ikhnesi tinos*, to tread in someone's footsteps (cf. *marcher sur les traces*!). But in the footsteps of what or of Whom? In the footsteps of Christ the *hupogrammos* (a word that occurs only this once in the New Testament). The *hupogrammos* was that line of writing written out by the Greek schoolmaster at the top of the schoolboy's wax writing tablet for him to keep copying out as handwriting practice. And the *hupogrammos* not only characteristically included all the letters of the Greek alphabet – so that Christ is here being pictured as an alphabetical entity, the whole of language's potential, all the alphabet from *alpha* to *omega* (as He is also seen in the *Revelation of St John*); it was also frequently a nonce-sentence composed by the schoolmaster for practice in the mere formation of letters rather than for sense, and one that commonly contained nonsense words, so that Christ becomes here also a non-referential, language-locked, riddling, enigmatical set of words or alphabetical bits, his writtenness a set of verbal *traces* corresponding oddly well to the Derrida-esque conception of the *traces* he believes language leaves in defiance of logocentrism.

The Christian idea of signs, then, looks as if it is able vigorously to embrace the dualism that Saussure announced (prior to renouncing it) and that Dictionary Johnson observed. The actual, rather than the mythical, Christian logocentrism is an affair in which meaning is held to look outwards to the world, but also inwards to the mysterious, elusive, darker life of signs, an elusiveness that can be thought of as going even as far as the alphabetically playful nonce-ness and nonsense of the *hupogrammos*. And this view of how words and signs work in the light of the meaning of Christ the *logos* and *semeion* naturally burgeoned into a faith in the Biblical text as having similar varieties of eloquence. The Scripture, for Andrewes as for other hermeneutes of Biblical writing before him and after him, was, in consequence of their perception of the multivalent Logos, a text quite saturated in multiplicities of signification. As Christ the Logos was conceived of as the word whose meaning are infinitely squeezable, inexhaustible, both historically and literally, so the Biblical text, whose constant reference was believed to be this christological *signatum* in all its possible aspects, became an absolutely multivalent text. The reader of Andrewes's sermons is frequently amazed at his hermeneutical ingenuity, at the way meaning is wrung again and again from the textual passages he chooses for examination.[18] It seems as if his exegetical squeeze can be prolonged almost indefinitely. 'A sign, this, nay, three in one, able to amaze any', he'll say, warming up to his analysis, but easily able – as he frequently demonstrates – to go on beyond a mere three sets of possible meanings. He's a sort of Malvolio, confident in the knowledge that if he reads it hard enough Maria's letter will make more and more sense: as Shakespeare's grotesquest interpreter has it, 'to crush this a little, it would bow to me'. And though he sometimes appears over-ingenious, Andrewes's practice never seems to become actually absurd. He may be thought of as putting on Jonson's learned sock and handling Walter Benjamin's curiously ambivalent gift, but he never quite gets to the yellow garters stage. He does indeed seem to be possessed of a theory of interpretation that produces much hermeneutical fruit.

For Andrewes – or Milton or Bunyan, or many another orthodox Christian exegete – the Biblical text, like the divine Logos, was of course quite special. No other texts approached the absoluteness of Scripture's meaningfulness. In the Bible – and here the assumptions of the Christian hermeneutes built on the hermeneutical assumptions and practices of their predecessors the Jewish rabbis – nothing at all was incidental, meaningless, no word of Scripture was wasted or disregardable. Every jot and tittle counted. But, equally obviously, it is not ridiculous for us to jump from the practice of Lancelot Andrewes to that of the letter-and poem-reading, cabbalistic Malvolio, for that is the kind of jump Andrewes's exegetical assumptions sanctioned: from sacred texts to secular ones. The overwhelming sense of the multivalence of Scripture overflowed: so that all scriptures, particularly those we think of as "Classics", caught the hermeneutical contagion of the Biblical text, even as the idea of the Logos had come to inform the sense of how words in general had their meaning. The Scriptures were historical, literal; they were also hermetic, cabbalistic, *hupogrammatical*. And so, potentially, were all texts. This is what logocentrism really means.

Borges, importantly, invites us to contemplate the extent to such assumptions. He knows very well that this Christian set of hermeneutical paths was an afforcing of the rabbis' ways with their stories and texts, their Bible, the 'Old' Testament, and also that these techniques of reading were passed on to unorthodox interpreters. In his extremely suggestive essay 'The

Mirror of Enigmas', Borges reflects on such ways of thinking about Scripture, and so about all texts, including the world itself, as a dazzling combination of the literal and the evasively hermetic, a line of thought developed with particular extravagance by the Cabbalists, and by Swedenborg, and by other Christian and post-Christian thinkers of an hermeneutical bent. Borges is talking particularly about Léon Bloy, the French novelist and mystic (1846–1917), a writer captivated by the world as a set of infinitely meaning and self-meaning texts. Bloy's thoughts along these lines were, Borges suggests, 'perhaps inevitable within the Christian doctrine':

> Bloy... did no more than apply to the whole of Creation the method which the Jewish Cabbalists applied to the Scriptures. They thought that a work dictated by the Holly Spirit was an absolute text: in other words, a text in which the collaboration of chance was calculable as zero. This portentous premise of a book impenetrable to contingency, of a book which is a mechanism of infinite purposes, moved them to permute the scriptural words, add up the numerical value of the letters, consider their form, observe the small letters and capitals, seek acrostics and anagrams and perform other exegetical rigours which it is not difficult to ridicule. Their excuse is that nothing can be contingent in the work of an infinite mind. Léon Bloy postulates this hieroglyphical character – this character of a divine writing, of an angelic cryptography – at all moments and in all beings on earth. The superstitious person believes he can decipher this organic writing....
>
> It is doubtful that the world has a meaning; it is even more doubtful that it has a double or triple meaning, the unbeliever will observe. I understand that this is so; but I understand that the hieroglyphical world postulated by Bloy is the one which best befits the dignity of the theologian's intellectual God.[21]

An absolute text: Cabbalistic, full of signs that are infinitely meaningful, offering to the ingenious interpreter alphabetical and numerological clues, and consisting of acrostics, anagrams, hieroglyphs, cryptograms, built on this indeed 'portentous premise of a book impenetrable to contingency'. And what Borges's thumbnail sketch of text as divine writing should remind one of is not only particular enthusiasms for the Cabbalistic intricacies of texts such as are manifested in Borges's own fictions and in the critic Harold Bloom's use of the instructive possibilities for a modern criticism of an assortment of Cabbalistic and Gnostic reading practices (his *Kabbalah and Criticism*, 1975,[22] and *Agon*, 1982, for instance, celebrate variously as hermetic hermeneutes the Gnostic heretic Valentinus, the Cabbalist rabbi Isaac Luria, and the great English re-reader of Scripture and Christian heretic the poet William Blake). Borges does forcefully look out towards Harold Bloom. But he also opens a window onto numerous other elements within the broad and busy field of post-structuralism and modernism/postmodernism generally that are not, at first sight, connected so obviously with the Cabbalistic.

Is it not, for example, as some such set of uncontingent textual absolutes as Borges describes that Sigmund Freud perceives the unconscious and its texts – what he called the work of dreams, the verbal slip, the pun, the joke – which are all at once texts, and models of texts and textual operations, that in their refutation of the idea that any figure is merely contingent, and so redundant for the reader or analyst, have provided the most fruitful of stimulants for all our modern taking of liberties in interpreting? (It's a belief that induces nightmare and even paranoia in the cautious reader such as Martin Price in his *Forms of Life: Character and Moral Imagination in the Novel*, 1983,[23] but that is sturdily taken aboard by more eager modernists such as Frank Kermode in his book *The Genesis of Secrecy: On the Interpretation of Narrative* (1976)[24] and his gathering *Essays on Fiction 1971–82*, 1983). Is this not also how Surrealism, the great post-Freudian enterprise (in which the notable re-reader of Freud, Jacques Lacan took an early and immese interest), perceives the unconscious. And how the consciousness-revealing, accident – defying existence of the art-works Surrealists specialised in – found-objects, ready-mades, *collage* and *bricollage* (cut-up poems and the like), art-objects made by 'ignorant collaboration' as in games of consequences (*le cadavre exquis*), shapes printed with random blots of paint (*décalcomanie*) – are thought of by their perpetrators and admirers as existing? Is this not also, effectively, how Ferdinand de Saussure assumed literature to have its being when he tried over the years 1906–9, to hunt out the anagrammatical meanings of poems ancient and modern, filling up very many notebooks at a task finally discarded as leading nowhere, but one which merged chronologically into the *Cours* on linguistics which offers a view of language curiously approximate to those anagrams. This is an enterprise of some attraction to Derrida, who is to be found in a footnote at the end of Ch. 2 of his *Grammatologie* thinking 'particularly' of these anagrams, and an effort repeatedly hailed by Vincent Leitch in his *Deconstructive Criticism* as post-structuralism done in advance, the proleptic 'end-point' of our current postmodern hermeneutics. And does not Borges's description remind one also and extremely strongly of James Joyce's *Finnegans Wake*, the most deliberately crypto-graphic, punning, alphabetically gamey text ever deliberately and consciously so manufactured in English – perhaps in any language? Does there not occur, in fact, a convergence just here in Borges's description of 'divine' textuality of the views of language and writing by anagrammatically-minded Saussure; by Freud who always acts implicity, and Lacan, who acts ex-plicitly as if the unconscious were structured like a language; by deferring (if non-deferential) anti-logocentrist Derrida; by Surrealism's art-revolutionaries, and in particular by Eugène Jolas, friend of Joyce and editor of *transition* magazine whose 'revolution of the word', a celebration of language's turn into a quasi-religious, magical, self-sustaining play of self-reference, has as its Exhibit Number One Joyce's 'Work in Progress', that is to say *Finnegans Wake*, the text regarded on all sides now (by for instance Stephen Heath in *The Nouveau Roman.* 1972,[25] and by Margot Norris in *The Decentered Universe of Finnegans Wake A Structuralist Analysis*, 1976,[26] by David Lodge in *The Modes of Modern Fiction* and by Jonathan Culler in his *On Deconstruction*, and so on and on) not only as the ultimate and quintessential modernist work, but also as the ultimate post-structuralist, post-modernist text.

What I'm suggesting, in other words, is that hereabouts, and along the lines of my third epigraph from Foucault, one has come upon something like a shared ideology for whole swathes of the modernist enterprise, even perhaps for all of it. I'm very well aware that explanations that seem to explain a very great deal, that offer keys to all mythologies, run the risk of not explaining anything very well. But the force of the con-vergences in and around that Borges essay is undeniable. Again and again what Modernism and its successors opt for – and in consequence of the straight rejection of Christian and/or Judaic beliefs and theology – is spurning of the dual-facing notion of language that Judaeo-Christianity helped build and has strongly propped up through the ages, and a settling lopsidedly (and in a completely or partially secularised spirit) into what is left of the mysticohermetic, Cabbalistic side of that one-time duality, the formerly more balanced Christian, (and Greek), and Jewish position. The bi-focussed Logos and the multivalent Scripture are thrown out in favour only are the imploding self-centred word and text. And where once the Cabbalists held that the hermetic meanings derived from their assumptions about the sacred text as absolute and non-contingent – meanings always enrichingly supplementary to the literal, historical meanings – believed that these interpretations revealed and proved a Divine authorship and also the self-sufficiency and uncontingency of that author God ('No science', claimed Pico di Mirandola in the fifteenth century, 'yields greater proof of the divinity of Christ than magic and the Kabbalah'), the structuralist/modernist/deconstructionist sense of language's inwardness and hiddenness, of *Les Mots Sous Les Mots* (as Jean Starobinski titles his took about Saussure's anagrammatical exercises, 1971),[27] the idea of language's cutting loose from literalism, history, reference and imploding into mere writtenness, is held to prove rather the self-generative autonomy, the autotelic, authorial power and life only of the verbal sign, of language itself.

Merely defining this aspect of the ideological texture of Modernism does not by itself argue the rightness or wrongness of the modernist views of language and writing that it touches on. But exposing an ideology's outlines is always important. It's even more important when that ideology is working to deny ideology and history. And whatever one thinks, in the end, of Saussure, or Eugène Jolas, or Joyce, or Derrida, or whoever, one can do worse than start by realizing that within the zones of the modernist frame that they, their followers and imitators variously inhabit and sustain, there has gone on a large-scale set of substitutionary acts, a giant serial act of parody or pastiche. And not only a swapping of one set of myths for a substitute set in a general way (as in, say, Yeats's visionary system, or Lawrence's religion of the blood), and certainly not just a vague Arnoldian exchange of old theology for new pseudo-theology, of old religion for new poetry – though these transactions have obviously occurred and understanding them is essential to understanding our culture – but much more particularly: a very specific exchanging of an old plenary sense of Scripture for a new but limitedly and limitingly partial sense of *écriture.*

*

The movement of Joyce's writing towards the post-structuralist practices of *Finnegans Wake* – the modern 'English' text most puzzling to orthodox interpreters (so far it's been unassimilable into established genres, according to Alastair Fowler in his encyclopedic *Kinds of Literature, An Introduction to the Theory of Genres and Modes,* 1983),[28] but the one most admired in recent hermeneutical circles, even if it does remain the most commonly unread text in the whole canon of literature written in English – this movement illustrates nicely the link between the modernist abandonment of realism, the opting for signs over *signata,* for signifiers over signifieds, and an attempt both to parody and to out-do the Christian idea of Logos and Scripture.

Joyce begins realist-wise with Ibsen, but Ibsen enhanced, as it were, by the theory of epiphany derived from the Christian theology of the Epiphany. In the New Testament story of the Epiphany the Magi attain a visionary perception that the child in the cratch is God. They observe that that Word coheres in the human body of Christ. For them the Word and the flesh collaborate in a revelation of divine glory. This human flesh contains the glory of the Word, and the glory of the Word grants infinite value to this piece of human flesh. And so, borrowing from theology, Stephen Hero 'believed that it was for the man of letters to record' such moments when by analogy they occurred in his life: to 'record these epiphanies with extreme care, seeing that they themselves are the most delicate and evanescent of moments'. There is some sense in the commonly held view that all of Joyce's work is a collecting and recording of epiphanic moments. Primarily, though, epiphany became for Joyce a doctrine for realism, for a glorious particularity in which the words on the artist's page are thought of as giving revelatory life to objects. Hence the discussion in *Stephen Hero* and *A Portrait of the Artist as a Young Man* of Aquinas's theory of the objects, the things, of aesthetic contemplation, and the illustration of epiphany by the extremely thingy Ballast Office Clock (in *Stephen Hero*) and the use of the butcher's boy's basket (in *A Portrait*).

But already in *Stephen Hero* Joyce was moving away from things as the basis of epiphanies, moving away from such *signata*, as it were, towards signifieds and signifiers as the objects of the writer's epiphanic efforts. 'By an epiphany he meant a sudden spiritual manifestation, whether in the vulgarity of speech [a signifier] or of gesture [referential *signatum*] or in a memorable phase of the mind itself [signified]'. From the start, then, of his thinking and writing Joyce was as interested in words as such – the Logos of the Epiphany – as he was in the world objectively given or subjectively perceived. So it's not surprising that *Dubliners* – correctly seen as 'a book of epiphanies' of the sort Stephen Hero pondered collecting and that James Joyce did in a manner collect – not only consists of Dublin life both realistically and impressionistically done, but is also filled with the talk of Dublin and, what's more, opens the volume's opening fiction with an almost programmatic set of reflections on the central position and the generative power of words themselves – words in the mouth, words in books, words that engender situations, events, behaviour, emotions, life and death:

He had often said to me: 'I am not long for this world', and I had thought his words idle. Now I knew they were true. Every night as I gazed up at the window I said softly to myself the word paralysis. It had always sounded strangely in my ears, like the word gnomon in the Euclid and the word simony in the Catechism. But now it sounded to me like the name of some maleficent and sinful being. It filled me with fear, and yet I longed to be nearer to it and to look upon its deadly work.

We have to keep reminding ourselves that *it* is, primarily, and right to the end of this passage, a word, and only secondarily a concept or a thing.

This strong sense of the primacy of signifiers, however, is one that the young artist has to mature into. As a child in *A Portrait*

Stephen Dedalus has a primitive, onomatopoeic sense that words and things are one, and that things give rise to the words for those things. He has no notion of Saussure's belief in the arbitrariness of the signifier. *Suck* was 'a queer word': its 'sound was ugly. Once he had washed his hands in the lavatory of the Wicklow Hotel and his father pulled the stopper up by the chain after and the dirty water went down through the hole in the basin. And when it had all gone down slowly the hole in the basin had made a sound like that: suck'. Likewise *kiss*: 'You put your face up like that to say good night and then his mother put her face down. That was to kiss. His mother put her lips on his cheek; her lips were soft and they wetted his cheek; and they made a tiny little noise: kiss'. But even this early in the linguistic education of Dedalus – the main subject of *A Portrait* – there is emergent another way of seeing the order of words and things. In the Wicklow Hotel, 'There were two cocks that you turned and water came out: cold and hot. He felt cold and then a little hot: and he could see the names printed on the cocks. That was a very queer thing'. Queer not least because it suggests that the *names* hot and cold are capable of producing hot and cold water, hot and cold physical sensations.

And the sense of the primacy of words – words as Logoi that become flesh, are the basis of things' becoming, because they precede things, come first – is what young Dedalus soon grows into. There's a transitional, epiphanic stage, in which words and things are thought of as enjoying co-responsive equality. The Director's mention of the French word for the Capuchins' dress, *les jupes*, makes Stephen think of stuffs and words for stuff:

The names of articles of dress worn by women or of certain delicate stuffs used in their making brought always to his mind a delicate and sinful perfume. As a boy he had imagined the reins by which horses are driven as slender silken bands and it shocked him to feel at Stradbrooke the greasy leather of harness. It had shocked him, too, when he had felt for the first time beneath his tremulous fingers the brittle texture of a woman's stocking for, retaining nothing of all he read save that which seemed to him an echo or a prophecy of his own state, it was only amid soft-worded phrases or within rose-soft stuffs that he dared to conceive of the soul or body of a woman moving with tender life.

Soft-worded phrases: rose-soft stuffs. But their equality is only temporary. Even within this reflection Dedalus is indicating the power of names actually to generate experience (smells); in other words he's hit on the originative, proleptic, predictive powers of language. And so the piety of a 'squad of Christian brothers' would not only be 'like their faces, like their clothes', but also 'like their names'. Hickey, Quaid, MacArdle and Keogh, the names have made the men. Just so, Stephen's own name is making him what he is. 'Stephanos Dedalos! Bous Stephanoumenos! Bous Stephaneforos!': 'Now, as never before, his strange name seemed to him a prophecy.... Now, at the name of the fabulous artificer, he seemed to hear the noise of dim waves and to see a winged form flying above the waves and slowly climbing the air'. His name, these words out of myth, text, fiction, precedent words, shape him as all the various words and texts in *A Portrait* shape him: the songs, rhymes, sayings, catechisms, litanies, the Bible and sermons, the texts of Dante and Aquinas, Aristotle and *The Count of Monte Cristo*, the words of Satan (*Non serviam*, I will not serve); even the graffiti on public lavatory walls (the cry of frustration before his sexual initiation with the whore 'was but the echo of an obscene scrawl which he had read on the oozing wall of a urinal').

And there is a yet further stage, in which its's suggested that words might be transcending even this potential for generating things and be properly apprehensible as things in their own right; in other words, that signifiers as such might grant the reality that Dedalus most craves, and do it all on their own:

He drew forth a phrase from his treasure and spoke it softly to himself: – A day of dappled seaborne clouds. The phrase and the day and the scene harmonised in a chord. Words. Was it their colours? He allowed them to glow and fade, hue after hue: sunrise gold, the russet and green of apple orchards, azure of waves, the grey-fringed fleece of clouds. No, it was not their colours: it was the poise and balance of the period itself. Did he then love the rhythmic rise and fall of words better than their associations of legend and colour? Or was it that, being as weak of sight as he was shy of mind, he drew less pleasure from the reflection of the glowing sensible world through the prism of a language many-coloured and richly storied than from the contemplation of an inner world of individual emotions mirrored perfectly in a lucid supple periodic prose?

And, clearly, the impressionistic, subjective, inner world that language is perfectly to mirror is already teetering on the edge of collapse into the inwardness of what is elsewhere (in the anatomy theatre episode) called 'mere words', or, as here, 'the poise and balance of the period itself.' Already in *A Portrait*, then, the way forwards to *Ulysses* and beyond that to *Finnegans Wake* is indicated: to *Ulysses* in which the life of the signifier is continually breaking away from the world of urban reference to enjoy its own life as verbal character, verbal subject; and, further down that road still, to *Finnegans Wake*, where language romps, rampages, even raves, ranged, arranged, disarranged and rearranged this way and that, a wildly multivalent spree of extravagantly multi-layered punning and multiplex *entendres*, loudly and continually self-referential, always eager to demonstrate that its significance begins and ends in words ('synopticked on the word') and in the building-blocks of words, the letters of the alphabet.

Ulysses demonstrates massively enough that the word and the text were in the beginning – whether the text is *Hamlet* or the Bible or the *Odyssey*, a religious hand-out, a newspaper, or any number of alluded-to texts, including the text of *Ulysses* itself – and that in this fiction's mock-heroic, textualized, scriptured Dublin what is has become so only by courtesy of that word, that text. Characteristically, in a bookshop in 'The Wandering Rocks' section Bloom turns the pages of sensational books; and the sweetly lascivious words turn into stimulatednesses of the flesh as surely as, say, Gertie MacDowell is determined by the trashy pages she's steeped herself in:

Mr Bloom read again: *The beautiful woman.*
Warmth showered gently over him, cowing his flesh. Flesh yielded amid rumpled clothes. Whites of eyes swooning up. His nostrils arched themselves for prey. Melting breast ointments (*for him! For Raoul!*). Armpits' oniony sweat. Fishgluey slime (*her heaving embonpoint!*). Feel! Press! Crushed! Sulphur dung of lions! Young! Young!

Bloom is shown, lengthily, painstakingly, to be always, in a sense, in a bookshop. His realities are continually derived from, and consist of, books, words, reading-matter. But *Finnegans Wake*'s dive into the womb of language is hardier and intenser yet. Where *Ulysses* breaks its verbal stuff into bits only from time to time, plays only with occasional alpha-beticism, *Finnegans Wake* has its pair of chief protagonists H. C. Earwicker and Anna Livia Plurabelle most persistently present on its textual stage as their initials A. L. P. and H. C. E., initials seeded diligently and randomly, a consciously encoded set of anagrammatical presences, right across the text's massive assembly of words. The reader of *Finnegans Wake* is plunged not *in medias res* but *in medios loquos* (398:8), and into a play of words reduced – by a repeated mono-euvre in which this text proves continually to be collaps-ing into metatext – reduced to basic alphabeticisms, so that repeatedly the art of letters that this text is concerned to demonstrate is shown to consist of the letters of the alphabet that compose all writing. Language ceases to be a window onto something, it turns its and the reader's gaze onto itself, its own stuff and substance. *Finnegans Wake* tells us it is *abcedminded* ('what curios of signs... in this allaphbed!', 18:17–18), *abecadarian* (198:20), *as simple as ABC* (65:27–28), a matter for *alphabetters* (107:9), and of *alphybettyformed verbage* (183:13). It demands of its readers *abecedeed responses* (140:14); it is not just to be appreciated but *Abbreciade[d]* (534:2). It's offered not to the sweet tooths that enjoy Huntley and Palmer's sweet animal or even alphabet biscuits, but to those who will chew and digest 'Huntler and Pumar's animal alphabites' (263: footnote 1).

These 'animal alphabites' are said to be 'the first in the world from aab to zoo'. Embedded as they are in a discussion of origins, it's clearly deducible that these biscuits signify that what comes first in all creation – what creates, in fact – is language. And the world that is created by language consists of language, is the alphabet *from aab to zoo*, from *a* to *z*. The alphabet is presented as precursor, generator, father; the womb in which reality, i.e. text, originates and come to birth is language, is the alphabet. And this is evidently what *Ulysses* was seeking to demonstrate in 'The Oxen of the Sun' episode where the growth of Mrs Purefoy's child in the womb and its subsequent parturition are parallelled with something like the development of the English language (the identification of the various stage and styles has never been an entirely convincing business). Something similar is going on in the 'Wandering

Rocks' episode we just noticed, where Bloom looks in a book and discovers embryos in it: 'Plates: infants cuddled in a ball in bloodred wombs like livers of slaughtered cows. Lots them like that at this moment all over the world. All butting with their skulls to get out of it. Child born every minute somewhere. Mrs Purefoy'. Babies come from wombs; wombs are in books; wombs are books. But if language and books are, under such considerations, female, maternal, Mrs Purefoys, where are the fathers of language, of texts? And the curious answer returned is, nowhere really. At least Joyce's texts try hard to banish the idea of fathers as generators of the word, the text, the fiction. Their Oedipal content is high, both manifestly and latently.

At the beginning of *A Portrait*, and seemingly cognate with Stephen Dedalus's very early notion that words are generated out of an intimately onomatopoeic relation with things, we are introduced into the text as into a story told by Stephen's father Simon:

Once upon a time ... there was ... a nicens little boy named baby tuckoo ...
His father told him that story: his father looked at him through a glass: he
had a hairy face.
He was baby tuckoo.

Simon fathers Stephen, and authors the story of Stephen. He looks at his son, his creation, through a glass: an eye-glass maybe, or a beer-glass, or maybe even the glass or mirror of St Paul and of Borges through which we are all said to look, *per speculum* (precisely 'The Mirror of Enigmas' of Borges's essay referred to earlier). So that Stephen appears here as the mirror image of his divine-like creator, in a relation of author and creation that is still close to the old reflexive notion of language and texts as mirrors held up to the world.

But the meaning of the 'glass' remains a puzzle. In fact its enigma reminds us that St Paul (and Borges) have us looking 'though a glass darkly', *per speculum in aenigmate*. And the relationship of Stephen and Simon Dedalus remains, like the relationship of every son with his father in Joyce's writing, an enigma, a matter of puzzle and of hermeneutical problem. In *A Portrait* this enigmatic relationship rapidly increases, especially when Stephen accompanies his father to Cork and goes into the Queen's College anatomy theatre in a quest for his father's initials – S. D., his own initials too – and finds instead of his father's name (as it were) something more disturbing, 'the word *Foetus* cut several times in the dark stained wood' of the desk. This word repeatedly cut into the desk proves generative: 'A vision' of the life of his father and his contemporaries, 'which his father's words had been powerless to evoke, sprang up before him out of the word cut in the desk [a Derrida-esque exchanging of the power of the spoken word for the even greater power of the written]. A broad-shouldered student with a moustache was cutting in the letters with a jack-knife, seriously'. Subsequently, Simon Dedalus finds the initials S. D. on another desk. But one meaning of the episode is fairly clear. Stephen came looking for a father, a writing-father to supplement the story-telling father with whom *A Portrait* opens, and found a foetus instead. In the matter of origins, foetus precedes father, and the word foetus, the written textualized word foetus at that.

The word *cut*, and the act of cutting, are curiously stressed. It is as if Stephen has been cut off from his father; as if the father has been emasculated, rendered powerless, castrated, cut off from paternality and the generator's precedence. And since Stephen was at first so emphatically not only his father's son but also his father's story, his utterance, his text, the implications for this text, and so for all texts, harden onto the notion of some sort of self-existence, self-subsistence, or at least of self-existence in a word – and a word of course written down, the written word. And this word not only cuts – and the Oedipal cut is the most unkindest cut of all – but its presence is a cut. And a cut-out word has a revealingly double-edged existence. It's both a presence (the presence of the word that is cut, the word *foetus*); and an absence (the wood that has been cut away to make the word). Which is highly apt to this cut word's signifying all at once the presence of the actually generative word, the written sign (the positive aspect of Derrida's *gramme*, the slash of the pen, the written gash) with all the power of life in it, and the cutting away, an erasure or obliteration, the *grammé* as negative act, emblematic of the absenting of the generative father whose presence dominated Stephen's most babyish thoughts about his own and his story's existence.

A son/text whose name, or at least initials and so identity, are the same as his supposed father's or author's; but a son/text cut off from that father, or that has been cut free of the authoritative originating power of that father; and a son/text generated from a word, or as a word, that has a precedent existence prior to any other generator and so is as it were its own (linguistic, textual) primogenitor: whatever other meanings we might wish these notions built around this incident to bear – (and my reading obviously differs somewhat from e.g. Maud Ellmann's more Lacanianized reading of this cutting: see 'Disremembering Daedalus: "A Portrait of the Artist As A Young Man"')[29] they do ring apparently clearly of Christian theology. And also, of course, of endless wranglings in the Early Church about the relation of God the Father to God the Son.

In his thinking and writing about fathers and sons/texts Joyce was most anxious not only to have his words and texts seen as versions of Christ the Son or Logos, but also as versions of Christ the self-generating, self-substantive Logos. And here it was heresy – or as is usual with heresy, heretical tinkerings with orthodoxy – that came to his help. In particular, out of the large roster of Christian heresies that Joyce interested himself in, it was Arianism in one form or another (and the histories of Christian heresy are notoriously vague about the exact details of the great heretics' aberrations) that he kept being drawn to as models and examples. Again and again in *Ulysses* the discussion reverts to Arius, the Bishop who wanted to drive a wedge between God the Father and Jesus the Son. The Son was not, in Arius's view, *consubstantial* with God, was not, as the anti-Arian Nicene Creed puts it: 'Unum Dominum Jesum Christum Filium Dei unigenitum. Et ex Patre natum ... Deum de deo ... Genitum non factum, consubstantialem Patri': 'One Lord Jesus Christ, the only-begotten Son of God, Begotten of his Father... God of God... Begotten, not made, Being of one substance with the Father....' This is, as it were, the orthodox thinking about father-son relations whose consolations Stephen Dedalus craves in *Ulysses* against the heterodox mockers among his friends. In that novel's opening section Stephen imagines 'A horde of heresies fleeing with mitres awry: Photius and the brood of mockers of whom Mulligan was one, and Arius, warring his life long upon the consubstantiality of the Son with the Father, and Valentine [Harold Bloom's Valentinus, I take it] spurning Christ's terrene body, and the subtle African heresiarch Sabellius who held that the Father was Himself His own Son. Words Mulligan had spoken a moment since in mockery to the stranger. Idle mockery'. 'Where is poor dear Arius to try conclusions?' Stephen asks himself in the 'Proteus' section, still pondering consubstantiality. And in 'Scylla and Charybdis', explicating *Hamlet*, Stephen sticks to orthodoxy: Hamlet is 'the son consubstantial with the father'. But all the time the rudely heretical voice of Mulligan counters orthodoxy with the creed of a mocker, an Arianism and Sabellianism gloriously mingled to divide the Father from the Son and to make the Son his own Father:

He Who Himself begot, middler the Holy Ghost, and Himself sent himself, Agenbuyer, between Himself and others, Who... fared into heaven and there these nineteen hundred years sitteth on the right hand of His Own Self....'

The word as self-begetter, self-sustainer, self-substantive. And even Stephen, still prone to orthodoxy, spurning such heretical notions, taking his own place in the fallen human face ('Wombed in sin darkness I was too, made not begotten'), has a vision in 'Proteus', sparked off by the sight of Mrs McCabe, the midwife, of a succession of births from a succession of wombs, a train of omphaloi, a whole human race of umbilical cords, which go back to the original Eve's womb in the Garden of Eden which turns out to be a primal womb or scene of language: 'strandentwining cable of all fresh. That is why mystic monks. Will you be as gods? Gaze in your omphalos. Hello. Kinch here. Put me on to Edenville. Aleph, alpha: nought, nought, one'. And this is not the orthodox divine creation of the world from nothing, it's creation from the alphabet. Language becomes God, in a process as circular as an omphalos or a womb. The telephone line to Edenville is a loopline: a loop of wombs, of words. 'In woman's womb word is made flesh', again and again, so 'The Oxen of the Sun' suggests, and the process is a 'successive anastomosis of navelcords': a self-feeding set of mouths, an invaginating, intussuscepting connection, a solipsistic hoopsnake beginning and continuing in language.

And this dwelling on the solipsistic, self-sustaining, circular existence of the verbal/textual offspring will keep leading *Ulysses* back, however unwelcomely this may be to Stephen, to Arius the heresiarch. And Arius's separation of son's being from father's, his refusal of the orthodox relation between the Son and the Father – which leads to the Sabellian conclusion (as interpreted by Joyce) that the Son if He be divine must have been his own father – unites with Stephen's reflections on that exemplary fiction that Byzantine orthodoxy put about on the subject of Arius's death. Arius was said to have had to break off in the middle of a triumphal procession through the streets of Constantinople in order to go the lavatory, and to have died there in the act of trying to relieve himself. But 'Beware', warns Stephen in Night Town, 'the last end of Arius Heresiarchus. The agony in the closet'. 'Where is poor dear Arius', as Stephen has it in 'Proteus', 'to try conclusions? Warring his life long on the contransmagnificandjewbangtantiality. Illstarred heresiarch. In a Greek watercloset he breathed his last: euthanasia. With beaded mitre and with crozier, stalled upon his throne, widower of a widowed see, with upstiffed omophorion, with clotted hinderparts.' The trier of heretical conclusions finds an uneasy death in an attempt to ease himself (*euthanasia*: easy death). But this degrading end in an effort to rid his body of degraded matter is also curiously circular: a least it's hintful of new potentials, new beginnings. The crozier, the word upstiffed, a reminder of phalluses, and the episcopal vestment (*omophorion*) only half conceals within its verbal folds the *omophore*, one of the Hindu elephants and the gigantic Manichaean omophore that were thought in ancient times to support the world upon their backs. Within this little fiction of an ending, then, there emerges a fiction of a beginning: Arius's closet – the solipsism of his unorthodox son, the enclosedness of the text within language – is not only a way of making an end, it contains within it the promise of new starts.

Generation: degeneration. One's not surprised to discover that Joyce, in the way of pornographers classically defined by D. H. Lawrence, persistently blurred the generative sexual emission into the degenerative anal release. Arius's was by no means the only closet Joyce liked entering and contemplating. As Molly Bloom eases herself, her thoughts of possible pregnancy ('who knows is there anything the matter with my insides or have I something growing in me getting that thing like that every week when was it last I Whit Monday yes its only about 3 weeks I ought to go to the doctor') run in and out of thoughts about urination and defecation and about the sexual pleasures associated by coprophiliacs with excrement ('What did he [the doctor] want me to do but the one thing gold maybe what a question if I smathered it all over his wrinkly old face for him with all my compriment').

The unstated wishes of the doctor were ones pretty freely stated by Joyce himself – he of the 'excrementitious intelligence', to use Lynch's phrase from *A Portrait* – in his heated correspondence with Nora in 1909 (and only released in 1975 in the *Selected Letters of James Joyce*, edited by Richard Ellmann).[30] Joyce revels, in a fashion that's extremely redolent of the most notorious poems of Jonathan Swift, in the stink and odours of Nora's sweat and farts and excrement. And unlike Swift he has no ambivalent feelings. He consciously enjoys the bad smells he rubs his letter's nose in. *Filthy, obscene, shameful, immodest, bad, dirty, dirtier, dirtiest*: the climactic rhetoric of his *filthy* (as he loves to label them) filthy fantasies and invitations mounts hectically. Copulation, orgasm, and excretion, the vocabulary for all three, and the prospect of Nora's voice joining his writing in the naming of these things, race-excitedly across his epistolary page, mixing and converging in an astonishing kaleidoscope of bodily functions in the body-obsessed text. 'I wish I could hear your lips spluttering those heavenly exciting filthy words, see your mouth making dirty sounds and noises, feel your body wriggling under me, hear and smell the dirty fat girlish farts going pop pop out of your pretty bare girlish bum and *fuck fuck fuck fuck* my naughty little hot fuckbird's cunt for ever.' And more, he wants to have sex with her while she actually excretes: 'Fuck me if you can in the closet, with your clothes up, grunting like a young sow doing her dung, and a big fat dirty snaking thing coming slowly out of your backside.' In these letters Nora's excrement enjoys the shape of James's phallus: the 'big fat dirty snaking thing', the 'fat brown thing stuck half-way out of her hole', becomes startlingly akin to 'his dirty red lumpy pole in through the split of her drawers and up up up in the darling little hole between her plump fresh buttocks.' The circle between the generative and degenerative is complete and, to Joyce, completely satisfying.

And, of course – for in Molly's and Nora's closets we are by no means as far removed from Arius's closet as might at first be supposed – the association of this closed, self-servicing cycle of generation-degeneration-generation with writing, the production and existence of words and of text, is made abundantly clear when we are taken into the solipsistic closet of Shem the Penman in *Finnegans Wake* (169ff). Shen's *stinksome* house, the Haunted Inkbottle, 'no number Brimstone Walk', the lair in which he writes – writes *Finnegans Wake* in an impressive metatextual flourish which purports to show how all texts are written – is a lavatory. In this noisy and noisome chamber whose 'soundconducting walls' mock the silences of Proust's sound-proofed room, Shem, shitty Arian heretic turned writer, writes in his own excrement – not ink but *inkenstink* – 'over every square inch of the only foolscap available, his own body'. And, awesome echo and parody of Arius-Sabellius's self-substantive Logos, Shem's cyclical (de)generative act is the production of all history, all life, because in Shem's extraordinary circle of textuality all life is held to consist. He and his text are the logos that is the ground of all being. He writes in his inkenstink all over his own body, we're told (185, 186), 'till by its corrosive sublimation one continuous present tense integument slowly unfolded all marryvoising moodmoulded cyclewheeling history (thereby, he said, reflecting from his own individual person life unlivable, transaccidentated through the slow fires of consciousness into a dividual chaos, perilous, potent, common to allflesh, human only, mortal) but with each word that would not pass away the squidself which he had squirtscreened from the crystalline world waned chagreenold and doriangrayer in its dudhud. This exists that isits after having been said we know'.

'This exists that isits after having been said': words, in other words, are all of existence. The words of this text posit and produce a chaotic existence: they undo God's creation, the ordered Logos – with its connectedly ordered syntax and grammar and semantics – of orthodoxy, transforming it into the faked, parodic de-creation, the logos of the heretical undoers of orthodoxy. *Dudhud* it's called here. It's the reply to Christian *Godhead*; it's what *Godhead* has been transformed into, a *dud*. And with Godhead go the creeds of orthodoxy: 'my dudhud dirtynine articles' (534:12) oust the Church of England's Thirty-Nine Articles of Religion. The new dirtynine articles are, the text goes on, 'articles of quoting'. But of course! For Shem, the perpetrator of the new logos and its text *Finnegans Wake*, demonstrates the new linguistics, the new textuality (both of them self-subsistent only within language, within text) by a tight inter-textual set of relationships, a relationship of destructive parody and heretical displacement (a Pelagianism, the heresy of human self-sufficiency, prompted and promoted by plagiarism, by – 'pseudostylistic shamiana ... piously forged palimpsests slipped ... from his pelagiarist pen' 181:36–182:3) involving the creeds, liturgies, formulae and Scriptures of the Christian Church.

Shem's 'each word that would not pass away', for example, is a version of Christ's assertion that his words would not pass away. Shem writes from his bowels, 'through the bowels of his misery, flashly, faithly, nastily, appropriately' (185:33–34), not only for Arian reasons but also because Christ acted from what the Authorised Version of the Bible calls the bowels of his compassion. Shem is 'the first till last alshemist' (184:34–35), because Christ is called in the last book of the Bible the first and the last, the Alpha and the Omega. The walls of Shem's closet are (183, 184) papered with writing – he lives only within writing, within words, 'once current puns, quashed quotatoes', 'borrowed plumes', 'alphybettyformed verbage' and the like. But the puns and the quotatoes prominently include puns on and quotatoes from the Biblical and other Christian stories: 'vivlical viasses', 'fallen lucifers', 'messes of mottage' (compare Jacob who sold his birthright for a 'mess of pottage'), 'blasphematory spits', 'lees of whine', broken wafers, unloosed shoe latchets, crooked strait waistcoats, fresh horrors from Hades', 'glass eye for an eye, gloss teeth for a tooth, war moans', 'longsufferings of longstanding': all corruptions of things Christian (Christ 'trod the winepress alone' on the cross; wafers are eucharistic edibles; John the Baptist felt himself 'unworthy' to 'loose' the shoe latchets of Christ; Christ came to make crooked paths straight; the way to heaven is 'strait'; Christ opposed the Jewish vengeance code of an eye for an eye and a tooth for a tooth; the Salvation Army newspaper was (and is) the *War Cry*; Christian teaching makes much of longsuffering). At the end of the passage about this *literatured* closet, we're told that Shem, 'self exiled in upon his ego ... writing the mystery of himself', is 'Tumult, son of Thunder'. His noisy closet is, of course, a thunder-box (thunder-boxes were commodes, or portable lavatories, slangily considered). But more, in the New Testament the Sons of Thunder were James and John in their vengeful, power-seeking role:Shem/James (and James Joyce was the son of John Joyce) is the sort of disciple Christ said that he preferred not to have. The son in the thunder-box.

And so one could go on. There's much more where all this comes from. And *Finnegans Wake* does go on and on, ballooningly, monstrously on, in this anti-Christian, heretical, blasphematory vein, to which it carefully and constantly calls the reader's attention. The realm of this text is the *supernoctural* (598:17). Its signs are *sacred scriptured sign[s]* (356:24–25). It is a *holycryptogram* (546:13), an *epistle*, or *epiepistle*, that is *our scripture* (121:21) and a *godsend* (269:17), travelling through the mails carried by postman Shaum, that is the *holy post* (237:20). It is willingly acting as the anti-Scripture that the Bible itself fears ('another Gospel that is not another'); it is *my otherchurch's in her light* (546:21), a new synoptic Gospel, the Gospel of Shem/James the son of John, 'Synopticked on the word' (367:17): 'Mattheehew, Markeehew, Lukeehew Johnheehewheehew! Haw! ... So, to john for a john, johnajeams, led it be!' (399:29–34).

'Renove that bible' is *Finnegans Wake*'s brisk imperative (579:10), recalling the story of Cromwell's impatience with the mace in the House of Commons, 'Take away that bauble': remove the Bible, the Biblical bauble, and put in its place a renovated Bible, in other words *Finnegans Wake*, an altogether more valuable text, by no means just a bauble. And as the Biblical Gospels are misprized, hostilely reread, distorted and displaced by *Finnegans Wake*'s busy substitutions, so also is every part of the Big Book. And particularly the Bible's beginning books. *Finnegans Wake* asserts the originating power of language in its secularized version of Scripture. So it is as anxious to take over from the beginning book of Genesis ('In the beginning God created...') as it is to take over from the New Testament's beginning texts, the Gospels, especially of course *St John* ('In the beginning was the Word'). So the Fall of Adam and Eve in the Garden of Eden takes place in a version of Dublin's Phoenix Park and their Original Sin is replaced by all of this text's many sexual misdemeanours and by the violences that also occur in the Park. The *felix culpa* becomes a set of *foenix culprit[s]* (23:16). The involvement of the sons of Noah, Shem and Japheth, in the sin of their brother Ham who looked upon his father's nakedness in *Genesis* – the Old Testament's primal Oedipal scene, if you discount Adam's earlier transgression against his author/father God – turns into the misdemeanours of Shem and the whole slate of voyeuristic pursuits that *Finnegans Wake* presents. As a confusion of tongues, at Babel/Babylon and on the Day of Pentecost, straddles the Old and the New Testaments, linking its old beginning with its new one, making Biblical beginning an affair of puzzling language and language puzzle and joining the Bible's two great opposed urban centres Babylon and Jerusalem in verbal chaotics, so Joyce's apocalyptic city-scape declares itself *our tour of bibel* (523:32).

The note of this vast piece of city literature literatured upon the Bible adopts the note of the Biblical writing about those antithetical great symbolic towns, and it's the note, the textuality, of babble: in *Finnegans Wake* pervasively the babbling of ALP the river-woman, which is just one of the rationales for the punning babble and Babel that the text comprises. The *confusium* of tongues here (15:12) is a redoing and undoing of Babel or of Pentecost: *no pentecostal jest about it* (99:21), a speaking in *diversed tonguesed* (381:20), a *pentecostitis* (130:9). (The pentecostal Holy Ghost, the dove of the Christ's baptismal scene, the creative Spirit of God brooding over the face of the waters in Genesis – a creature absorbed into the airborne preoccupations of Stephen in *A Portrait* and obsessively recurrent in *Ulysses* as the sacred pigeon (for example in the 'anastomosis of navelcords' passage in 'Oxen of the Sun') – is granted a freshened existence as *Finnegans Wake's* Hen, 'that original hen' (110:22), the layer and the reader of the

text (a lay-reader one might call her), who puts 'hen to paper' and
so is both the womb and the site of 'pigeony linguish' (584:4)
'Lead, kindly fowl!(112:9).) The density of this book's play with
Biblicism is visible as soon as the reader enters it, in its early play
with the early books of the Bible, its endeavour to go beyond
them, to outwit the Pentateuch and rebuild it (and the tower of
Babel) within a zealously marginalising intent, to outdo by
redoing that old Babel blasphemy:

Bygmester Finnegan, of the Stuttering Hand, freemen's maurer, lived in the
broadest way immarginable in his rushlit toofarback for messuages before
joshuan judges had given us numbers or Helveticus committed deuteronomy
(one yeastyday he sternely struxk his tete in a tub for to watsch the future of his
fates but ere he swiftly stook it out again, by the might of moses, the very water
was eviparated and all the guenneses had met their exodus so that ought to
show you what a pentschanjeuchy chap he was!) and during mighty odd years
this man of hod, cement and edifices in Toper's Thorp piled buildung supra
buildung pon the banks for the livers by the Soangso ... Oftwhile balbulous,
mithre ahead, with goodly trowel in grasp and ivorioled overalls which he
habitacularly fondseed, like Haroun Childeric Eggeberth he would caligulate
by multiplicables the alltitude and malltitude until he seesaw by neatlight of the
liquor wheretwin 'twas born, his roundhead staple of other days to rise in
undress maisonry upstanded (joygrantit!), a waalworth of a skyerscape of
most eyeful hoyth entowerly, erigenating from next to nothing and
celescalating the himals and all, hierarchitectitiptitoploftical, with a burning
bush abob off its baubletop and with larrons o'toolers clittering up and
tombles a'buckets clottering down (4, 5).

And from the beginning of Finnegans Wake right to its end,
Biblical characters, incidents, writings from end to end of the
Holy Scripture, from *guenneses* to *apolkaloops* as Joyce's text
has it, are all liberally absorbed and with extreme license
transcended. Moses the law-giver and the Books of his Law are
transformed into *this new book of Morses*: the Moses code (more
rigid than the Napoleonic one) is now a sort of Morse code
(123:35) – a cryptic text with (of course, given Joyce's intense
interest in rectums) a *recto* as well as a *verso* side (123:36). The
cryptic passages of Holy Scripture are adopted to bring home
and strengthen the cryptic passages of this *écriture*. The reader is
invited to read *Finnegans Wake* as a version, for instance, of
Daniel's vision:

(Stoop) if you are abcedminded, to this claybook, what curios of signs (please
stoop), in this allaphbed! Can you rede (since We and Thou had it out already)

its world? It is the same told of all. Many. Miscegenations on miscegenations. Tieckle. They lived und laughed ant loved end left. Forsin. Thy thingdome is given to the Meades and Porsons. The meandertale, aloss and again, of our old Heidenburgh in the days when Head-in-Clouds walked the earth. In the ignorance that implies impression that knits knowledge that finds the nameform that whets the wits that convey contacts that sweeten sensation that drives desire that adheres to attachment that dogs death the bitches birth that entails the ensuance of existentiality. But with a rush out of his navel reaching the reredos of Ramasbatham. A terriculous vivelyonview this; queer and it continues to be quaky. A hatch, a celt, an earshare...(18).

Finnegans Wake feeds grandly in fact, on the Biblical texts. *Credo* becomes *Greedo*; rosary beads become *grocery beans*; the daily bread of the Lord's Prayer becomes *daggily broth*; scripture becomes *scripchewer* (411). This text's God-directed Oedipus Complex is indeed an *eatupus complex* (128:36). Shem's excremental ink is the result of a lot of chewing over of Biblical materials. It's also the result of having swallowed a lot of liturgical stuff. 'His hungry will be done! On the continent as in Eironesia' (411:11) *Finnegans Wake* repeatedly offers variants like this on the Lord's Prayer (always seeking to replace the paternal addressee of the orthodox Paternoster by the maternal Hen/Anna, or by Shem the Son, or by language itself), just as it repeatedly does its own undoing versions of all sorts of other parts of the litanies, offices, services of the Church (baptisms, marriages, funerals), of benedictions, of the whole apparatus of Holy Days, saints, prophets, priests, arks, temples, tabernacles, synagogues, sermons.

And these greedy ingestings and reworkings of the words of the Bible and the Christian tradition are all centred in the text's, and Shem's liturgical and credal (mis)appropriation of the Logos Christ's activity and status in their marriage of Biblicism with the post-Biblical: 'My unchanging Word is sacred. The word is my Wife, to expanse and expound, to vend and to velnerate, and may the curlews crown our nuptias! Till Breath us depart! Wamen.... The ring man in the rong shop but the rite words by the rote order!... That mon that hoth no moses in his sole nor is not awed by conquists of word's law...if he came to my preach...[etc]' (167, 168). A marriage ceremony of the word, a preaching, an amalgamation of ritual and poetry (the right words in the right order varies Coleridge's famous definition of poetry as 'the *best* words in the best order'), the

declaration of writing's new sacredness, of a new legal regime of
the word, 'word's law'. Law and reading keep converging in the
Joycean text: at least we're encouraged to suppose and perceive
their convergence by that most interesting passage in Beckett's
essay in *Our Exagmination*[31] on the subject of the etymology of
the Latin word *legere*: *lex* (a gathering of laws), i.e. *Law*, giving
rise eventually to *legere*, to read, which is traditionally the
following of textual, verbal laws. And the reader is being offered
here a new law by a new Logos, Shem the new Christ, the self-
fathering Son, 'excruciated ... bound to the cross of your own
cruelfiction' (192:18), a form of crucifixion that aims to achieve
not justification but only *Just a Fication* (241:36). No wonder,
then, that such christological concepts and claims are repeatedly
applied to *Finnegans Wake*'s doings, that its status as a
crossword puzzle, a linguistic game, a verbal parcel simply there
for the unpacking, or parsing, a *crossmess parzel* (619:5) has
strong overtones of Christ's birthday celebrations, Christmas,
and of the Word on the saving cross of the crucifixion, a Calvary
that became the occasion of the church's celebratory
feasts – messes or masses, and that the verbal play of *Finnegans
Wake* (play both as game and as theatre) is presented as
theological or post-theological play: a *pantheomime* (180:4), a
theogamyjig (332:24).

It's small wonder, either, that Berkeley, the Irish Bishop who
sited the guarantee and ground of reality in the mind of God, is
displaced by Archdruid 'pidgin fella Balkelly' who comes on
(in what is, admittedly, a particularly knotty passage even by
Finnegans Wake's standards, 611, 612) to insist on a God-less
ontology ('he savvy inside true inwardness of reality'), an
inwardness readily absorbed into the mind, as it were, of the
text, 'the Ding hvad in idself id est'. Significantly, Balkelly is
opposed by what appear to be the reactionary arguments of
'Same Patholic', an orthodox Catholic whose name recalls the
unchanging conservatism of the followers of St Patrick, who
pushes orthodox linguistic opinions: reality, he argues, mirrors
God ('his fiery grassbelonghead all show colour of sorrelwood
herbgreen': i.e. (Irish) grass is green because the Christian God
is an Irishman and green with the colour of Irish nationalistic
fervours), and language mirrors that divinely sustained reality
in a set of *sound sense sympol[s]*. But this divinity is made

ridiculously autocratic in an accelerating rush of abusive titles (High Thats Hight Uberking Leary, Exuber High Ober King Leary, Most Highest Ardreetsar King, High High Siresultan Emperor, Highup Big Cockywocky Sublissime Autocrat); and the orthodox linguistic theory He is alleged to sustain is declared to be too *sympol* in its notion of language symbolizing the world, i.e. not clever enough. The 'mind', the inwardness of language and the text, is not a symbol of the real world anymore than the inwardness of 'the real world' is a reflection of the mind of God. If there be any Berkeleyan Godlikeness it's now all textual.

The mind of James Joyce was, of course, as Cranly gibed at Stephen Dedalus in *A Portrait*, 'supersaturated with the religion in which you say you disbelieve'. And even if Joyce had had few, or no, ulterior intentions in deploying such material, he would doubtless still have quoted, parodied, reworked, blasphemously redone the Biblical and Catholic text in which he had been brought up. Joking James found it natural to be a Joking Jesus. But *Finnegans Wake* and the *oeuvre* of which it is the extraordinary culmination (a *culmen*, or summit, dedicated to the *culs, cula*, or backsides that preoccupy it), take us beyond the accidental debris and detritus of a Christian childhood and education, and beyond the mere love of jesting blasphemies. Joyce, we discover, did indeed imagine himself to be, like Shem, a writing Christ. In September 1905, for instance, in a letter to his brother Stanislaus that denounces the literary world (and *The Literary World*) for not noticing his genius, he says that he must 'get rid of these Jewish bowels I have in me yet' (more bowels!) and he then addresses to a vague deity a prayer for an un-Christlike revenge upon the Judases who annoy him (an angry prayer, 'not identical', he says, with the soothing prayer offered on the Acropolis by Ernest Renan, another lapsed Christian and a learned delver into languages who for his own part tried to undo and re-do the life of Jesus):

Give me for Christ' sake a pen and an ink-bottle and some peace of mind and then, by the crucified Jaysus, if I don't sharpen that little pen and dip it into fermented ink and write tiny little sentences about the people who betrayed me send me to hell. After all, there are many ways of betraying people. It wasn't only the Galilean suffered that.

'Ah Jolas', Joyce is said to have said when Jolas guessed what *Work in Progress* was finally to be titled, 'you've taken something out of me', thus revealing that writing, and particularly writing *Finnegans Wake*, was for him a kind of signmaking akin to Christ's own performing of miracle-signs (Jesus felt that 'virtue' had 'gone out of' Him when the hem of his garment was touched and health was so gained by the woman with the 'issue of blood'). And if Joyce was, in such wild surmises, a rival to the Divine Logos, his largest textual endeavour fell readily into place as a usurping Scripture. The *Wake*'s cryptogrammic, anagrammatical secrets, designed to give curious readers endless Biblical pause, its *sigla* conscious of their close kinship with the charts of Hebrew letters drawn up by the Cabbalists to show the hermeneutical rules by which the Biblical mysterium was to be unlocked (see, e.g., Christian D. Ginsburg's *The Kabbalah: Its Doctrines, Developments and Literature, An Essay*, 1865, 49–56), its repeated plunge into the hinterlands of language, into and (even) beyond alphabeticism, into a condition previous to regular grammar and syntax and word-formation, the *pre-*, *pro-*, *proto-*, *fore-*, *arch-*, *epi-*, and *ante-* condition of language that so many of *Finnegans Wake's* vocables announce, the text's craving for *decomposition* (614:34), for the *abnihilisation of the etym* (353:22), *Nomomorphemy* (599:18), for the scrambled linguistic condition of the hupogrammatical Christ: none of these are unselfconscious or accidental. As Justius says to Shem (188):15–19): 'condemned fool, egoarch, hiresiarch, you have reared your disunited kingdom on the vacuum of your own most intensely doubtful soul. Do you hold yourself then for some god in the manger, Shehohem, that you will neither serve nor let serve, pray nor let pray?' Stephen Dedalus's Satanic *Non serviam* was a private act of defiance against Catholic belief, mother, and all priests and other Fathers of the Church. Shem's text is not so much a private retreat, but rather a challenging public act of massive displacement, In 1937 Ezra Pound referred to *Work in Progress* as *'transition* crap', 'that diarrhoea of consciousness', which is apt enough. He also called it 'Jheezus in progress', which is apter still (letter to Hilaire Hiler, 10 March 1937).

God in the manger; Jheezus in progress; No cods before Me
(579:21–22). The wishes of James Joyce and *Finnegans Wake*
are clear. But wishes must not be taken for accomplishments,
especially in dreams and in a text which purports like *Finnegans
Wake* to be a very long piece of Freudian nightwork. So one
has to ask whether *Finnegans Wake* actually fulfills its ambitions. And whether the self-perceived nature and ambitions of
the other would-be absolute modernist textualities I have related
to Joyce's project – Freud's pun-world, his dreaming texts,
Saussurean anagrammaticalising linguistics, Surrealism's defiant setting aside of contingency – hold water. It seems evident
that in quite fundamental ways they do not, and the house that
Jolas built is only (in a suggestion of the *Wake* itself) 'the hoose
that Joax pilled', Jolas's hoaxing joke or jokey hoax (369:15).

The modernistic ludus may think of itself as a strong and
adequate displacement of the old God-centred logocentrism
('Play', as Edward Said puts it in his *Beginnings*, 1975, 'which is
another way of characterizing the totality of structures in
language as they reflect one another, is supplementary to
absence').[32] *Les plaisirs du texte*, of the text secularized and
modernist, think of themselves as ruling very nicely in the
absence of God. But the quest for this sort of ludicity, this post-
sacred lusiveness, proves troublingly elusive and is perhaps in
the end even quite delusive. It has always been difficult for
sober Christians, let alone religious sceptics, to accept the non-
contingent absoluteness of God's world and God's Word or
Textuality – (Borges: 'It is doubtful that the world has a
meaning; it is even more doubtful that it has a double or triple
meaning'). It's harder still to accept the absoluteness of
Finnegans Wake or any other of the modernist texts. At
least – and in the fashion of those theologicans and Biblical
critics who have long urged on Christians a different hermeneutics from the Cabbalists or their modern half-sisters the
fundamentalists, a hermeneutics that will respect the historical
(ideological, anthropological, biographical) contingencies that
have gone into the Bible's many stages of writing and layerings
of interpretation—one does want to mention a few basic
hurdles to any argument about the absoluteness of Joyce's
most massive production.

If, for instance, the mind of this text is uncontingent, if its

words are a steep dive into the a-historical linguistic inwardness of mere signifiers, how are we to account (to take only a
clutch of the most obvious examples) for the presence of such
twenties and thirties phenomena as *Kodak* (171:32) and
bungaloid (471:12), sky-signs (4:13), BBC broadcasts and
radio language generally (359f), Heinz beans (*Heinz cans
everywhere*, 581:5, just one more of HCE's manifestations),
Groups (Oxford Groups and the like (365:20), the Thirties
hiking/shorts/outdoor cult (437), a Belisha beacon (267:12),
Hitler's road-building ('them new hikler's highways',
410:7–8); for the presence of Marx (365:20), O'Duffy of the
Irish Fascist Blueshirts (84:13–14), Auden (279: footnote),
Woodbine Willy and Choorney Choplain, i.e. Charlie Chaplin,
(351:12–13) and the publisher of *Ulysses*, John Lane (408:33);
or for references to *Our Exagmination* ('what sublation of
compensation in the radification of interpretation by the
byeboys', 369:6–7), or to Eliot's *The Waste Land* ('Shainti and
shaunti and shaunti again!', 408:33–4). Such historical allusions are almost innumerable in *Finnegans Wake*. The many
intertextual references to bits of literature, titles and authors
and contents of books can be, of course, at a pinch, winkled
away from history proper – though even here it's patently hard
to rinse the dyes of history off many large particular intertextual presences that figure in *Finnegans Wake* such as
Proust's *A La Recherche*, Wyndham Lewis's *The Childermass*
(355:34), Freud's *Interpretation of Dreams* ('an interpidation
of our dreams', 338:29), Eddington's *The Expanding Universe*
(410:17), titles from *Dubliners* (186) to name only a handful of
the many prominent modern literary allusions that pack this
text, even if it were possible to argue (which I doubt) that the
use of the Bible, the Book of Common Prayer, Shakespeare,
Virgil, Sterne, Tennyson and all the other texts and authors
that have (as we say) entered the language is somehow cleansed
of the taint of the historical, the vexatious diachronic.

Finnegans Wake simply would not exist were it not for the
pre-existence of historical texts and historical phenomena
anterior to itself as text. Dublin, the Phoenix Park, the
Irishman at the Crimean, have become signifier, metaphor,
pseudo-reference all right; but these textual presences are
inseparable from metonym, signified, reference. An army of

puns – such as *Finnegans Wake* indeed is – can only march by courtesy of its stomach-full of predigested linguistic formations. The pun is a parasite. 'Say mangraphique, may say nay por daguerre!' (339:23): yet another textual pronouncement conveys a metatextual comment, about its own mere Writtenness (man(u)-graphicism) and its distance from nineteenth-century photographic realism (Daguerre was an early pioneer of photography, memorialized in the early photographic process of the daguerreotype). But this metatextual sentence is also strikingly a calque, as all puns are in some sense calques, built on the famous words of the observer of the Charge of the Light Brigade at the Crimean War, 'C' est magnifique, mais ce n'est pas la guerre!' As a critical commentary on *Finnegans Wake* this is wittily apt enough. But my immediate point is the line's linguistic and hermeneutic dependence. To read it at all, you need to know about the line it's calqued on; you need, like it is, to be schooled in the doxas of English and French syntax; and you need a sophisticated awareness of the endless critical discussions that have gone on about literary realism, especially in the novel. In other words, this moment of self-declaring *écriture* is indissolubly steeped in historically formed conventions and historical informations. As David Lodge puts it in his *Modes of Modern Writing*, the punning of *Finnegans Wake* is as jumpy as can be, defying sense and the logics of semantics. But -and one wants to rescue his point from the throwaway observation he makes of it – *Finnegans Wake* would have been unintelligible – an outpouring of a truly uninterpretable pentecostal glossalalia – if the historically given orders of grammar had not been obeyed: 'Grammar – the code of combination – is still largely intact. If number and concord are not always strictly correct, word-order (the most important single feature of English syntax) is generally regular ....'

History, context, the given phenomenological realities (discovered realities or invented ones), that exist in and around and before the written letter, and are there before the writer's hand seizes the pen, have a way of re-arriving like this in even the most determinedly post-modernist of scenes: whether in the arrays of precursor poets and interpreters who constitute Harold Bloom's new versions of literary history as angst and

Oedipalism, or in Foucault's archives, or in Barthes's *Tel Quel* affinities and in his 'codes', or in Derrida's repeated admissions (in *Positions*, 1972) that analyses are always made in history and that his work is only possible 'dans une situation historique, politique, théorique, etc., très determinée', or (to case one's eyes lower down the ranges of our modernist pundits) even in the devoted, minute historiography of the post-war deconstructive movement against history which books like Leitch's *Deconstructive Criticism* conduct with such an astonishing eye for detail. Leitch and other hod-carriers of this particular 'revolution' – unaware just how historically conditioned and historically referential their exuberant celebrations of the floating signifier are, and specially unaware of the implications of their blithe repetitions about logocentrism – simply do not know how to cope with this persisting survival of the diachronic, contextual dimensions. 'There is no effort is Miller's project to step abruptly outside the historical enclosure' (Leitch, p. 195). 'For Miller, as for Derrida, there can be no escape outside the tradition' (Leitch, p. 194). Thus Miller and Derrida are left dangling between the begrudged idea that history might be inescapable and the hostile implication that they're not trying as hard as they ought to get their minds and their analyses out of the historical fix and into the 'nothingness' that lies behind the text and the 'world as text'. The irresolution and the difficulty are of Leitch's and all the other not sceptical enough anti-logocentric ideologues' own devising. It's hard to work up much sympathy for the plight they've thus carefully backed their interpretative juggernaut into.

NOTES

1   Ferdinand de Saussure, *Cours de Linguistique Générale*, eds. Charles Bally, Albert Sechehaye and Albert Riedlinger, 1915; trans. W. Baskin (New York: Philosophical Library, 1959); repr. London: Fontana, 1974.
2   J. Derrida, *De La Grammatologie* (Paris: Minuit, 1967); trans. G. Spivak, *Of Grammatology* (Baltimore: Johns Hopkins, 1974).
3   C. MacCabe, *James Joyce and the Revolution of the Word* (London: Macmillan, 1978).

4	J. Hillis Miller, *Fiction and Repetition* (Cambridge: Harvard University Press, 1982).

5	J. Hills Miller, 'The Two Allegories' in ed. M. W. Bloomfield, *Allegory, · Myth, and Symbol* (Harvard English Studies, No. 9, 1981).

6	J. Hills Miller, 'Stevens' Rock and Criticism as Cure', *Georgia Review*, No. 30, 1976, pp. 330–48.

7	J. Derrida, *L'Écriture et la différence* (Paris: Seuil, 1967); trans. A. Bass, *Writing and Difference* (London: Routledge & Kegan Paul, 1978). *Marges de la philosophie* (Paris: Minuit, 1972); trans. *Margins of Philosophy* (University of Chicago Press, 1983). *Glas* (Paris: Galilée, 1974). *Living On: Border Lines*, in H. Bloom *er al, Deconstruction and Criticism* (New York: Seabury, 1979).

8	J. Hills Miller, 'George Poulet's "Criticism of Identification", in ed. O. B. Hardison, *The Quest for Imagination* (Cleveland University Press, 1971). 'On Edge: The Crossways of Contemporary Criticism', *Bulletin of American Arts and Sciences*, Jan. 1979.

9	D. Donoghue, *Ferocious Alphabets* (Boston: Little, Brown, 1981).

10	J. Culler, *On Deconstruction* (London: Routledge & Kegan Paul, 1983).

11	D. Lodge, *The Modes of Modern Writing* (London: Arnold, 1977).

12	F. Kermode, *Essays on Fiction 1971–82* (London: Routledge & Kegan Paul, 1983).

13	ed. R. Young, *Untying the Text* (London: Routledge & Kegan Paul, 1981).

14	V. Leitch, *Deconstructive Criticism* (London: Hutchinson, 1983).

15	J. Derrida, *Positions* (Paris: Minuit, 1972); trans. A. Bass, *Positions* (University of Chicago Press, 1981).

16	Saussure, *op. cit.*, esp. pp. 16–17, & pp. 67–9.

17	R. Barthes, *Image-Music-Text* (London: Fontana, 1977), ed. & trans. Stephen Heath.

18	Lancelot Andrewes, de. G. M. Story, *Sermons* (Oxford: Clarendon Press, 1967).

19	T. S. Eliot, 'Lancelot Andrews', in *Selected Essays* (London: Faber & Faber, 1934).

20	S. Fish, 'Structuralist Homiletics', Part I, chapter 8, *Is There A Text In This Class?* (Cambridge: Harvard University Press, 1980).

21	J. L. Borges, 'The Mirror of Enigmas', in *Other Inquisitions* (New York: Washington Square Press, 1966), pp. 131–4.

22	H. Bloom, *Kabbalah and Criticism* (New York: Seabury, 1975). *Agon: Towards a Theory of Revisionism* (Oxford University Press, 1982).

23	M. Price, *Forms of Life: Character and Moral Imagination in the Novel* (New Haven: Yale University Press, 1983).

24	F. Kermode, *The Genesis of Secrecy* (Cambridge: Harvard University Press, 1979).

25	S. Heath, *The Nouveau Roman* (London: Elek, 1972).

26	M. Norris, *The Decentred Universe of 'Finnegans Wake': A Structuralist Analysis* (Baltimore: Johns Hopkins University Press, 1978).

27	J. Starobinski, *Les Mots Sous Les Mots* (Paris: Gallimard, 1971); trans.

O. Emmett, *Words Upon Words* (New Haven: Yale University Press, 1979).

28   A. Fowler, *Kinds of Literature* (Oxford: Clarendon Press, 1982).

29   M. Ellmann, in ed. R. Young, *op. cit.*, Part III, Chapter 9.

30   ed. R. Ellmann, *Selected Letters of James Joyce* (London: Faber & Faber, 1975).

31   ed. S. Beckett *et al*, *Our Exagmination Round his Factification for Incamination of Work in Progress* (London: Faber & Faber, 1929; new edn, 1972).

32   E. Said, *Beginnings* (Baltimore: Johns Hopkins University Press, 1975).

2 Author–Reader–Language: Reflections on a Critical Closed Circuit

David Morse

Like the dislodgement of Milton, the institutionalization of English literature as an academic discipline was effected with remarkably little fuss. The role of English has been that of a successful usurper, replacing the Classics as the focus of a humanistic education. The price of that usurpation in intellectual terms has been high, because the key assumptions about what constituted a humanistic education were never seriously questioned. English could take the place of Classics, indeed assume the mantle of Classics; for as the study of Greek and Roman authors might appear increasingly arid and remote from the ordinary business of life, so contrariwise it seemed self-evident that the literature of one's own language was accessible, relevant, immediate. But while those who teach Classics have been forced to acknowledge their cultural remoteness and place a historical and sociological understanding at the centre of all attempts to reconstitute the Graeco-Roman world, English has been left to shoulder the humanist burden, which is the tactical and principled, refusal of history. It is tactical because the study of texts in a vacuum is pedagogically simpler, and makes them the more readily adaptable to contemporary didactic purposes; it is principled since the perennial goal of an élite education has been to show, from Plutarch to Goethe, that great men can never be touched, tainted or soiled by the environment in which they are raised. Whether man of action, statesman or artist, whether Nelson, Pericles or Shakespeare, the moral is 'to thine own self be true', where such truth is to be interpreted as a release from the shackles of history. The practice of literary criticism centres

52

repetitively and recurrently around notions of the author, the reader and of language that seek to deliver literature from the banality – and density – of the quotidian.

In general terms the belief the writer transcends his time is one of considerable antiquity, but I believe the particular version of it that enjoys currency has its sources in the Weimar 'Classicism' of Goethe and Schiller. Both were afflicted by the anxiety of the modern; they feared that the degraded world in which they lived might prove disabling and incapacitating for the production of great art. While, arguably Homer, Sophocles and the sculptor of Laocoön merely expressed the spirit of a noble culture, the modern artist was forced to struggle against the grain. So, paradoxically, a classical ideal is also romantic because it predicates a cleavage between the artist and society, and because it turns the artist into a superman. In Goethe's eyes, the romantic writer simply reflects a social malaise, the classic writer distances himself from it. This interpretation left its mark on figures as diverse as Arnold and Nietzsche. Schopenhauer's *Parerga and Paralipomena* offers a representative formulation:

With artists, poets, and authors generally, one of the subjective infections of the intellect is also what we are accustomed to call ideas of the times or at the present day 'consciousness of the times', and thus certain views and notions that are in vogue. The author who is tinged with their colour, has allowed himself to be impressed by them, whereas he should have ignored and rejected them. Now when, after a shorter or longer spell of years, these views have vanished entirely into oblivion, his works of that period which still exist are deprived of the support that they had in such views and then often seem to be inconceivably absurd, or at any rate like an old calendar. It is only the absolutely genuine poet or thinker who rises superior to all such influences.[1]

Art and true poetry are always born from an immaculate conception. Schopenhauer is no doubt that poetry situates itself on the ground of the eternal.

The inaugurating document of modern literary criticism was Eliot's essay 'Tradition and the Individual Talent'. In this essay Eliot synthesized, or violently yoked together, the ostensibly disparate influences of Arnold and Mallarmé. Eliot took from Arnold his sense of culture as 'the best that is known and thought in the world;[2] from Mallarmé, his notion of the poem as a self-contained highly wrought art object. The artist is at once the repository of a cultural tradition and a miraculous medium of transcendence. But, of course, Arnold and Mallarmé also have much in common. Both react against romantic self-expression, both disdain the vulgarity and confusion of the world. For Arnold the highest duty of both poet and critic is the study of perfection and this, in the spirit of the founders of monastic institutions, means turning aside from a complacent, petty and sinful world. Of the education of the poet Arnold writes in his introduction to the poems:

As he penetrates into the spirit of the great classical works, as he becomes gradually aware of their intense significance, their noble simplicity, and their calm pathos, he will be convinced that it is this effect, unity and profoundness of moral impression, at which the ancient poets aimed; that it is this which constitutes the grandeur of their works, and which makes them immortal. He will desire to direct his own efforts towards producing the same effect. Above all, he will deliver himself from the jargon of modern criticism, and escape the danger of producing poetical works conceived in the spirit of the passing time, and which partake of its transitoriness. [3]

The passage is suffused with the ideals and language of Winklemann – the values and goals of art are unchanging, all that can change is the possibility of their realization. The modern artist in turning his back on the 'false pretensions of his age', in cleansing his mind of all pettiness may yet be great. But criticism, too, may lift itself into the realm of spirit and pure intellect; such, Arnold insisted in 'The Function of Criticism at the Present Time', is both its task and moral duty:

It is because criticism has so little kept in the pure intellectual sphere, has so little detached itself from practice, has been so directly polemical and controversial, that it has so ill accomplished, in this country its best spiritual work; which is to keep man from a self-satisfaction which is retarding and vulgarising, to lead him towards perfection, by making his mind dwell upon what is excellent in itself, and the absolute beauty and fitness of things. [5]

Arnold's suggestion that poetry might take the place of religion is well known, yet its full implication, that literature is to be moralized, morals aestheticized, is rarely pondered. The suggestion that art should lead towards perfection makes obscure yet all-embracing claims on art which it is very doubtful that art could satisfy, on even the most lenient of constructions. Yet with Arnold this shades into the implication that art actually does this. But the strange corollary is that the artist could not fulfil this moral function if he were actually to write about his own time. Eliot, of course, does write about his own time nevertheless, as in *The Waste Land*, there is the distinct implication that he could not do so without the heritage of a rich cultural tradition against which it can be weighed in the balance and found wanting. He can write of such things precisely because he is not of it himself. The myth of the poet as adumbrated by T. S. Eliot is a latter-day reincarnation of the theory of the King's two bodies: the poet as ordinary everyday individual, a person very much like you or I, is merely the vessel of a miraculous creative mind that transmutes base metal into gold, and filters out everything that is personal, experiential and contingent. At first sight it would seem we have simply a restatement of the Romantic imagination in impersonal terms, but the implications go deep. For the artist can have no prejudice, no bias, no convictions, no politics, no bugbears or bees in his bonnet, even if the ordinary everyday self does. And perhaps not even this should; the ideal is to be like the dehydrated Henry James of Eliot's projection, with a 'mind so fine that no idea could violate it'.[6] Art, poetry, creativity, by definition involves a severance from the actual historical world. The Fisher King turns his back on the arid plain.

Such a position is always implicitly Romantic because it was Romantic literature that adumbrated such a hypothetical place for itself; but in Eliot's criticism the journeying boat of the visionary imagination was replaced by a filament of platinum that seemed too austere to carry such connotations. It was Lionel Trilling who reclaimed the Romantic spirit in *The Opposing Self*, but in terms far more absolute than the Romantics themselves had used. Trilling did not simply assert the power of the writer to struggle against his time, for such an endeavour would always carry with it the risk of simplification and vulgarity; what he posited was the ideal of a spirit, utterly free, undetermined and untrammelled:

Somewhere in our mental constitution is the demand for life as pure spirit.
    The idea of unconditioned spirit is of course a very old one, but we are probably the first people to think of it as a realizable possibility and to make that possibility part of our secret assumption. It is this that explains the

phenomenon of our growing disenchantment with the whole idea of the political life, the feeling that although we are willing, nay eager, to live in society, for we all piously know that man fulfills himself in society, yet we do not willingly consent to live in a particular society of the present, marked as it is bound to be by a particular economic system, by disorderly struggles for influence, by mere approximations and downright failures.[7]

Arnold, of course stands directly behind this argument, both in the spiritual claims he makes for literature and in his disdain for the anarchy and confusion of a mass culture. For Trilling, it is literature, above all, that can give substance to the dream of a withdrawal and turning aside from the world. With Wordsworth as one of his privileged instances of its tangibility, Trilling invokes:

an intention which is to be discerned through all our literature – the intention to imagine, and to reach, a condition of the soul in which the will is freed from 'particular aims', in which it is 'strong in itself and in beatitude'. At least as early as Balzac our literature has shown the will seeking its own negation – or, rather, seeking its own affirmation by its rejection of the aims which the world sets before it and by turning its energies upon itself in self-realization. Of this particular affirmation of the will Wordsworth is the proponent and the poet.[8]

The longing for transcendence is one that poet and reader share. In Trilling's visionary and quasi-Hegelian perspective, Romantic poetry is but a shadowy adumbration of an impulse towards freedom that can finally come to its fruition in the age of Eisenhower.

In Trilling's criticism the relations established between Romantic literature and psychoanalysis are crucial; his intellectual position is established by weaving a web of connections between them. The conjunction was certainly apposite, for Freud's whole theory is grounded in a sense of the predicament of the individual in relation to culture as it is expounded in Romantic literature. In his essay 'Freud and Literature' Trilling significantly sidestepped the disparaging implications of some of Freud's comments on literature in order to stress Freud's brotherhood with the Romantic imagination. What Trilling calls 'a simple humanitarian optimism',[9] by which he means a politics of the Left, whether in its New Dealer or Communist versions, has proved inadequate because of 'the smallness of its view of the varieties of human possibility, a kind of check on the creative faculties'.[10] By contrast, 'In Freud's view of life no such limitation is implied.'[11] Imagining is to be left to the imagination. In his essay,' Freud: Within and Beyond Culture', Trilling elucidated further grounds for optimism in Freud's work: if literature created the possibility of a self beyond culture, Freud's sense of biological drives in man provides it with scientific support. The assertion of the absolute autonomy of the individual self by Kant, Goethe and Schiller is strangely reborn in the depths of the unconscious, in what Trilling styles: 'a hard, irreducible, stubborn core of biological urgency, and biological necessity, and biological *reason*, that culture cannot reach.'[12] – but which, perhaps not surprisingly, he does not actually designate 'the unconscious'. Through Freud, traditional élitist aspirations can be voiced anew and reiterated with a conviction that proclaims the diversity of the sources by which it is underwritten. Trilling slides from the modern use of the word 'culture' back to a usage that implies self-cultivation and self-development, so that true culture becomes all that finally negates culture, a ladder of liberation that can finally be kicked away:

This intense conviction of the existence of self apart from culture is, as culture well knows, it noblest and most generous achievement. At the present moment it must be thought of as a liberating idea without which our developing ideal of community is bound to defeat itself. We can speak no greater praise of Freud than to say that he placed this idea at the center of his thought.[13]

Yet despite Trilling's conviction and sense of assurance he nevertheless seems to undermine himself: for if what he states is genuinely the case why must he urge it upon us as a 'liberating idea'? Perhaps it is the idea that is all important.

To the idea of a writer freed from all cultural restrictions and restraints corresponds a reader who similarly distances himself from the ambience of his own day. The poet is no longer a man speaking to men but an isolated individual addressing a small and deeply isolated élite. In the work of I. A. Richards, the poet is seen as an expert in communication whose skills call for readers who are correspondingly sensitive and skilled. In *New Bearings in English Poetry* Leavis insists:

The potentialities of human experience in any age are realized only by a tiny minority, and the important poet is important because he belongs to this (and has also, of course, the power of communication).[14]

At a point in time half a century later what seems positively startling is that Leavis should perceive membership of an élite group as absolutely crucial for poetic greatness, taking precedence even over the writer's facility with words, 'his habit of seeking by the evocative use of words to sharpen his awareness of his ways of feeling, so making these communicable.'[15]

It is this tiny minority that is in possession of significant and enduring values – the task of the poet is to give them full and adequate expression. The way in which author, reader and poetic language are linked together can be brought out by Leavis's comments on Pope. Through the medium of poetry Pope is able to reach out across time and to separate himself from his own: 'Pope's greatness, we remind ourselves is of such a kind as to enable him to transcend his age.'[16] A scholarly apparatus of footnotes that seeks to explain the *Dunciad* is superogatory: 'The poetry doesn't depend upon them in any essential respect.'[17] The dimming of the referentiality of the *Dunciad* is a positive asset, for it can now be read as *poetry* instead of as an historically situated and allusive discourse that sends the reader away from the words on the page:

For eighteenth-century readers it must have been hard not to start away continually from the poetry to thinking about the particular historical victim and the grounds of Pope's animus against him; for modern readers it should be much easier to appreciate the poetry as poetry – to realize that Pope has created something the essential interest of which lies within itself, in what it is.[18]

Like a powerful sea hawk the poet shakes the droplets of the contingent from his wings and soars into the purest empyrean, where true comprehension lies. Along with many other critics of the time, Leavis takes it for granted that the modern reader, by virtue of his scrupulosity – and, one might add, his ignorance – is afforded a peculiarly privileged position for the study of poetry.

I. A. Richards in *Practical Criticism*, by displaying at length the inaccurate, irrelevant and inconsequential nature of many responses to the reading of poetry made it indispensable that the reader be seen as a *skilled* reader. But this skill is never seen as requiring specific knowledge or historical understanding in a context of poetry as effective communication. What is called for is attentiveness and concentration, like listening to a rather weak signal on the radio. In Richards's model of good communication it is never entirely clear where the onus lies; on the one hand it is up to the writer as a skilled communicator to control the responses of his readers; yet, at the same time, the reader has to be on his guard against rambling off along a path of blurred and highly subjective associations. The dual thrust of Richards's theory comes out in his statement: 'Keats, by universal qualified opinion, is a more efficient poet than Wilcox'[19] – so that, as it were, there can be no doubt at all about Keats's effectiveness, since that is the testimony of those who know what effectiveness is. By the same token, presumably, it would take a person well-versed in electricity to know that he had received a powerful electric shock. Richards is in no doubt that in the human animal there lurks a strong propensity to like bad poetry, and that only good poetry can cure it. In a way this is up to the poet:

The dangers are that the recollected feelings may overwhelm and distort the poem and that the reader may forget that the evocation of somewhat similar feelings is probably only a part of the poem's endeavour. It exists perhaps to *control and order* such feelings and to bring them into relation with other things, not merely to arouse them.[20]

But it is also up to the reader who must strenuously endeavour to derive out the demon within:

The alluring solicitancy of the bad, the secret repugnancy of the good are too strong for us in most reading of poetry. Only by penetrating far more whole-mindedly into poetry than we usually attempt, and by collecting all our energies in our choice, can we overcome these treacheries within us. That is why good reading, in the end, is the whole secret of good judgement'.[21]

So poetry can win us for the good against the grain of our own nature, but only through a long and strenuous novitiate of 'practical criticism'.

The problem of the relationship of good writing to good reading, the question as to whether the writer was able to control the response of the reader vexed, mystified and bemused the New Criticism. Empson, closest to Richards, was in no doubt that he could. Imagery, according to Empson was a crucial mode of compulsion:

> The only way of forcing the reader to grasp your total meaning is to arrange that he can only feel satisfied if he is bearing all the elements in his mind at the moment of conviction; the only way of not giving something heterogenous is to give something which is at every point a compound.[22]

But would the average reader have been half-nelsoned in the direction of readings as ingenious as those of Empson himself – presumably not, so even here a skilled and receptive reader is implied. For Wilson Knight, the true reader is a passive reader who gives himself up totally to the experience that poetic language offers; he invokes 'That consciousness we can enjoy at will when we submit ourselves with utmost passivity to the poet's work.'[23] Both L. C. Knights and D. W. Harding try to find a formula that will straddle the gap. In his *Explorations*, Knights asserts: 'Read with attention, the plays themselves will tell us how to read them';[24] while Harding, with even-handed justice argues:

> Failing to get the response we hope for from our hearers is admittedly a failure in speech, and can scarcely be counted a success in literature, whether it results from the author's failure to guide the reader's response or the reader's failure to take that guidance.[25]

In all these elaborate discussions, the odd implications of the élitist position they assumed were scarcely considered. It would appear that a Shakespeare play communicates more effectively than an Edgar Wallace thriller. The argument, of course is that the Shakespearean use of language is more disciplined than that of Edgar Wallace, but the problem of arguing Shakespeare's superiority in terms of communication is that it leads to the assumption that we will fully understand it if only we give ourselves up to the language. That an unprepared spectator might attend a performance of *Love's Labour's Lost* and be hard-pressed to understand a line scarcely enters into their moralistic calculations.

Skilled reading becomes a trans-historical discipline that can purge its exponent of all bias, prejudice and error. Derek

Traversi in his *An Approach to Shakespeare* stands as confidently before his images as Ranke before his documents:

> Even in the case of a single word, or an isolated image, there is a constant need of discipline if we are not to read our own interests into Shakespeare's; and yet the word and the image through which its relations are multiplied are obviously the simplest units at our disposal. Working on the basis offered by a dispassionate attention to verbal quality, it may be possible to reinterpret the critical discoveries of the past, of whatever period, and to clear them of at least a portion of the partiality which they owed to historical circumstance; and we may even aspire, in some degree, to the correction of our own partiality.[26]

Attendance to the texture of language brings with it a special kind of authority. The critic in Wimsatt's definition is a 'teacher or explicator of meanings'.[27]

Thinking about language, and especially poetic language, is the core of the New Criticism's endeavour and its intellectual legacy. Here again Richards was influential, since it was his distinction between the language of science and the language of poetry that shaped all subsequent discussion. Science dealt with facts, poetry dealt with feelings; scientific language was denotative, while in poetry connotation was more crucial; science made statements, while poetry deployed ambiguity, irony, paradox. With hindsight, it can be seen that while the concern to identify the distinctive features of poetry was productive in directing attention to the complexities and perplexities of language, the need to define poetry through its difference from other types of activity produced quite excessive restrictions on what poetry either could be or was. In searching for an impregnable position from which to defend poetry against the assaults of scientific rationalism, the new apologists for poetry gave up too much territory, and, as the surrounding countryside was ravaged, stood helplessly by within the safety of city walls. Poetry became a very tenuous and fragile, though subtle, thing. In the first place, since it was the province of science to issue authoritative pronouncements about the real world – and since, presumably, less authoritative pronouncements would not do – the task of the poet was primarily to report on his own subjective experiences. Yet even here there were dangers and pitfalls for the expression of feeling risked sentimentality and mawkishness and hence became bad poetry, while experience itself was nothing if not transformed and transmuted in the processes of composition. While Richards's successors could not accept the pejorative connotations of such terms used by Richards as 'emotive language' and 'pseudo-statement', they nevertheless implicitly accepted his idea that poetry depends on beliefs that are 'objectless, which are not about anything or in anything'.[28] In this way the theory of Richards and the example of Mallarmé proved mutually reinforcing. Secondly, the concern to define poetic language and to distinguish it from prose produced not always acknowledgement assumptions about pure poetry. If prose is expository and referential, then poetry cannot be limited to this; so Pope is not to be seen as commentator on his age, but as a contriver of vivid images and startling juxtapositions. Poe's suggestion that poetry was primarily a matter of moments and flashes and that there could be no genuine poem over a hundred lines found a ready echo. Part of the objection to Milton was not that he had written *Paradise Lost* in Latin, but that he had written a very long poem that could not be poetry all the way through. The New Critics reduced all literature to poetic language; such notions as ode, epic, novel, play were effaced as all longer works were subsumed under the title of 'dramatic poem'. So there can be no awareness of the cultural and historical specificity of literary forms, of the context in which they figure, the audience to which they are addressed, the expectations they arouse, the ideology and values they articulate. 'Poetry' is what the eighteenth century understood by 'The Sublime'. Finally, poetry could not concern itself with ideas, since this was the province of philosophy – or even religion. Richards insisted that the poet should not make assertions, but positively refrain from so doing. Here Richards and Eliot were in agreement, since Eliot felt that Keats ruined the 'Ode on a Grecian Urn' by collapsing into an assertion at the end. Yet the general worry about philosophy was odd, since it is hard to see why it should have exclusive possession of ideas; there are ideas that animate politics, fishing, the study of language, business, the law, driving, gambling – in fact, the whole range of human activity, whether profound or trivial. The valid perception that poetry is not purely propositional slipped and skidded into an absurd anathema directed against ideas in general, prompted as much by a suspicion of the prophetic claims of the Romantic poets as by a mistrust of ideology. Moreover, the enterprise was doubly questionable, because these critics knew very well that not merely poetry in general, but even the poetry they singled out for explication and praise was riddled with ideas, beliefs and assertions – and, contrariwise, I will go so far to assert, could not have been poetry without them – so that their privileged method of reading, as it paraded its scrupulous analysis, was simply a way of pretending that these ideas were not there.

The differentiation of the language of poetry from the language of science had very complex and far-reaching ramifications. For if poetic language is not that of clear, direct and unambiguous statement; if, in the modern period especially it tends to a compression, density and obliquity verging on obscurity; and if the writing of poetry involves a juggling with the plurisignificative possibilities of language, then it becomes increasingly difficult to imagine that the poet exercises the degree of control that Richards had posited. The poet instead of triumphantly planting his flag on the summits of meaning, appears dangerously perched on the lip of a volcano; the all-powerful magician increasingly figures as a blundering sorcerer's apprentice, whose spectacular effects may be as much the product of inadvertence as design. This alarming prospect is opened up by John Crowe Ransom in the final Essay of his *The New Criticism*, 'Wanted: "An Ontological Critic".' The thrust of this essay is to serve as a corrective to Richards and to place the science/poetry distinction on what Ransom believes to be a more satisfactory basis. By defining the poem as an icon, Ransom seeks an understanding of the poem as a created object like a painting, rather than in terms of communication. By stressing what he calls the 'ontological dimension' of poetry he seeks to restore the cognitive dimension to poetry that Richards had substantively denied:

Poetry intends to recover the denser and more refractory original world which we know loosely through our perceptions and memories. By this supposition it is a kind of knowledge which is radically or ontologically distinct.[29]

Ransom's definition of a poem as 'a loose logical structure with an irrelevant local texture'[30] recalls the denotation/connotation distinction; but since the poetry is in the irrelevant texture, then a diminution of logical structure seems implied, in the spirit of Eliot's:

The chief use of the 'meaning' of a poem, in the ordinary sense, may be ... to keep his mind diverted and quiet, while the poem does its work upon him: much as the imaginary burglar is always provided with a bit of nice meat for the household dog.[31]

For Ransom, indeterminacy – that is to say, irrelevant local texture – is crucial to a definition of the poetical and, in traditional poetry at least, it is produced by rhyme and metre. Apparently echoing Eliot's trope, Ransom writes:

It is a discourse which does not bother too much about the perfection of its logic; and does bother a great deal, as if it were life and death about the positive quality of that indeterminate thing which creeps in by the back door of metrical necessity.[32]

Ransom draws a distinction, however, between an indeterminacy 'that means inaccuracy and confusion' and a higher indeterminacy that opens up 'a new world of discourse'.[33] And in fact, at this point, Ransom turns the tables, privileging structure over texture, by showing how indeterminacy drives the logic out of passages from Wordsworth, Pope, Milton and Marvell. However, Ransom subsequently praises the indeterminacy of part, at least of Marvell's 'To his Coy Mistress':

As for Marvell, we are unwilling to praise or to condemn the peccadilloes of his logic.... This is all overshadowed, and we are absorbed, by the power of his positive particulars, so unprepared for by his commonplace argument.[34]

This teasing paradox comes as something of an anti-climax. Ransom goes on to associate positive indeterminacy with the use of images, which would then seem to imply that rhyme can only be deleterious. In modern poetry, he argues, the poet seeks indeterminacy directly, while eschewing rhyme: 'The effect is an ontological density which proves itself by logical obscurity.'[35] According to Ransom, what characterizes the work of the important modern poet, such as Pound, Eliot, Tate or

Stevens is 'the perfect poetic phrase' which stands 'isolated in the context of indeterminacy'.[36] So it would seem that this pure poetry is somehow the product of a poetic indeterminacy yet somehow to be distinguished from it. Indeed, in this concluding reference, indeterminacy appears as that which has to be negated. The see-saw of alternation cannot, apparently, be evaded.

In his preface to *The New Criticism*, Ransom cited R. P. Blackmur as an exemplary modern critic, but whereas in Ransom questions of indeterminacy and logical obscurity take the form of a theoretical puzzle, in Blackmur's reading of poetry they acquire disturbing and puzzling evaluative implications. Blackmur acquired great influence as a critic because he tackled the difficulties and opaquenesses of such modern poets as Yeats, Eliot, Stevens and Hart Crane head-on in a commentary that was subtle, discriminating, illuminating and authoritative. Blackmur had not only assimilated the methods and concepts of the New Criticism: he was able to deploy them flexibly and unobtrusively in a way that gave the reader confidence that criticism was fully able to pick up the gauntlet that modern poetry had thrown down. Blackmur seemed acutely aware that poetry involved a complex balancing act, as daunting as riding a unicycle across a tightrope. In Yeats, the meanings so multiply and proliferate that any notion that they are under control seems quite unthinkable:

There are meanings over the horizon, meanings that loom, and meanings that heave like the sea-swell under the bows, and among them, when you think of them all, it is hard to say which is which, since any one gradually passes through the others.... To elaborate further is vain waste, for with what we have the context begins to draw the meanings in, and begins to illustrate, too, in passing, to what degree the poet using this mode of language cannot help ad libbing, playing, with his most inevitable-seeming words: he cannot possibly control or exclude or include all their meanings.[37]

Whether to celebrate such an unconstrained play of language is, for Blackmur, always a difficult question; indeed, it cannot be responded to in such programmatic terms. It is a matter of nice judgement and calls for all the powers of discrimination that the critic is capable of. In the case of a lengthy discussion of Stevens' use of the word 'funest' (in 'Of the Manner of

Addressing Clouds'), Blackmur suggests that it somewhat stretches the dictionary sense of the word, and his comments imply that to do this may be a risk, an undesirable verbal nullity. However, Blackmur concludes that it is justified in this case because it does signify in this specific context:

The meaning so doubles upon itself that it can be understood only in context. It is the context that is stretched by the insertion of the word funest; and it is that stretch, by its ambiguity, that adds to our knowledge.[38]

Blackmur validates the 'nonsense' of Stevens' 'Disillusionment of Ten O'Clock' as follows:

The statement about catching tigers in red weather coming after the white nightgowns and baboons and periwinkles, has persuasive force out of all relation to the sense of the words. Literally, there is nothing alarming in the statement, and nothing ambiguous, but by so putting the statement that it appears as nonsense, infinite possibilities are made terrifying and plain. The shock and virtue of nonsense is this: it compels us to scrutinise the words in such a way that we see the enormous ambiguity in the substance of every phrase, every image, every word.[39]

So Stevens' poem is not simply nonsense, but a meta-statement about the nature of language itself, in which the absence of sense as clear and unproblematic meaning exhibits all the more clearly the vertiginous and destabilizing possibilities that language can generate. Blackmur continues:

The edge between sense and nonsense is shadow thin, and in all our deepest convinctions we hover in the shadow, uncertain whether we know what our words mean, nevertheless bound by the conviction to say them.[40]

This is a dark saying itself in more than one sense. On the one hand, Blackmur suggests that sense is barely snatched from the flames of nonsense and obscurity, but that it is nevertheless retrieved; on the other, he intimates that our belief that we do know what we mean is simply necessary for our existence and amounts to little more than a whistling in the dark. So this edge is both an edge and not an edge, marking the desire to believe an edge exists. And Blackmur in deciphering poetic obscurity is forced to acknowledge that his decipherment is as much an act of faith as the poet's ciphering. The critic rises to a poetic ambiguity of his own.

Yet Blackmur can be critical of poetic difficulty and obscurity, and it is by no means certain that he abandons the New Critics' concern with the ordering, controlling and disciplining role of the poet. In his essay 'A Critic's Job of Work' Blackmur alludes with apparent approval to the coadunative power of the Romantic imagination – 'the power of imaginative apprehension, of imaginative co-ordination of varied and separate elements'[41] – yet his own analysis of language seems to hint at the words' corkscrewing and wriggling out of this unificatory grasp. For instance: Blackmur is critical of the poetry of Hart Crane because he does not feel that Crane is in control of what he is doing. Crane's phrase 'ripe/Borage of death' may carry positive or negative connotations, or both at once; but Blackmur feels that the whole endeavour has become too undecidable to be praiseworthy:

> In any case a guess is ultimately worthless because, with the defective syntax, the words do not verify it. Crane had a profound feeling for the heart of words and how they beat and cohabited, but here they overtopped him; the meanings in the words themselves are superior to the use to which he put them. The operation of selective cross-pollination not only failed, but was not even rightly attempted. The language remains in the condition of that which it was intended to express: in the flux of intoxicated sense; whereas the language of the other lines of this poem here examined – the language not the sense – is disintoxicated and candid. The point is that the quality of Crane's success is also the quality of his failure, and the distinction is perhaps by the hair of accident.[42]

By his reference to 'the flux of intoxicated sense' Blackmur adopts the tone of Eliot or Leavis towards Shelley: Crane has got carried away with language, his perceptions are blurred, he is using words without really knowing what they mean. Certainly Crane has often been seen as a latter-day Shelley. But since Blackmur has granted the poet's right to difficulty and obscurity, which many critics do not, his task is to distinguish good from bad obscurity, as Ransom's was to distinguish good from bad indeterminacy. Moreover, since Blackmur has conceded that the poet cannot control all the implications of the words he uses, how can he baulk at the multiple significances generated by Crane. Crane is criticized for his defective syntax, yet Blackmur would have to concede that such tortuous syntax is characteristic of modern poetry. So what we are left with is

Blackmur's seat-of-pants feeling that with 'funest' Stevens just got it right and with 'borage' Crane just got it wrong.

But of all the New Critics it is Cleanth Brooks (as in *The Well Wrought Urn*) who is most disposed to emphasize the problematic nature of language and the dilemmas and puzzles bound up with the poet's task. Brooks himself is by no means a difficult critic, especially if we compare him with either Blackmur or Ransom, for he makes a particular effort to be understood by the reader. His methods of reading become the more accessible because they are brought to bear on some of the best-known texts of English poetry. However, it was felt by many of his contemporaries that Brooks, in making 'paradox' a defining characteristic of poetry, both over-extended the notion and applied it to a range of verse where its relevance was by no means evident. Brook's method amounted to treating all poetry as if it were metaphysical poetry. With Brooks's criticism, the thrust of a stress on the autonomy of language becomes manifest: it offers a space within which the critic can assert his freedom to interpret. Although at the time of the original publication of the essays collected in *The Well Wrought Urn* a stress on the writer's intention had not yet been designated a fallacy, it is certainly anti-intentionalist in spirit, since Brooks suggests that paradox is *there* in the poems he discusses regardless of whether the poet knew it or not, or whether others find his interpretation surprising. Brook's starting point is the familiar distinction between the language of science and the language of poetry: in poetic language the connotative predominates since the poet does not so much designate as set verbal implications against one another:

The tendency of science is necessarily to stabilize terms, to freeze them into strict denotations; the poet's tendency is by contrast disruptive. The terms are continually modifying each other, and thus violating their dictionary meanings ... the poet has no one term. Even if he had a polysyllabic technical term, the term would not provide the solution for his problem. He must work by contradiction and qualification.[43]

Like Ransom, Brooks sees metaphor and imagery as generating a volatility in languages. As the author lays trope on trope the effect is of patchwork or crazy paving rather than the Royal Road of logic. Metaphor by its very nature involves asymmetry:

> The poet must work by analogies, but the metaphors do not lie in the same plane or fit neatly edge to edge. There is a continual tilting of the planes; necessary overlappings, discrepancies, contradictions. Even the most direct and simple poet is forced into paradoxes far more often than we think, if we are sufficiently alive to what he is doing.[44]

In this way, Brooks lays the ground for his subsequent displays of practical criticism: there is to be no appeal to assumptions about simplicity, for the language of poetry is inherently complex. The process of writing generates slippages and discordancies that it is the task of the critic to analyse. Brooks's most sustained attempt to argue for the disruptive effects of language is the essay, 'Wordsworth and the Paradox of the Imagination'. The essay is thick with the buzzwords of the new criticism: irony, ambiguity and paradox; yet Brooks also concedes that these are neither values we associate with Wordsworth, nor even devices that Wordsworth would want to use. So if these effects can be demonstrated in the poem – against the grain, as it were – this will be decisive proof that Brook's understanding of how poetry functions is correct. Brooks concludes the essay by saying:

> Even the insistence on paradox does not create the defects in the 'Ode' – the defects have been pointed out before – but it may help to account for them. Indeed, one can argue that we can perhaps best understand the virtues and the weaknesses of the 'Ode' if we see that what Wordsworth wanted to say demanded his use of paradox, that it could only be said powerfully through paradox, and if we remember in what suspicion Wordsworth held this kind of poetic strategy.[45]

What Brooks is hinting at here is that it *is* paradox that is responsible for the most complex features of the poem, but Wordsworth through his unawareness of this cannot at the same time help tripping up over his own feet. Yet Wordsworth's obliviousness at the same time permits him to write more finely than he knows, to load every rift with ore in spite of himself:

> The poem, furthermore, displays a rather consistent symbolism. This may be thought hardly astonishing. What may be more surprising is the fact that the

symbols reveal so many ambiguities. In a few cases, this ambiguity, of which Wordsworth, again, was apparently only partially aware, breaks down into outright confusion. Yet much of the ambiguity is rich and meaningful in an Empsonian sense, and it is in terms of this ambiguity that many of the finest effects of the poem are achieved.[46]

Thus, Brooks deliberately skirts many of the more widely canvassed explanations for poetic excellence: that it is the product of conscious intention and meticulous poetic craft, or that it can be explained either by the workings of the unconscious or through the deep well of the imagination. For Brooks, both what he admires and what he criticizes in the poem can be attributed to the paradoxical workings of language.

The New Criticism was never altogether rejected or overthrown; it simply faded away. Indeed, it may very well be that it is precisely because the spirit of the New Criticism was never exorcized that it perpetually returns to haunt the living. Although the criticism produced since 1970 – stemming above all from five texts of the early 1970s: Paul de Man's *Blindness and Insight* (1971), Fish's *Self-Consuming Artifacts* (1972), Derrida's *La Dissémination* (1972), Bloom's *The Anxiety of Influence* (1973), and Iser's *The Implied Reader* (1974) – believed itself to inhabit an entirely new cultural world, it appears less as a new departure than as a completion of the project of the New Criticism. In Bloom's terms, the deconstructive and readerly perspectives constitute a *tessara*, where, in his definition we need only substitute critic for poet:

A poet antithetically 'completes' his precursor, by so reading the parent-poem as to retain its terms but to mean them in another sense, as though the precursor had failed to go far enough.[47]

But these later critics (from whom I omit Derrida, who has served to confirm these trends, but does not himself, altogether belong to them) have quite genuinely gone further down the same road and have thrust aggressively towards the conclusion from which the New Critics nervously held back, like the usurper who assumes the role of regent because he is not altogether sure whether he dare yet wear the crown. The critic now confidently claims as his birthright a sovereign power over the text – a text, which already exiled from its historical context by the good offices of the New Critics, is now lined up, helpless and trembling before a bloodstained wall. And yet the author still has a curious value, no longer as a flamboyant spiritual presence or as a self-effacing magician, but rather as a limit, boundary and fence. Why, one wonders, if the author's mastery of meaning is denied, as the Act of Enablement of the critic, does Paul de Man so insistently point an admonitory finger at the writer; and why, on the face of it, should Derrida in 'Le Double Séance' mention Mallarmé by name over 120 times? The deconstructive strategy is a far more problematic and uncertain enterprise than its practitioners recognize because a positing of authorial control is quite as essential as any subsequent undoing, for the compelling reason that what isn't done, can't be undone. To read de Man on Shelley is to experience a shock of recognition, since the argumentative moves so closely resemble Brooks on Wordsworth. Just as Brooks discerns in *'Intimations of Immortality* 'a rather consistent symbolism' that nevertheless 'breaks down into outright confusion', so de Man, discussing *The Triumph of Life*, insists that Shelley's imagery of light is 'extraordinarily systematic' – 'And still, this light is allowed to exist in *The Triumph of Life* only under the most tenuous of conditions.'[48] For Brooks as for de Man the integrative project of the Romantic poem is undermined by language itself, so the symbol does not have the power it claims. If Wordsworth's Ode is 'about the synthesising imagination', nevertheless in it 'basic ambiguities . . . assert themselves'.[49] In *The Triumph of Life*,

the figure of the rainbow is the figure of the unity of perception and cognition undisturbed by the possibly disruptive mediation of its own figuration.[50]

Both critics are participants in a prolonged war in twentieth-century criticism against alleged Romantic claims to a possession of prophetic truths, but the attribution to the Romantics of such an unquestioning belief is by no means as certain as they would wish to believe; to substantiate it would require a much more extensive argument. In considering the claim that Wordsworth and Shelley have disrupted their own meaning, the question is just who is doing the positing. For Brooks and de Man need first of all to set up a stable interpretation before they undermine it: we might equally consider that they have misrecognized the trajectory of Romantic poetry, and that their own intellectual commitments to paradox and deconstruction should lead them to be wary of erecting such a privileged interpretation in the first place. In the final analysis the main purpose that the invocation of 'Wordsworth' and 'Shelley' serves is to designate a site of error that can be displaced by the critic as a site of wisdom. If the author is not thus negatively invoked, then deconstruction can scarcely take place.

It would involve no solecism to say that with Harold Bloom's *The Anxiety of Influence* the notion of the author is deployed in a stronger form. It is Bloom who continues the exaltation of the transcendent genius who rises above all cultural determinations, yet he does so so imperiously that it is Emerson rather than Eliot whom he calls to mind. Yet the *Anxiety of Influence* is evidently a meditation on 'Tradition and the Individual Talent' in which Eliot's formulation of the relationship of the poet to his predecessors is filtered through a reading of Freud and Nietzsche. We are back with the thin and etiolated sense of tradition proposed by Eliot, in which a poet's relation to his predecessors is decisive, where poetry appears as the passing of a sacred flame from one great name to another, and where the poet already writes from within the cultural museum. As to the status of this legacy, Bloom is troubled and yet strangely sanguine. The poet calmly rewriting the canon in conformity with his own practice is transformed into an anxious, competitive and obsessive figure, somewhat redolent of the American literary marketplace, who is engaged in nothing less than titanic struggle for his very right to exist. Yet in *aprophades*, the most suggestive of his categories, Bloom seems to take up Eliot's suggestion that 'the most individual parts of his work may be those in which the dead poets, his ancestors, assert their immortality most vigorously.[51] For Bloom, the poet is defined through rejection and incorporation, through a rejection that makes incorporation possible. But thought-provoking as Bloom's analysis of this process often is, it is so abstract, so lacking in any sense of cultural density, that the commanding figures of his strong

poets seem like stone warriors perennially poised to do battle in
the dusty recesses of the Vatican, tireless yet meaningless
Laocoöns. If Arnold and Eliot still define the writer against his
age, with Bloom the age itself is obliterated. So although
Bloom abjures all history, we have to recognize that he
nevertheless does offer a cultural history in which poets
themselves construct and constitute their world. Glossing a
paragraph from Nietzsche that itself established a passage
back to Goethe, Bloom affirms the myth of the self-created
individual: 'The genius is *strong*, his age is *weak*. And his
strength exhausts not himself, but those who come in his
wake.'[52] Yet while it must be conceded that this myth of the
self-created individual was perhaps the one consolation which
Nietzsche could not do without, it should nevertheless be noted
that Nietzsche *does* explain the great man historically in the
passage Bloom quotes – in a manner very reminiscent of
Carlyle's 'explanation' of the French Revolution. But for
Bloom as for Eliot, it is imperative that the writer assume his
burden in an isolated and solitary majesty, in a self-consciously
heroic and sculptural pose. The reductiveness and vulgarity of
Bloom's cultural history only becomes fully apparent when he
glosses Shelley's famous statement:

Poets, not otherwise than philosophers, painters, sculptors, and musicians,
are, in one sense, the creators, and, in another, the creations of their age.
From this subjection, the loftiest do not escape.

– as follows:

Shelley's subjection, as he knew, was to the precursor who had created (as
much as anyone had, even Rousseau) the Spirit of the Age[53]

– that is, Wordsworth. With Bloom, the epistemological
implications of that loose and idealistic way of speaking, in
which the Age of Shakespeare or of Wordsworth and Coleridge
is invoked, finally come home to roost. For how can we deny
that these ages are not theirs when our very nomenclature
insists upon it. Nor is Bloom alone in this. In M. H. Abram's
Natural Supernaturalism also, Wordsworth becomes the complete articulation and embodiment of the spirit of the age,
though he stands not so much on a pedestal as at the

intersecting point of circles, ellipses and spirals. Yet in all Bloom's compulsive melodrama and family romance, it is extremely hard to discern why poetry should matter, what it offers the reader or whether it has anything to say. Though Bloom is very far from the old-fashioned literary biographer, it is nevertheless the case that what the poet actually writes has to play second fiddle to compelling tales of 'anxiety' and 'influence' where we watch the poet struggling to get free with all the absorption that might once have been devoted to a silent movie heroine, tied to the railway tracks. When Bloom is called upon to validate the poetry he so endlessly fictionalizes, he can offer nothing better than a reprise of Richards' pseudo-statement:

The marking, the will-to-inscribe, is the *ethos* of writing that our most advanced philosophers trace, but the knowing is itself a voicing, a *pathos*, and leads us back to the theme of presence that, in a strong poem, persuades us ever afresh, even as the illusions of a tired metaphysics cannot.[54]

Poetry, it seems can give back what Derrida has taken away. But if Derrida's view of language is correct, it is hard to see how that could be either possible or praiseworthy, or why, with such an end in view, anyone should ever bother to read it. It was certainly not for this that the Victorians took editions of the Romantic poets with them on their rambles; or on such grounds that modernist critics felt that poetry *mattered*. Bloom's apology for poetry is even limper than that of Richards, and inescapably reflects the posture of the academy, where poetry matters for the very good reason that it is *set*: inscribed not in a real historical world but in the curriculum.

A concern with the role of the reader has been an important concern of much recent criticism. Although reader-response criticism is itself a phenomenon of the 1970s, most of its practitioners would acknowledge Wayne Booth's *The Rhetoric of Fiction* (1961) as a significant precursor, although they themselves would adopt a more active, not to say aggressive, interpretation of the reader's role than Booth himself was prepared to. But Booth's rhetorical approach foregrounded the interaction between author and reader as a dynamic process and drew attention to the nature of the reading experience. Booth is prepared to talk about the kind of things a reader is interested in, even if he is inclined to suggest that they coincide with the concerns of the novelist he or she is reading: of *Emma*, for instance, he says: 'Like the author herself, we don't care about the love scenes.'[55] Without privileging one or the other, Booth may be said to have paved the way for Wolfgang Iser, since as Susan R. Suleiman points out in her introduction to *The Reader in the Text*: 'The implied author in Booth's scheme has a counterpart in the "implied reader" '[56] Booth's work is peculiarly instructive as a landmark for a bird's eye view of the development of Anglo-American critic-ism, because it demonstrates the transmission of the values of the New Critics into a later age. Booth's project of analyzing how the author imposes his meaning, announced at the outset, clearly echoes Richards and his British successors:

My subject is the technique of non-didactic fiction, viewed as the art of communicating with readers – the rhetorical resources available to the writer of epic, novel, or short story as he tries, consciously or unconsciously, to impose his fictional world on the reader.[57]

In frankly confessing that he had excluded from the work any consideration of their social and cultural context:

I am aware that in pursuing the author's means of controlling his reader I have arbitrarily isolated technique from all the social and psychological forces that affect authors and readers. For the most part I have had to rule out different demands made by different audiences in different times.[58]

Booth at least made the partiality and restrictiveness of his approach apparent, justifying such omission on pragmatic grounds. But there is far more to this strategy than mere pragmatism, for American criticism has consistently chosen to focus on what it chooses to call 'technique' and has firmly driven past every last exit to history, while often proclaiming its desire to visit there one of these days. In its day, Booth's work was more innovative than the foregoing might suggest, partly because American critics had tended to avoid the com-municative model and had preferred to view the poem as object, icon or urn; partly because talk of rhetoric was thought to be crude and simplistic; and partly because *The Rhetoric of Fiction* was itself part of a major shift away from the analysis of poetry towards the analysis of prose fiction. The strengths as much as the blindspots of *The Rhetoric of Fiction* illuminate a whole tradition. Booth's analysis of narrative techniques, perceived as ways of persuading and influencing the reader is in detail often immensely suggestive; yet it never seems to occur to Booth that these same techniques are bound up with a specific phase of European culture and with the development of a mass audience, so that to address this issue might well have been a first rather than a last step – but it's rather one postponed until the Greek Calends. Booth's treatment of the drama is important, since plays rarely possess anything that can give the authorial point of view with authoritativeness, despite prologues, epilogues and *raisonneurs*. Booth has no compunction speaking about Greek drama, since the chorus seems to lend weight to his general case, yet drama considered more generally would seem to render problematic Booth's propositions about how literary works come to be understood. Clearly the dramatist (and equally, of course, poet, essayist and novelist) produces his work in a particular ideological and cultural setting, within interlocking literary, political and philosophical or religious discourses which already make conditions for understanding. But he has many specifically literary devices at his disposal that Booth does not mention or seriously consider: the use of stereotypes, the deployment of narrative structures that are familiar, and which have already been the subject of conflicting interpetative emphases, the foregrounding of characters perceived as dissonant, marginal or in opposition to the class or group that constitutes its primary audience. Informed audiences rarely require the guidance that Booth takes to be indispensable, but in doing so he is able to filter out altogether the very complex nature of this intellectual construction – which only *masquerades* as an immediate relation.

Although fully conversant with the Anglo-American literary tradition, Wolfgang Iser writes within a German cultural context where the emphasis on hermeneutics has always involved recognition of the historicity of texts as much as their interpretation. Iser's argument is that the novel involves a questioning of the normative values established in society:

Norms are social regulations, and when they are transposed into the novel they are automatically deprived of their pragmatic nature. They are set in a new context which changes their function, insofar as they no longer act as social regulations but as the subject of a discussion which, more often than not, ends in a questioning rather than a confirmation of their validity.[59]

Simultaneously, in his construction of it, this is an opening up to the relativity of cultures and the historical distance:

Linking these essays is one dominant, and it seems to me, central theme: discovery. The reader discovers the meaning of the text, taking negation as his starting-point; he discovers a new reality through a fiction which, at least in part, is different from the world he himself is used to; and he discovers the deficiencies inherent in prevalent norms and in his own restricted behaviour.[60]

Yet, however admirable this might be, its realization in Iser's work is distinctly problematic. The very oddity of Iser's suggestion that norms no longer have a regulatory function when they appear in a novel itself gives one pause. Is slavery merely hypothetical as Harriet Beecher Stowe writes about it in *Uncle Tom's Cabin*? Does the coercive force of the Gulag Archipelago slacken as Solzshenitsyn questions it in *One Day in The Life of Ivan Denisovich*? Iser might well reply that these are not norms, but institutions; but such a reply would only serve to indicate how void of substantive content the notion of norms is, how glib the assumption that a real world can be placed in brackets. 'Norms' as a concept is doubly vexing because it permits the familiar glissando from past to present. For the questioning of norms, even assuming that novels question norms as much as Iser supposes, and that this is the most cogent way of construing their activity, is very different for a reader who shares in or observes such norms than for one who does not. Although Iser has subsequently tried to give greater recognition to this difference (in *The Act of Reading*), it still remains bound by the terms of its initial construction – that is, fiction is an imaginary realm, where the real world is suspended, and into which everyone can enter, as a reader. In the final analysis, Iser would seem to be saying little more than that people get something out of reading, without ever being able to say precisely what. For the invocation of such a trans-historical 'implied reader' necessarily cancels and suspends the distance between the successive generations of readers who encounter a work that continues to be read.

The emphasis on the role of the reader in the 1970s was given a much broader significance by Jonathan Culler's *Structuralist Poetics* (1975), which, as well as offering an overview of intellectual developments in France, at the same time offered a restatement or rehabilitation of the notion of skilled reading, which had been so central to the practice of the New Criticism. Although Culler has been accused with some justification (by Frank Lentricchia in *After the New Criticism*[61]) of simply recuperating and assimilating structuralism to established norms and of bypassing its more challenging implications, Culler's role on the American critical scene has been a generally constructive one. Culler figures as a citizen of the world rather than as a narrow pounder of campus circuits. In endeavouring to be fair and open-minded – some might say too open-minded – he has if anything taken too great a burden upon his shoulders, by trying simultaneously and continuously to interpret structuralism, semiotics and deconstruction to an American public. With the important exception of Fredric Jameson, Culler has done as much as anyone to challenge the presumptions, dogmas and presuppositions of current critical practice. In his invaluable recent essay 'Beyond Interpretation' in *The Pursuit of Signs*, Culler has dared to question the automatic assumption that the primary task of criticism is the interpretation of isolated texts:

To read is always to read in relation to other texts, in relation to the codes that are the products of these texts and go to make up the culture. And thus, while the New Criticism could conceive of no other possibility than interpreting the text, there are other projects of greater importance which involve analysis of the conditions of meaning. If works were indeed autonomous artifacts, there might be nothing to do but to interpret each of them, but since they participate in a variety of systems – the conventions of genres, the logic of story and the teleologies of employment, the condensations and displacements of desire, the various discourses of knowledge that are found in a culture – critics can move through the texts towards an understanding of the systems and semiotic processes which make them possible.[62]

But even now the traces of his earlier positions are still to be seen – as in his invocation of the institution of literature, which owes more to Northrop Frye than anyone else – and regret-tably Culler has not so far produced such a work of historical and semiotic positioning himself. In Culler's critical activity there have been opportunities missed as well as opportunities taken, and his preponderate influence, exerted through *Structuralist Poetics*, has been to reinforce the anti-historical conviction that reading and writing are simply sophisticated techniques.

The most radical implications were drawn from reader-response criticism by Stanley J. Fish, who, in his earlier essays appeared to argue that textual meaning was solely determined by 'the reader' – though my very formulation indicates how slippery and doubtful this notion had become. For such a reader might to both here and now, and in the distant past, and hypothetically both at once, a real person and a hypothetical (even metaphysical) construct. The reader was feeling the strain. But Fish later assigned such authority to interpretative communities, though without much considering that this, like all authority, might require some further intellectual justifi-cation. By comparison with many of the critics I have discussed, Fish, in his works on seventeenth-century literature, *Surprised By Sin* and *Self-Consuming Artefacts*, is quite conscious of 'background' and period; and in his influential essay, 'Literature in the Reader' he even appeared to argue for an historical understanding:

In its operation, my method will be radically historical. The critic has the responsibility of becoming not one but a number of informed readers, each of whom will be identified by a matrix of political, cultural and literary determinants. The informed reader of Milton will not be the informed reader of Whitman, although the latter will necessarily comprehend the former.[63]

But the very formulation gives the game away. The critic, by donning his seven league boots and magic cloak, can transform himself at will and travel through space and time, effortlessly picking up all the cultural threads without even dropping a single stitch. What conceivable meaning can be given to the suggestion that the informed reader of Whitman necessarily comprehends the informed reader of Milton, when they inhabit worlds that are so utterly disparate? The simple explanation is that Fish's sense of history is very like that of Harold Bloom, so that to know Whitman is also to know his poetic predecessors. In his recent essays, 'Is There A Text in This Class?', and 'What Makes an Interpretation Acceptable?', Fish has been concerned to argue against attempts to restrict and constrain interpretation and to insist that interpretation cannot be evaded; but the title of the former, 'Is There A Text in This Class?' and the conclusion of the latter, 'Interpretation is the only game in town',[64] point to the myopia of Fish's apparently freewheeling approach. For Fish cannot think that a class could ever concern itself with anything but *a text* or imagine that it might address itself to questions of genre, discourse, semiotics. And would interpretation still be the only game in town or another game altogether if it did not squint from a distance at this fetishized object? It is this cult of the text that really is the only game in town.

If language is a crucial for contemporary literary criticism as it was for the New Critics, this is very largely due to the influence of Jacques Derrida, whose complex, diffused and delayed reception in England and America has been curiously reminiscent of his own conception of language. Derrida's own intellectual formation, a triangulation of Heidegger, Husserl and Nietzsche, has been very different from that of the Anglo-American critical tradition yet there are undoubted parallels. The New Critics defined poetry in opposition to science and philosophy; Derrida uses literature to criticize metaphysics, developing Mallarmé's conception of poetry as a practice of writing, resisting both reference and ideas. Ringing down the century we hear Mallarmé's legendary demolition of Degas, who, when he complained that he could not write poetry because he never got any ideas, was informed with decisive finality that poetry was made out of words. Although Derrida's positions are by no means reducible to the influence he has exerted across the Atlantic, it is difficult to resist the conclusion that part of his appeal for contemporary American critics has been that in his work, (to cite Emerson) their own, if not rejected, at least half-forgotten thoughts return 'with a certain alienated majesty',[65] endowed with an apparent philosophical authority, which they had hitherto lacked.

Derrida's argument that has most readily found an echo has been his claim that the author can exert no mastery over

language; and if this is taken to be the nub of the matter then
here, at least, I am in agreement with Derrida. The idea that the
author should and could control both language and the
reader's response too it, in the way The New Critics envisaged
(or even E. D. Hirsch's insistence on willed authorial meaning)
has always been deeply unconvincing, and has led its proponents into insoluble and fatal conundrums. But, in skirting
this particular deep intellectual snowdrift, we are by no means
obliged to follow Derrida into another still deeper. Preparatory
to pointing an alternative route it is necessary to examine the
case of Derrida in greater detail.

It is certainly significant that Derrida established himself as a
critic of the writing of others, of Husserl, Lévi-Strauss,
Saussure, to mention only the most obvious names. But, of
course, these were impressive scalps. Derrida's method was to
subject particular passages from these writers to a searching
scrutiny in order to show contradictions and hiatuses in their
argument. Derrida has forced on our attention the intellectual
claims of rhetoric, once seen as an archaic and out-moded
discipline, by foregrounding in all types of writing their
techniques of persuasion as distinct from their pretensions to
truth. And there can be no doubt but that this strategy will
exercise a continuing influence; that many other authors will be
read as Derrida has read Freud and Lacan. Here Derrida has
opened up a new path – it is only a pity that he has not taken
this a step further and recognized that rhetoric must itself be
contextualized, that its functioning depends on a particular
network of ideological presuppositions that rhetoric plays on
and invokes. But, of course, this would not be Derrida's
project. Yet in Derrida's early writings the critique itself
appears somewhat problematic since the position from which
the critique emanates is by no means clearly defined. I take the
very existence of *Positions* as testimony to that fact. Un-
fortunately, Derrida's articulation of such a position or
positions persistently involves wild, totalizing generalizations
on the basis of two or three instances that makes it difficult to
resist the conclusion that Derrida, in Isaiah Berlin's terminology, is a hedgehog masquerading as a fox. Who, but
Derrida, would attempt to ground an entire interpretation of
Western culture in a brief, unpublished and unfinished essay by

Rousseau? Who, but Derrida, would articulate a whole theory of language on the basis of a prose poem by Mallarmé? Derrida's elusiveness is achieved through his speed and dexterity as an intellectual quick-change artist, as he instantly swaps gown and mortarboard for a garish carnivalesque attire. Derrida as critic of others demands the utmost rigour and seriousness, but when his own position is at stake he responds with jesterlike insouciance and mockery. While it is impossible not to relish the performance, such irresponsibility can scarcely be to his advantage in the long run. Derrida's current credibility, such as it is, still depends on his earlier work, yet from his present position or non-position, its force is largely dissipated. What are we to make, for example, of the following comment, in a footnote to *Positions,* on Jacques Lacan: 'I read this style, above all, as an art of evasion.'[66] Leaving aside Derrida's own art of evasion, the criticism seems well founded, but by what right can Derrida say this? In an endless sliding of signifiers, which Lacan himself also emphasized, who is to say where dissemination and the play of the signifier leaves off and downright evasion begins? It seems to me that Derrida does not now, and indeed did not have then, the terms in which to criticize Lacan. Particularly so when Derrida's own language is slippery in the extreme and when such self-coinages as 'grammatology' and 'logocentrism' have constantly variable ambitions. In devising these terms Derrida, of course, claims to know what they mean and, equally, he would insist that they are not to be understood as old-fashioned stable concepts; nevertheless Derrida's own ability to communicate is at stake and it scarcely meets the case to try, as Derrida does, to dismiss communication as a reductive and simplistic illusion. Derrida has progressed, if that is the word, from a critique of metaphysics to a rejection of philosophy, on to something which, if not pataphysics, appears as a sophisticated anti-intellectualism, in which ingenious wordplay endeavours to eliminate all traces of thinking.

To understand the appeal Derrida has exerted, it is necessary to situate his work in the context of Paris in the 1960s, notoriously the age of structuralism and also *les événements* of 1968. Derrida's critique of a metaphysics of presence seemed to link the most important intellectual tendencies of the period,

Saussurean structural linguistics, Marxism and psycho-analysis, while at the same time going beyond them. It was a period when it was in vogue to speak of language in extremely generalized terms and to imagine that absolutely every conceivable intellectual issue could be posed and resolved in terms of 'language'. This was partly because Lévi-Strauss had urged the claims of structural linguistics as master discipline for the human sciences; and partly because both Chomsky and Lévi-Strauss sought to relate language to culture-free structures of mind. History could be left behind because Sartre was passé and because the work of both Saussure and Lévi-Strauss had a markedly anti-historical thrust. Not the least convenience of Saussure's work for Derrida as a benchmark and reference-point is that the avoidance of history can simply be taken for granted and does not even need to be seriously argued. Saussure as a professor of linguistics had good grounds for defining language as a system of differences, but only then could it have been assumed, as Derrida does, that all function-ing of language can be reduced to such a linguistic under-standing of it; in which language can have differences and yet not possess any boundaries. There is no sense of the way in which language is to be broken up into various types of discourse, as economic, legal, religious, journalistic, etc.; of the ways in which language can vary from context to context, as slanging match, funeral oration, sales pitch; of the sub-languages of specific social groups, as breaker jargon, soul talk, R. A. F. slang; of such formalized modes as ode, science fiction, tragedy, dissertation. So that the error of the New Criticism is repeated. When language is thus totalized, all distinctions disappear; Barthes, for example, blandly speaks of 'bourgeois language' as if every word in the language dripped with their values so that the working class could have no speech. Saussure's strategic move becomes an unquestioned axiom. Language becomes completely abstract and idealist, utterly divorced from the world, people and circumstances that give it anchorage, pertinence and meaning. And no one does this more thoroughly than Derrida. His mangle is the most devastatingly efficient: after his endeavours, language, hardly surprisingly, becomes an endless deferral and referral, where any attempt to focus meaning can only figure as an illusion. Of

course, in some very general sense, if we are speaking of
language in the abstract and not about the way in which it
functions in society, if we posit language itself as a system, then
the entire language, hypothetically, must be our frame or
reference. But as Henry James said: Really, universally, relations end nowhere';[67] at some point a circle must be drawn:
the fact that any deployment of language in any context
ultimately depends on much else does not mean that we must
either totalize with Derrida and Spinoza, or admit defeat. In any
particular context language always carries a directed charge of
meaning that is necessarily dissipated when cycled and recycled
through such a medium as Roget's Thesaurus. Hence rhetoric as
a weapon in the hands of the deconstructionists can only
boomerang: for what is rhetoric if not a message formulated
with a specific audience in mind. But Derrida is writing in an era
of totalizations and his own aims to subsume all others. His
notion of 'logocentrism' can take the place of the Marxist
concept of ideology, his 'différance' supplant Lacan's
psychoanalytic approach to language. If society and the individual subject are emptied out, so much the better. And if
Derrida's totalization is the emptiest, that only goes to show that
it is the most radical. The appeal that Derrida's writing has
exerted is founded not so much on his actual arguments about
'logocentrism' or even on his idiosyncratic interpretation of the
implications of structural linguistics, taken, where convenient,
as contemporary gospel, but on his potent suggestion that by
embracing this doctrine, modern man can heroically and finally
give up all his illusions. As René Girard has written: "The
modern intellectual is a romantic soul who likes to think of
himself as the boldest iconoclast in history."[68]

Derrida tries to avert the dangers of a metaphysical tradition of 'logocentrism' with its illusions of presence through
his own understanding of language as 'différance'. Language
for Derrida, as for Wittgenstein, and indeed for Hegel before
him, traps us into attributing a real existence to that which we
posit; but whereas Wittgenstein and Hegel try to steer us away
from specific illusions, for Derrida the whole enterprise is
illusory from start to finish. But Derrida's notion of 'logocentrism' does not merely invoke an imaginary cultural history
that Derrida scarcely attempts to substantiate, it creates the

thing it would deconstruct through the suffix of an *ism*. Derrida's deep distrust of ideas recalls Eliot and Mallarmé; the persistent implication is that those who trade in ideas must be inherently crude and simple-minded. As so often in the twentieth century, we are asked to shrink away in horror at the putative tyranny of concepts, and Derrida finds in literature the same release and relief that it afforded the New Critics:

> The emergence of this question of literarity has permitted the avoidance of a certain number of reductions and misconstruings that always will have a tendency to re-emerge (thematicism, sociologism, historicism, psychologism in all their most disguised forms).[69]

Ostensibly 'différance' permits us to be more attentive and perceptive, but we must not be misled: Derrida's 'différance' is the very opposite of what it appears to be, for like Spinoza's substance it runs everything together and makes differentiation impossible. Moreover Derrida's rhetoric works a binary opposition which he himself claims to have deconstructed. On the flimsiest of grounds and through a chain of unyielding assertions, Derrida asks us to accept a view of language that contradicts absolutely everything in our experience, to accept on his authority that our sense that language is indeed stable is merely phenomenal, dissemination the underlying and inescapable fact. Yet this stability in language can be demonstrated in a manner that simultaneously exposes the abstractness of Derrida's discussion. In their book *Cunning Intelligence in Greek Culture and Society*, Marcel Detienne and Jean-Pierre Vernant show how *mêtis*, as cunning intelligence or informed prudence, functions within the context of Greek culture. They show that *mêtis* is located within a network of concepts:

> The term *mêtis* is associated with a whole series of words which together make up quite a wide, well-defined and coherent semantic field.[70]

They also argue that its meaning remains stable over an extraordinarily long period of time:

> From the carpenter to the general, the politician to the doctor and the blacksmith to the sophist, the fundamental characteristics of *mêtis* remain unchanged throughout Antiquity....
> Over more than ten centuries the same, extremely simple model expresses skills, know-how and activities as diverse as weaving, navigation and

medicine. From Homer to Oppian, practical and cunning intelligence, in all forms, is a permanent feature of the world.[71]

We should note that not only is the notion of *metis* bound up with particular activities and professions, it is crucially defined through mythological narratives, since Metis is the first wife of Zeus: it is Zeus, above all, who possesses *mêtis*. Every culture is defined by such linkages between concepts, mythological structures and practical activity; and to grasp such inter-relations is the essential and inescapable task of the human sciences. Moreover, Derrida's own work offers an instance of this: his 'Le Pharmacie de Platon' (despite his determination to belabour the reader with paradoxes) shows an awareness of the Greek lexicographical field and significantly draws on Jean-Pierre Vernant's *Myth and Society in Ancient Greece*. Derrida's view of language can be seen as an inversion of Zeno's paradox. According to Zeno, if we take an arrow at any point in its flight, it is at rest; so it follows that motion can only be an illusion. For Derrida, contrariwise, it is the incessant motion of language that is real, and the apparent moment of rest that is an illusion. Language is a heaving, inchoate, churning sea that never finds a shore. Structuralism in its Lévi-Straussian incarnation has often been compared with Kantianism, and the analogy offers still more interesting parallels. For just as Schopenhauer, though accepting Kant's structuring under-standing, sees all life lying beyond it as an endless, blind striving of the will; so Derrida, beyond a structuralism perceived as the last gasp of logocentrism, sees language as an unceasing flux. Is it accidental that both lead their disciples towards a pessimistic mysticism?

For Derrida, 'Signature Événement Context', a paper delivered at a philosophical conference in Montreal in 1971, on the theme of 'Communication' was in all respects a crucial confrontation.[72] He faced a persuasive rival critique of propositional philosophy in the work of J. L. Austin as well as in the burgeoning fields of communication studies and semiotics – and like the Brave Little Tailor, Derrida would slay all three at a single blow. But even read in the most indulgent fashion – and Derrida never asks to be read in any other way – the essay falls very far short of its pretensions. For even if we were to accept all of Derrida's arguments on the subject of citationality, it by no means follows that the invocation of context has been discredited once and for all. But Derrida characteristically makes the most grandiloquent claims for even the most meagre of debating points, and in furtherance of his ends has no hesitation in using the most unscrupulous argumentative methods, on the one hand belabouring straw men, on the other resorting to cloudy obliquities and evasions. But even his claims that writing breaks with its context, that it involves

the disruption, in the last analysis, of the authority of the code as a finite system of rules; at the same time, the radical destruction of any context as the protocol of code.

that

a written sign carries with it a force that breaks with its context, that is, with the collectivity of presences organising the moment of its inscription. This breaking force is not an accidental predicate but the very structure of the written text.[73]

are highly dubious; not least because they gloss over the processes whereby written texts from the Koran to the American constitution acquire a symbolic and prescriptive significance in the first place. The issue is not simply that texts are open to interpretation or that they cannot answer back – though we cannot disregard the fact that an author may subsequently respond to certain queries and objections, as Derrida himself did in *Positions*. It is that Derrida's imaginary moment of rupture from some originary context is nothing more than a romantic fiction. My own response to Derrida is admittedly no longer bonded to a particular winter's afternoon when I sat at a pine table behind a typewriter, now and then glancing out of the window at a hotel called "Sunnyside" across the street; but that is because its context is an intellectual debate in which Derrida features prominently. If taken seriously, Derrida's claim that context cannot supply the protocols of code would mean that there could no understanding or meaning at all. For all his parade of scepticism no one is more closely wedded than he is to the dogmatic certainties of the dictionary – and thus to assumptions about transcendental meaning which he purports to reject. The understanding of context that he offers is simplistic and reductive. In the first place, sentences are their own context. Secondly, what a text is and what a text can mean is very much bound up with the signifying context in which it figures, and that can vary as much contemporaneously as subsequently. There is no given and self-evident context. Contexts are always constructed and plural. They are ways of reading, understanding, assessing and evaluating. They are matters of definition. Even a contemporaneous reader of Blake's *Jerusalem* who could fully identify Blake's perception of his role and situation in the writing of that poem, would still have his or her own way of contextualizing it and thus grasping it in a certain way. Contexts cannot be envisaged independently of the people who are involved in them, or from their perception of them or from the purposes that animate them. The only conceivable way in which we can think of a text's breaking with context is that it should remain literally and perennially unread. Derrida's corybantic simulation of such a liberated word in his subsequent *Limited Inc abc* ... (a cavalier riposte to the critique of John R. Searle) can scarcely sustain its argumentative burden through mimesis; and in any event it would have to reckon with the challenge offered by Bakhtin's essay, 'Discourse in the Novel,' which offers a more penetrating analysis of the contextualizing nature of Derrida's own performance:

We cannot, when studying the various forms for transmitting another's speech, treat any of these forms in isolation from the means for its contextualized (dialogizing) framing – the one is indissolubly linked with the other. The formulation of another's speech as well as its framing (and the context can begin to prepare for the introduction of another's speech far back in the text) both express the unitary act of dialogic interaction with that speech, a relation determining the entire nature of its transmission and all the changes in meaning and accent that take place in it during transmission.'[74]

All conceptions of the author's control and mastery of language, of willed and determinate meaning amount to a misconstruction of the problem. To say so may seem to imply a systematic denigration of the author's struggle with language, but all that is involved is the postulate that an analysis of meaning cannot take the author as its starting point. Social meanings are organized in large-scale discursive structures, they are bound up with distinctive ideological configurations, they involve codes and patterns of signification that circulate through many different texts and contexts. Literary texts, above all, are extremely complex and derivative texts; however it may seem to the writer confronting a blank sheet of paper, the literary work is *never* originary, but always a gesture at second, third, fourth, fifth, sixth remove. Literary texts figure as an interlacing of codes. They are articulations on top of articulations. And there is a very real sense in which an artwork's location with a particular genre and in relation to a specific cultural context *already* gives a meaning to the work before an engagement with it even begins. So the belief in the author's control over language, though harmless enough if not pressed too far, has concealed and deeply élitist implications: the author's meaning becomes something created *ex nihilo*, that is totally idiosyncratic, that is firmly locked and enclosed within the text. But the complexity of a text is not intrinsic: rather it is constructed through its interface with other texts and semiotic systems. The difficulty of such representative modern works as Joyce's *Ulysses*, Pound's *Cantos* or Mallarmé's *Igitur* is not solely a matter of ellipsis or syntactical obscurity, though this cannot be underestimated, but is bound up with an intricate allusiveness to such works as *The Odyssey*, the tales of Poe, *Hamlet*, or Golding's translation in 1567 of Ovid's *Metamorphoses*. An analysis of such a multi-faced social, cultural and ideological positioning of the text offers no finality. It seeks an understanding that is not viewed as an unveiling or grasping of the object in all its intrinsic quiddity, but as a constant and mobile process of *scanning*. It is a dynamic conception of knowledge, not a static and rigidified one. Yet to grasp the text in all its historicity has paradoxical effects, for it comes nearer and recedes simultaneously, bringing feelings in which pathos and elation are strangely mixed.

In his poem 'L' Albatros', Baudelaire likened the poet to a great seabird, who pays for his ability to soar away on colossal imaginative flights with a crippled existence in the social world:

Le poëte est semblable au prince des nuées
Qui hante la tempête et se rit de l'archer;
Exilé sur le sol au milieu des huées,
Ses ailes de géant l'empêchent de marcher.

By a symmetrical inversion it seems to me that the critical tradition I have been discussing, in its lack of historical imagination, may be likened to a cluster of penguins, jammed together on a rocky promontory, who are fully in agreement that the place where they so stiffly stand together is the only place to be.

NOTES

1 Friedrich Schopenhauer, *Parerga and Paralipomena*, trans. E. F. J. Payne (Oxford: Oxford University Press, 1974), Vol. II, pp. 66-7.
2 Matthew Arnold, *Lectures and Essays in Criticism*, ed. R. H. Super with Sister T. M. Hoctor (Ann Arbor: University of Michigan Press, 1962), p. 283.
3 Matthew Arnold, *On the Classical Tradition*, ed. R. H. Super (Ann Arbor: University of Michigan Press, 1960, pp. 12-13.
4 *ibid.*, p. 14.
5 Arnold, *Lectures*, p. 271.
6 Frank Kermode (ed.), *Selected Prose of T. S. Eliot* (London: Faber & Faber, 1975), p. 151.
7 Lionel Trilling, *The Opposing Self* (London: Secker & Warburg, 1955), pp. 90-1.
8 *Ibid.*, p. 150.
9 Lionel Trilling, *The Liberal Imagination* (London: Secker & Warburg, 1951), p. 56.
10 *Ibid.*, pp. 56-7.
11 *Ibid.*, p. 57.
12 Lionel Trilling, *Beyond Culture* (London: Secker & Warburg, 1966), p. 115.
13 *Ibid.*, p. 118.
14 F. R. Leavis, *New Bearings in English Poetry* (London: Chatto & Windus, 1932), p. 13.
15 *Ibid.*
16 F. R. Leavis, *Revaluation* (London: Chatto & Windus, 1936), p. 114.
17 F. R. Leavis, *The Common Pursuit* (London: Chatto & Windus, 1952), p. 88.
18 *Ibid.*, pp. 88-9.
19 I. A. Richards, *Principles of Literary Criticism* (London: Routledge & Kegan Paul, 1925), p. 206.
20 I. A. Richards, *Practical Criticism* (London: Routledge & Kegan Paul, 1929), p. 239.
21 *Ibid.*, p. 305.
22 William Empson, *The Seven Types of Ambiguity* 3rd edn (London: Chatto & Windus, 1953), pp. 238-9.

23 G. Wilson Knight, *The Wheel of Fire* 4th edn (London: Methuen, 1972), p. 7.
24 L. C. Knights, *Explorations* (London: Chatto & Windus, 1946), p. 5.
25 D. W. Harding, *Experience into Words* (London: Chatto & Windus, 1963), pp. 173–4.
26 D. A. Traversi, *An Approach to Shakespeare* 2nd edn (London: Sands, 1957), pp. 6–7.
27 W. K. Wimsatt, *The Verbal Icon* (London: Methuen, 1970), p. 34.
28 Richards, *Principles*, p. 280.
29 John Crowe Ransom, *The New Criticism* (Norfolk, Conn.: New Directions, 1941), p. 281.
30 *Ibid.*, p. 280.
31 T. S. Eliot, *The Use of Poetry and the Use of Criticism* (London: Faber & Faber, 1933), p. 151.
32 Ransom, *op. cit.* pp. 302–3.
33 *Ibid.*, p. 303.
34 *Ibid.*, p. 316.
35 *Ibid.*, p. 335.
36 *Ibid.*, p. 336.
37 R. P. Blackmur, *Language as Gesture* (New York: Harcourt, Brace, 1952), pp. 113–4.
38 *Ibid.*, p. 224.
39 *Ibid.*, p. 226.
40 *Ibid.*
41 *Ibid.*, p. 389.
42 *Ibid.*, p. 314.
43 Cleanth Brooks, *The Well Wrought Urn* (London: Dobson, 1949), pp. 8–9.
44 *Ibid.*, p. 9.
45 *Ibid.*, p. 138.
46 *Ibid.*, p. 115.
47 Harold Bloom, *The Anxiety of influence* (New York: Oxford University Press, 1973), p. 14.
48 Harold Bloom, Paul de Man *et al., Deconstruction and Criticism* (London: Routledge & Kegan Paul, 1979), p. 57.
49 Brooks, *op. cit.*, p. 136.
50 Bloom *et al., op. cit.*, p. 58.
51 T. S. Eliot, *Selected Essays* 3rd edn (London, Faber & Faber 1951), p. 14.
52 Bloom, *op. cit.*, p. 51.
53 *Ibid.*, p. 104.
54 Harold Bloom, 'Auras: The Sublime Crossing and the Death of Love', *Oxford Literary Review*, Vol. 4, No. 3, p. 19.
55 Wayne Booth, *The Rhetoric of Fiction* (Chicago and London: University of Chicago Press, 1961), p. 266.
56 Susan R. Suleiman and Inge Crosman, eds., *The Reader in the Text* (Princeton: Princeton University Press, 1980), p. 8.
57 Booth, *op. cit.*, Preface.

58   *Ibid.*
59   Wolfgang Iser, *The Implied Reader* (Baltimore and London: Johns Hopkins University Press, 1974), p. xii.
60   *Ibid.*, p. xiii.
61   Frank Lentricchia, *After the New Criticism* (London: Athlone Press, 1980), pp. 103–12.
62   Jonathan Culler, *The Pursuit of Signs* (London: Routledge & Kegan Paul, 1981), p. 12.
63   Stanley Fish, *Is There a Text in This Class?* (Cambridge, Mass. and London: Harvard University Press, 1980), p. 49.
64   *Ibid.*, p. 355.
65   Ralph Waldo Emerson, *Collected Works* Vol. II, *Essays: First Series* ed. Slater, Ferguson, Carr (Cambridge, Mass. and London: Harvard University Press, 1979), p. 27.
66   Jacques Derrida, *Positions*, trans. A. Bass (London: Athlone Press, 1981), p. 110.
67   Henry James, *The Art of the Novel*, introduced by R. P. Blackmur (New York: Scribner's, 1962), p. 5.
68   René Girard, *Violence and the Sacred* trans. P. Gregory (Baltimore and London: Johns Hopkins University Press, 1977), p. 130.
69   Derrida, *op. cit.*, p. 70.
70   Marcel Detienne and Jean-Pierre Vernant, *Cunning Intelligence in Greek Culture and Society* trans. J. Lloyd (Hassocks: Harvester Press, 1978), p. II.
71   *Ibid.*, p. 307.
72   Jacques Derrida, Signature Event Context, *Glyph* I, p. 180.
73   *Ibid.*, p. 182.
74   M. M. Bakhtin, *The Dialogic Imagination* ed. M. Holquist, trans. C. Emerson and M. Holquist (Austin and London: University of Texas Press, 1981), p. 340.

3   Representation and the Colonial Text: A Critical Exploration of Some Forms of Mimeticism*

Homi Bhabha

To re-integrate himself with worldly actuality, the critic of texts ought to be investigating the system of discourse by which the 'world' is divided, administered, plundered, by which humanity is thrust into pigeonholes, by which 'we' are 'human' and 'they' are not, and so forth. We will discover that even so innocuous a discipline as philology has played a crucial role in the process. Most important, we should be intent upon revealing the secrecy, the privatizations of texts whose circumstantial thickness and complicity are covered by the other-worldly prestige of art or of mere textuality.

Edward Said: *Diacritics* Fall, 1976.

I

Beginning, as Edward Said has coined it, has two faces: 'One which I shall call temporal and transitive, foresees a continuity that flows from it ... the other kind of beginning [which I shall call] intransitive and conceptual ... is very much a creature of the mind, very much a bristling paradox ... because it challenges continuities that go cheerfully forward with their beginnings obediently affixed – it is therefore something of a necessary fiction.'[1]

The deep ambiguity which is commensurate with beginning, with speaking or writing *in the first place* – the division between the subjects of the enunciation and enounced – is resolved in the discourse of literary history through the inception of an 'origin' whereby history turns to a kind of myth, and the problem of beginning is resolved as the progressive distinction between past and present. The authority of the past is finally authored (and authorized) in the present. Histories of the novel

93

from Leavis's *The Great Tradition* to Lukács *The Historical Novel*, from Auerbach's *Mimesis* to Barthes' early *Writing Degree Zero*, all these are historicist and teleological: a chronological ordering of the history of the novel, while establishing, at the same time, the relationship of the Novel and History, in terms of an organic, progressive approximation of reality, the accuracy of reflection. Produced in this way, both Literature and History, as well as the history of literature, enable a perspective of essential order, coherence, culmination and Culture. There is an undeniable collaboration between historicism and realism. In the face of the spatial and temporal disunity in beginning, in the act of writing, it is as if the possibility of establishing a history of narrative, or indeed the narrative of history, depends on a view of textuality which Bergonzi describes as:

'the ideology that sustained the novel for the first two centuries of its existence, its belief in unmediated experience, in originality and individuality and progress.[2]

It is this link between the order of literary history and the unmediated originality of its texts that I want to establish and explore. We find it in Leavis's estimate of Lawrence, in his conception of Tradition: what lives so supremely in Lawrence's work, Leavis believes, is the central ethical and religious tradition he shares with George Eliot. But whereas George Eliot's record of an 'essential English history was enlivened by the ethical, Lawrence's work is impassioned by the religious, his sensuous, moving power of revelation.[3] Here we have it then, the possibility of a history of literature driven forward by the progressive discovery of the essentially unmediated nature of reality in its works. And we find it again, despite Iris Murdoch's belief in the radical contingency of reality, in her fine phrases:

Real people are destructive of myth.... When we think of the works of Tolstoy or George Eliot... we are remembering Dolly, Kitty, Stiva, Dorothea and Casaubon.[4]

It is there in W. J. Harvey's four constitutive categories – Time, Identity, Causality and Freedom – which constitute reality and elude any ideology;[5] and it is even there in Wayne Booth's assessment of Beckett's bleak irony, for if, he argues, the mouth speaks, then that is a sufficient sign of reality, a mark of human order and courage.[6] It occurs so often, this link between historicism and realism, between the plausibility of linear order and coherence in history and the immediate evidence of the real in Literature, that Edward Said's conclusion is just:

The central purpose of the western novel is to enable the writer to represent characters and societies more or less freely in development. Characters and societies so represented grow more and more in the novel because they mirror a process of engenderment or beginning and growth possible and permissible for the mind to imagine. Novels, therefore, are aesthetic objects that fill gaps in an incomplete world: they satisfy a human urge to add to reality by portraying (fictional) characters in which one can believe.[7]

Much of the criticism that deals with Third World literature in English sees the problem of representing the colonial subject at this mimetic level. The unmediated reality that an authentic literary tradition must ideally reveal – the mark of its originality – it is argued, can hardly be written in a language and literature of colonial imposition. The historical and ideological determinants of Western narrative – bourgeois individualism, organicism, liberal humanism, autonomy, progression – cannot adequately reflect, for instance, the Caribbean environment, as Wilson Harris describes it, steeped 'in such broken conceptions as well as misconceptions of the residue and meaning of conquest.'[8] The discourses and institutions of English Literature can only provide a dim and refracted light, that casts a shadow on an alien culture. 'The vision was alien', Naipaul writes:

It diminished my own and did not give me the courage to do a simple thing like mentioning the name of a Port of Spain street.... It helps in the most practical way to have a tradition... the English language was mine; the tradition was not.[9]

The irony is complete when we remember Iris Murdoch's statement, 'A novel must be a house fit for free characters to live in',[10] and then remind ourselves of *A House for Mr Biswas* – the desperate wish to be accommodated, to defy a primal lack, but the object of desire is always deferred. What the narrative achieves at the end is denied by its opening, and there is, within that novel, a real problem of beginning, originating, creating.

However, although the refractions of a Western tradition are accepted as ironical (if not tragic), the demand for a literary tradition, a history, is put in exactly the same historicist and realist terms – the familiar quest for an origin that will authorize a beginning. *Trinidad*[11] and *The Beacon* which published the earliest West Indian short stories, insisted on the use of local settings, speech, character, situations and conflicts, and warned against the use of foreign literature which would create inauthenticity. And so, the early barrackyard stories of C. L. R. James and Maynard inaugurated the history of West Indian literature with an emphasis on the unmediated value of text and reality.

There is, however, another way of raising the issue of the representation of the colonial subject which questions the collusion between historicism and realism. It proposes that the category of literature, as of its history, is necessary and throughly mediated: that its reality is not given but produced; its meanings transformative, historical and relational rather than revelatory; its continuity and coherence underscored by division and difference. This other view demands quite another notion of the historical inscription of literature and entails a critique of representation as simply given.

When Edward Said says that the plenitude of narrative 'fills the gaps' in an incomplete world, he hints at a theme I want to explore. And there is much more than a hint in Anthony Giddens's comment, appropriate to the 'writing' of both historicism and realism:

It is not too fanciful to suppose that the development of writing underlies the first emergence of the *linear time consciousness* which later in the West became the basis of historicity as a feature of social life.... Its very linearity as a material form perhaps encourages the consciousness of the elapsing of time as a sequential process, leading from one point away to another point in a progressive manner.[12]

Writing as the *filling* of a *gap* (is it the gap between beginnings?); linear time consciousness as the effect of the sequential practice of writing; teleology and unity, progression and coherence as convention-bound, formal productions – all these notions give writing a materiality, a productive position, where before we saw only *through* it to the reality or Truth beyond. There are intimations here of the *construction* of the unity of the sign (as opposed to its primordial 'givenness'), and the resulting stability of the signified which, paradoxically, suggests the possibility of its arbitrariness, that is, the irony of its repression of discontinuity and difference in the construction of 'sense', those modes of meaning that we call realism and historicism. What we are made aware of immediately, is that the values of historicism and realism, the 'unmediated' and sequential progression to truth, the originality of vision – what Leavis would call the wholeness of their resolution – are historical and ideological productions without any of the inevitability that they claim. They are necessary fictions that tragically believed too much in their necessity and too little in their own fictionality. They are historical in the sense that Giddens locates such practices of writing – such concepts of consciousness and truth – in the post-feudal West, associating them with development of the ideas of tradition, hermeneutics, historiography, and dissociating them from ascriptive, traditionalist cultures where writing may be mythological, and time-consciousness is cyclical. They are ideological in the sense in which the discourses of historicism and realism manifestly deny their own material and historical construction. Their practices can be seen as unmediated and universal because the unity of tradition lies in an absolute presence – a moment of transcendent originality. Listen to Leavis on Lawrence in the assessment that follows. In the act of establishing Lawrence's originality, Leavis subtly, associatively establishes that the English writer has a prior claim to the direct presentment of Reality:

We cannot help feeling that it comes with peculiar directness from the centre of Lawrence himself. Here is Lawrence whose genius is to be the antithesis of the inventor of the Houyhnhnms and Yahoos. It is in such places as these that we realize with special force how inseparable from such creativeness as Lawrence's, how essentially of so un-Flaubertian an art, is the un-Flaubertian attitude towards life; the reverence that in its responsiveness is courage and vitality.... We see and take the vibration... the direct concrete presentment.[13]

Differences of genre, mode, structuration; differences in historical and ideological determinants; the diversity of cultural and social practices; the changing institutions and discourses of Literature – everything that makes the text of history and literature systemic and ideologically mediated is rendered transparent before the direct concrete presentment, 'As if it were afraid to conceive of the "other" in the time of our own thought' – Foucault writes of historicism:

Continuous history [and Realism, we may add] is the indispensable correlative of the founding function of the subject: the guarantee that everything that has eluded him may be restored to him; the certainty that time will dispense nothing without restoring it in a reconstituted unity; the promise that one day the subject ... will once again be able to appropriate ... all those things that are kept at a distance by difference....'[14]

To represent the colonial subject is to conceive of the subject of difference, of an-other history and an-other culture. This requires a notion of literary representation that does not conceive of the problem of representation as the presentation of *different* images of the colonial, some more progressive than others. It requires an end to the collusion of historicism and realism by unseating the Transcendental subject, the *origin* of writing as linear time consciousness. It denies its teleology, the natural and necessary unfolding of meaning and consciousness, by conceiving of writing as a signifying practice. That is to say a process which conceives of meaning as a systemic production within determinate institutions and systems of representation – ideological, historical, aesthetic, political. It is crucial for our purposes that this does not permit meaning to be recuperable through a direct reference to the 'origins' of mimetic reflection or authorial intention. For to remove the possibility of an 'unmediated reality' is to re-introduce the division in the two aspects of beginning. It is to suggest that the relation between beginning as temporal and transitive, and beginning as conceptual or 'critical' is not an immanent or universal link, but a productive and transformational, indeed, ideological relationship. It demands a theoretical self-consciousness of those critical practices which in claiming to restore the 'natural' and 'reasonable' meanings of texts, are in fact engaged in strategies of naturalization and cultural assimilation which make our readings unwillingly collusive and profoundly uncritical.

One of the major operators in the cultural reproduction of texts and the constitution of the order of *Literature* is, not surprisingly, literary criticism. It is the discourse by which texts are systematized, synthesized and signified, within a range of cultural institutions. It is the history of colonial difference as it is represented in three major critical traditions – Leavisian Universalism, Nationalist criticism[15] and Althusserian ideological analysis – that this essay explores. It is a history which is hidden in those unifying titles such as 'Commonwealth Literature' of 'The Caribbean Tradition' which may have a ring of truth, but it is only the shrill school bell that establishes a discipline and guards its boundaries defensively.

II

The major debate that has shaped our view of 'colonial literature' and identified the concepts by which we read it and write about it has been 'image analysis'. In using this term, I refer first to a philosophical method and an ideological problematic, rather than, as would be usual, an identifiable critical tradition. I propose to show that the debate between the Universalist and Nationalist critics which constitutes the major controversy around the question of colonial literature, is fought essentially on the same aesthetic ground.

Both are representationalist theories and share a problematic form within which their questions are posed. It is a predominantly mimetic view of the relation between the text and a *given* pre-constituted reality. This entails the classic subject/object structure of knowledge, central to empiricist epistemology which further installs the structure of the essential and the inessential.[16] Part of these familiar couples is that characteristic method of inquiry of traditional criticism, the question of appearance and reality, which functions on the basis of what Paul Hirst describes as knowledge as the *recognition* of given objects. From such a concept of textual reference, it follows that the representation – the literary text – becomes the image of the represented – the given reality – which as the essential, original source determines the form and action of its *means* of representation. The effect of such a placing of the text/reality, in terms of the subject/object structure of knowledge, traps the text within what Derrida calls a violent hierarchy 'organised by the privileged term (Reality) to which the other term (the Text) is both necessitated and subordinated.'[17] It is at this point that the question of evaluation, the necessary issue of mimetic adequacy, is posed as providing the normative knowledge of the text. The 'image' must be measured against the 'essential' or 'original' in order to establish its degree of *representativeness*, the correctness of the image. The text is not seen as *productive* of meaning but essentially reflective or expressive – as Hirst says of ideology in a functionalist context, neither a discourse nor a practice, but a form of recognition. Such analysis is largely content-oriented. The main question that is asked of the production of the image, the significant knowledge allowed of it, is in relation to the pre-given model or original. The text as a *form of recognition* is the central term of a critical discourse which Macherey character-izes 'as a drive to grasp the content of the narrative directly, independently, immediately.'[18] It is broadly within these empiricist terms – in Althusser's formulation, 'the abstraction by the subject of the essence of the object. Hence the knowledge of the object is part of the object itself'[19] – that the discourses of Universalist and Nationalist criticism circulate and pose the questions of colonial difference and discrimination.

  Dr Kenneth Ramchand (whose work, *The West Indian Novel and Its Background*, is the classic introductory text to many Anglophone Caribbean Literature Courses) makes a plea for Leavisian standards in Caribbean criticism, – against the work of Nationalists like Sylvia Wynter and Gordon Rohlehr whose analysis he says, 'belongs to a tradition of . . . naive, pretentious socio-political and racial cultural generalization that passes for literary criticism in the West Indies.' After suggesting that Leavis's essay on *The Irony of Swift* should be the model for a critique of Naipaul, he tries to rally Caribbean critics around the Leavisian endeavour:

to create a consciousness throughout . . . society that literature matters as literature, not as a substitute for something else; and that literary criticism is a craft calling for maturity, intelligence and sensitivity to the organization of words on the page.[20]

This much vaunted concern for the concrete and particular 'words-on-the-page,' the practical criticism of *Scrutiny*, denies the cultural and historical basis of the *literary*, the thing it purports to defend. Consequently it denies the grounds on which to pose the question of the 'colonial' in literary representation. For that is fundamentally a problem of the signification of historical and cultural difference. The opposition set up between the literary as a unique verbal experience and its 'socio-political' appropriation is a combative act to preserve, it is claimed, the specificity of the literary form. But this conscious separation of the literary from other discourses, this act of exclusion is in itself ideological in its claims to neutrality and innocence, and prepares the way for the appropriation of the text as the object of a *moral* discourse that claims universality for its imperatives. The sense of the 'appropriate' which establishes the universality of aesthetic judgement through the operation of taste is inseparable from the appropriateness of moral judgements, since they share, Roger Scruton argues, 'standards of practical reasoning generally'.[21]

Both discourses are centred in the essentialist unitary subject – for aesthetics depends on an identity that establishes the consistency of taste, and ethical discourse is equally dependent on identity as the basis of moral judgement and responsibility. Recognizing the 'literary' as the words-on-the-page is given the positivist imprimatur of recognizing 'fact' as the guarantee of the essential meaning of the text revealed in an intrinsic act of criticism; it is seen as an appreciation as against the prescriptivism of the Nationalist critics. However, as Macherey points out, the empiricist fallacy consists in the representation as an aesthetics of mere reception, what is the necessary refusal of the text in criticism. That is, it disregards the necessary discontinuity between text and criticism created by the presence of the other, the always elsewhere which ratifies critical judgement.[22]

The *problematic of recognition* which refuses that essential discontinuity therefore refuses to account for the knowing subject or the object known. But these discursivities, necessary to any critical theory, are refused: criticism as a *practice* of reading becomes, as Mulhern recognizes in *The Moment of Scrutiny*, 'a form of intuitionism of moral values';[23] and the text as a *practice* of writing becomes an essentially spiritual reality, a logos: at once word and its existence. So the material *specificity* of how language works, which is the way the 'words on the page' as systems of significations produce the text (a setting up of subject-positions from which literature is read and sense is *made*) – evaporates in the religiosity of immanent, universal meanings that Leavis proposes and Ramchand echoes. Equally, the exclusiveness of this notion of literature denies its specificity as a practice of writing, the meaning of which is constructed in a process of reference and difference in relation to other ideological and historical discourses which constitute its conditions of existence and intervention. The Great Tradition seals its value (and its fate) in an exchange, aptly described by Leavis as 'That is so, is it not?'; Terry Eagleton reads this exchange-value in another relevant way:

[It is the] alienation of the historically specific which permits one lonely abstraction to encounter, and be equalized by another, in a self-closing circle from which the material has been abolished...the valuable reader is constituted as valuable by the texts which he constitutes as such; ideological value is projected into the Tradition....[24]

The crisis in literary and cultural values that would ensue from a reading based on questions of historical, cultural difference and racial discrimination as constituting meanings that we may read as 'racist' or 'culturally imperialist' or 'neo-colonial', *within* the Great Tradition, generally throws such a regime of criticism and culture into disarray. Differences of class, gender, race and contradictions as evinced in the struggle for hegemony, which constitute the text of politics and history are always superseded in the quest for universal meanings. Such questions, then, will be repressed in the affirmation of a Transcendental Human Nature – the unifying category of Universalism – where, as Abbott writes:

the recognition of difference is procured in an innocence, as a 'nature'; recognition is continued as primary cognition, spontaneous effect of the 'evidence' of the *visible*....[25]

The '*evidence* of the visible'; the spontaneous value of the words-on-the-page; all these evocations of aesthetic auton-omy are, in fact, the ideological conditions for its repro-duction. The effectiveness of such an enterprise is to valorize a specific literary – cultural practice and inscribe within it a particular political and social value, under the guise of pure criticism. It should come as no surprise, then, that the Leavisian method that Ramchand so enthusiastically recom-mends for a free criticism of Caribbean colonial literature is imbued with an ideological and cultural reference that would make its use critically prescriptive with a marked neo-colonialist emphasis. For, despite his brilliant insights, Leavis was the most parochial and nationalist of critics. It was the work of *Scrutiny* that transformed the free-floating Eurocentricism of Arnold's dialectic of the Hebraic and Hellenic and of Eliot's notion of Tradition, and gave them a specific *national* reference to the lost word of seventeenth-century *England* and its literature. The concept of unified sensibility conjured up ever more a moral and psychical harmony that 'now survive[s] in *potentia* in *England's* inherited literary language'. The concern for language that Ramchand proposes as a way of freeing literature from prejudice and conviction can hardly be elaborated in Leavis's committed terms. For him the English Language was essentially the 'language of Shakespeare ... (formed) in a *genuinely national* culture ... rooted in the soil.' The 'unity' that Leavis sought, was again 'the very spirit of the language – a spirit that was formed when the English people who formed it were pre-dominantly rural.'[26]

It is from within this Universalist problematic that an eminent critic has judged the importance of Achebe's *Things Fall Apart*, in the passage that follows:

What is significant is that he transcends his African world, embodies a conception of civilisation which has a root in reality, grasps what is *humanly* significant so that we are easy with it and not strained by it.

And Achebe is surely right when he observes of this Leavisian discourse:

In the nature of things, the work of the western writer is automatically informed by universality. It is only others who must strive to achieve it. As though universality were some distant bend in the road you must take if you travel far enough in the direction of America or Europe.[27]

Universalism does not merely end with a view of immanent, 'spiritual' meaning produced in the text. It also interpellates, for its reading, a subject positioned at the point where conflict and difference resolves and all ideology ends. It is not that the Transcendental subject cannot *see* historical conflict or colonial difference as mimetic structures or themes in the text. What it cannot conceive, is how it is *itself* structured ideologically and discursively in relation to those processes of signification which do not then allow for the possibility of whole or universal meanings. The representation of the colonial subject presupposes that signification is ideological and constructed through the systemic play of difference. What Achebe's critic shows quite clearly is that within a Universalist problematic criticism exists only to resolve the material significations of historical and cultural difference into a deeply ethnocentric transcendence. The colonial text of racial and cultural otherness must be exceeded if it is to be genuinely meaningful.

For anti-colonialist, anti-racist 'Nationalist' criticism, image-analysis leads to the issue of stereotypes, which usually demands a mimetic reading, frequently sociological, performed principally in terms of two concepts central to its ideological and narrative strategy. One is 'character', and the other is a form of narrative closure, a process achieved through the articulation of Barthes' hermeneutic and proairetic codes. It must be stressed that the coherence of character as the strong mimetic centre of narrative resolves and occludes what Barthes calls the text's 'festival of effects'; its productivity, its network of codes and their transformations. However, as I mentioned earlier in relation to writing as 'linear time consciousness', solving the text's problem of identity by referring its representations to a pre-given reality, results in a mode of criticism that emphasizes the signified as independent of the *means* of its representation. Iris Murdoch's recuperation of a range of texts as a *musée imaginaire* of favourite folks, cited earlier, is a case in point.

Within a realist problematic, such a character-based reading privileges one element or code of the text. It compacts the essentialist nature of the narrative discourse, by repressing any knowledge of it as a complex, articulated systems of signification. It makes of 'character' the sign of the 'sociolect', the *vraisemblable*, what is most easily naturalizable and recognizable as the 'individual'. Consequently such criticism represses the ideological and discursive *construction* of racial difference. Moreover, its ready reference to the unitary individual or 'character' rather than the social group which cannot be so easily 'subjectified' or unified, makes an individual and ethical problem of racism, instead of recognizing its historical and political significance.

The evaluation of the image – the *status* of the question of difference and discrimination – is engagingly paradoxical within this tradition. The Nationalist critic caught in the problematic of image analysis, speaks against one stereotype but essentially, and inevitably, for another. The static nature of 'stereotype-analysis' – which is the image caught outside the process of the text – demands that the derogatory stereotype must be replaced by positive ('Nationalist') images, which oppose the *undifferentiating* liberal humanist discourse of Universalism. The Black image must correspond to an emergent Black consciousness: it must be more complex, less hidden from history and vividly distinct in its textual figuration. In practice – both critical and creative – the Black image is often the elaboration of a given socialist-nationalist thesis of liberation. In the cultural field, it is frequently accompanied by Lukacsian emphasis on 'typicality' and 'totality', which shares with Leavis a preference for realist signification.

The demand that one image should circulate rather than another is made on the basis that the stereotype is *distorted* in relation to a *given* norm or model. It results in a mode of prescriptive criticism which Macherey has conveniently termed the normative fallacy, because it privileges an ideal 'dream-image' in relation to which the text is judged. The only knowledge such a procedure can give is one of negative difference because the only demand it can make is that the text should be other than itself.

The prescriptivism of much Nationalist or anti-racist criticism re-presents the problem of difference and discrimination as the problem of image and its distortion. It shares with Universalist criticism what I described earlier as the basis of image-analysis – *a problematic of recognition.* 'Distortion' is the recognition of 'difference' in relation to the pre-giveness of an affirmative image which constitutes the primary cognition, of which the literary text is only a secondary elaboration. The demand then is merely for the replacing of one content with another, until through a process of 'correction' the right image is produced. Literature as a discourse or practice, engaged in a form of transformative 'work' is effaced, and the succession of images – a question of the *history* of textual signification and ideological struggle – becomes the moralist rectification of a 'given' essence. The construction of the colonial as a sign of difference within the production of literary discourses is a perspective denied within this critical tradition. The problem of *representing difference* as a problem of narrative can only be seen, within this kind of critical discourse, as the demand for *different representations.*

The critical discourse that I have called 'ideological analysis' is formulated to deconstruct the empiricist problematic we have just encountered. It refuses the epistemological dependence on a pre-given Transcendental subject, which functions as both origin and end, guaranteeing discursive coherence. It does so by proposing a break between the knowing subject and the object known, which is the space where Althusserian Marxism makes its intervention. It is through the transformation of what was posed in Hegelian Marxism as the *problem* of false consciousness into a *problematic* of ideology, that the Althusserian revision has opened up a rich seam for the analysis of cultural formations and their practices. The distinction turns on the change in the status of *representation.* In classical Hegelian Marxism, ideology is seen as the problem of refraction, a superstructural miasma or false consciousness that the science of Marxism could 'see through' to reveal the real structural foundations. The problematic of ideology asserts the necessity for a system of representation as the medium necessary for the interpellation of the subject in its relations to its 'real' conditions of existence. This reformulation claims to have displaced the reductive economistic and historicist tendencies in Marxist analysis and put in their place the notion of ideology as having a 'relative autonomy' of function. Ideology is then a practice that is transformative in constructing its own 'real' and its realm of effectivity is, in Lacanian terms, the domain of 'imaginary' identifications.

Art, which is an effect of ideology, has its authentic practices, its specific categories of transformation, and therefore its own autonomous productions. It is in the projected *closures* of ideology that the effectivity of the *practice* is best seen; it is the contradictory coherence of ideological closure that is crucial to this form of analysis. Ideological closure – as indeed the resolution of the work of art within this problematic – re-presses or displaces 'contradiction', which is the point at which the 'real' of history exceeds art. For the textual representation of contradiction is, in the last instance, the tension of the text's own insertion in capitalist relations of production. As re-latively autonomous, then, the practices of art or literature are elaborated in complex and intricate systems of representation analogous to Freud's mechanisms of the dream-work. Structurally they can be over-determined or displaced, de-centred as they are by an *absence* which is doubly determined. Literature functions at once as the trace of the repression of the contradictions of late capitalist history as well as the textual 'working over' of that repression. In Freudian terms, it is not a forgetting but a forgetting of the forgetting. However relatively autonomous literary practice may be, however perspicacious its 'distantiating' aesthetic effect in revealing contradictions in and between ideologies, the *objectivity* of literature lies in its function of producing those ideological identifications which secure the political conditions of capitalist reproduction.
For instance Pierre Macherey writes:

So the objectivity of literature is its necessary place within the determinate processes ... in which the effectivity of the ideology of bourgeois education is realized.[29]

It then becomes the function of the scientific practice of Marxism, to decentre ideology by making its absence speak. Similarly, critics who work within the tradition of ideological analysis, see it is as their function to transform the repressions of the text, its 'articulate silences', into a form of knowledge.

Unlike image-analysis where the knowledge of the *production* of the text is limited to the question of its reflection and evaluation, ideological analysis proposes textual signification as the articulation of the historical in the form of literary representation. The politics of signification are not seen as a prescriptive construction or an authorial intention working on the 'outside' of the text. Literature and History, mediated by the concept of ideological practice, are part of an internal relationship; a process of that internal contradiction which, Macherey suggests, constitutes literature as an ideological form. In resolving and resituating ideological conflict, Literature provides a foregrounding of the devious operations of 'Ideology-in-General',[30] in the very act by which it forestalls the unmediated emergence of Historical contradiction in the field of representation and the imaginary.

Henri Mitterand's ideological analysis of a passage from Céline's *Journey to the End of the Night* is one of the few theoretically sophisticated studies of colonial discourse.[31] He explicitly resists taking the text on the simple mimetic level, for he is interested in clarifying its *ideological content*. Mitterand proposes to expose the contradictory construction of the 'text-in-between' the racist discourse of the European merchant and the ambiguous Christian discourse of Bardamu, the narrator.

Using structural models Mitterand shows how various codes in the text – (principally those that Barthes would classify as the hermeneutic, proairetic and symbolic codes) – articulate a discourse of degradation of which the dominant connotation is racism. The commercial transaction between a *colon* and a native, which constitutes the action of the narrative, ideally demands two free individuals participating in a fair exchange, but, as Mitterand shows, this is inevitably contradicted by its location within an exploitative colonial system. Observing the silence and powerlessness of the Africans, Mitterand concludes that they are deprived of the two fundamental signs of communication and exchange within Western society – words and money – both of which are monopolized by the European in the Colonial context. This contradictory commercial practice – where peremptory exchange becomes peremptory barter – is the dynamic of the narrative. It is 'staged' in the ambiguous discourse of the narrator Bardamu, whose participation in the racist act is balanced and made enigmatic by his satiric narratorial distance from the values of the merchant's colonialist discourse. Bardamu's narrative authority is a result of what Mitterand sees as the discourse of Christian ideology which maintains an explicit silence when confronted by racist discourse, but mediates the passive silences of the oppressed and gives them – between the lines – a stoicism and dignity. This establishes the *presence* of the natives, while the operations of racist colonial discourse *efface* them. The narrator's final line – 'You'd have said that they were trying to understand what had happened to them' – is read by Mitterand as a 'mark of resistance'. The deciphering of the codes of oppression is the first act of liberation.[32]

Within the narrator's discourse, reformist, sentimentalist and pious at best, scorn and pity, disgust and complicity are not incompatible. It is the function of ideological analysis to identify the internal distancing of racist ideology achieved through satire and ambiguity. This Mitterand does by showing how the political issue of colonialist exploitation is represented as an overdetermined instance of the moral problem of racism. Such a decentring finally restores the textual real to its objective conditions:

The silence regarding the political wheels of colonization, the background structures of metropolitan power. . . . In short, it is the silence about the true system and history of colonization.[33]

One of the central problems of ideological analysis is apparent here: the science of the text is founded on a functionalist view of the literary effect. Like other forms of ideological practice within Althusserian Marxism, aesthetic practice, which produces the literary effect, has an intriguing materiality.

To assess the innovatory potential of Althusser's theory, we must come to terms with a crucial paradox in his concept of Ideology. It amounts to saying, in his own words, that Ideology-*in-general* is historyless, but specific ideologies have a history of their own. It is as if to conceive of a living, materialist history of Ideology as a differential and diachronic practice, Althusser has to first construct a monument to its eternal presence. This paradox represents a symptomatic moment in

Althusser's articulation of structuralism and Marxism, setting, the scene for what, post-Hirst, is recognized as the functionalism of Althusser's concept of ideology.

To deconstruct the 'expressive totality' and teleology of the Hegelian – Marxist dialectic, Althusser, introduces a 'decentred totality' constructed through a system of differential *practices* – economic, political, ideological, theoretical. Ideology-in-general is a concept inscribed in the subjectless discourse of theoretical practice, and introduces into the system an invariant structure and function. Such a structuralist move is crucial to the argument despite the problems it entails for a Marxist theory. It enables Althusser to conceive of the *space* of Ideology-in-general as historyless or omni-historical, thus permitting a functionality without the necessity of any notion of the expression or transmission of a substantial *content* – class, economy, etc. Ideology-in-general *as* theoretical practice does not participate in interpellation – the siting/sighting of social subjects – which is the *practice* through which *specific* ideologies develop a relatively autonomous history of their own. Althusser is then able to avoid reductive forms of determinism, without confronting the real issue of the hierarchy and priority of determinate instances. He sidesteps this crucial problem in his Marxist-structuralist mutation, which is the concept of the social totality as a 'structure-in-dominance'.[34]

For Althusser's theory of ideology the determinism of the economic as class struggle 'in the last instance' is not the reflection of a pre-given *content*. It is a much more sophisticated mode of representation which is *the specific reproduction of a general function* which makes possible the *imaginary* relation of individuals to the real relations in which they live. Ideological formations and their effects – literature, for instance – are relatively autonomous in two significant ways. Firstly, by taking the question of mediation seriously, there is an acceptance of ideology as constituting a necessary illusion which then makes an allusion to the reality of class struggle (Althusser's formula, ideology = illusion/allusion). Secondly, there is an initial and partial acknowledgement of the heterogenous construction of ideological effects, distributed across a range of sites and structures of interpellation, – both regimes of representation and Ideological State Apparatuses (School, Church, media, etc.).

Despite Althusser's notions of a decentred social formation and the autonomy and materiality of representation, the inherent distancing function of Literature, placed eternally between Ideology and Science, denies Literary practice a properly transformative role. Literature transforms the materials of its production only to *re-produce* the function of Ideology-in-general; its articulation and address are caught in the 'imaginary' of its mirror – relation to the supervening reality of Ideology-in-general. Ideological analysis resists the material practices of the text as a process by which heterogeneous discourses are 'produced' in different modes of writing. It cannot conceive of textuality as the transformations of ideology within differentiated modes of address, producing practices of writing as *literatures* rather than an invariant Literature.[35] Despite its interpellation of ideological subjects for its reading or 'reproduction' the address of the text is, in the last instance, to the unitary subjectless discourse of Science. This results in an 'essentialist' deep structural search for the dominant textual discourse, its silences, and their position in relation to the critical science which produces a 'materialist' knowledge. The reader is then essentially 'given', outside the process of the text, not positioned as its effect at the crucial point of articulation and address.

There is also a teleological impulse in ideological analysis which produces a final 'closure' in providing a *science* of the text. This amounts to a denial of the rich and suggestive structure of productivity assigned to both literature and ideology which enables their articulate silences to speak in many wondrous tongues – overdetermined, metaphoric, displaced, metonymic.... The 'not-said' of the text may then be read as the 'given' which an Althusserian symptomatic reading, 'completes' with the knowledge of its history and thus makes the text consumable. Looked at like this. Historical Materalism would be the *ideal* normative text, and consequently ideological analysis would participate in that same manoeuvre of refusal-and-appropriation which Macherey considers to be the paradigm of empiricist criticism. The materiality of the text – its production of contradictions and fissures – is then merely the necessary operation of its ideological effect, which scientific criticism will later integrate into a higher metadiscursive unity. 'The textual-real', Eagleton writes, 'is related to the historical real as the product of signifying practices whose source and referent is, in the last instance, history itself.'[36]

It is problematic to conceive of signifying practices on the basis of a notion of History which, if not an 'expressive totality', is still a 'decentred totality', teleological and normative in the last instance. This results in a system of binary oppositions in Eagleton's work – textual or pseudo-real *vs* historical real, Ideology *vs* Science – which flaws an otherwise rich and ambitious encounter with the materiality of signifying practices. The 'not-said' which is the quiddity of the literary text, its distancing effect, is the mark of 'certain determinate absences which *twist* its various significations into conflict and contradiction.'[37] But the notion of *twisting* implies a normative position of equivalence where the signifier is finally absorbed into the signified, which further weakens the original claim for the literary as a relatively autonomous transformative practice. The 'excess' of signification, of 'fictionality', is finally normalized when it finds its referent in its function as ideological effect. This is, then, to constitute a new sign which is 'historical' but no less unitary.

This leads us back to Mitterand's analysis, and especially to the concept of *language* within ideological analysis. I think it can be fairly said that Mitterand's reading is essentially a sophisticated Marxist-structuralist mimeticism in that he is illustrating what he himself describes as ideological *contents*. In his analysis, language – the very material of literary practice – is seen as a *theme* within the text, merely the *instrument* of social relationship reflected in the text. Its effectivity as a material condition of textuality and as a site of the problem of representation is never considered or questioned. This is apparent in the way his analysis works to continually locate the 'essence' or 'the last instance' of the ideological content within the play of the literary discourse, ignoring the text's articulation of ideological discourses and modes of address. So the 'theatrical' *mise-en-scène* in which the colonial transaction takes place is read reductively: 'The discourse of commerce forms the ideologized version of the art of spoilation in this specific situation i.e. the colonial situation.'[38]

Mitterand's concept of colonial discourse, marks an advance in the debate on the representation of the colonial subject. The naive mimetic relationship between language and social reality is exceeded by Mitterand's analysis of the complex narrative function of colonial discourse: the contradictory articulation of Christian piety and the commercial imperatives of colonialist racism which, in repressing the 'political', produces a moral discourse that closes the narrative on a note of irony rather than impaling it on an alienating open-endedness. The value of literature does not lie in its evocation of an unmediated reality, but in the predisposition of its torsions (to continue Eagleton's sense of the 'twist' of signification) to a 'symptomatic' reading which reveals the colonial situation. What is troubling here is that the subjectless discourse of science that produces the reading, is itself effaced and, consequently, the relation of literary signification to its historical determinants reverts to a necessarily allegorical relationship.[39] Unlike the mimeticism of image-analysis, ideological analysis has no faith in a transparent, unmediated reality. However, in the shadow-play between ideology and science, it does assume that distortions and miscognitions of representation are in fact the baroque excrescences of a relentless historical rationalism; that, in the last instance, the former can be 'read off' from the latter.

What is jeopardized for critical analysis is what interests us most. That is, the process through which, in relation to social and institutional practices, and within the 'inter-text' of other discourses, literary signification 'fixes' its significations – a fixing that makes meaning stable and fastens the subject in a position of intelligibility. If meaning is fixed pre-emptively in Ideology or Reality or History, then there is the danger of slipping back into Derrida's violent hierarchy of Subject and Object. The concepts of discourse and signifying practice, with their emphasis on the systematic, arbitrary construction of the sign, and their rejection of a metadiscursive will to knowledge,

do not allow me to pose the text as an object 'outside' ideology nor as an object 'inside' ideology, but rather as one of the crucial points of the articulation of the ideological and of the relations between the imaginary and the symbolic on which ideology turns.[40]

III

The appropriation of *A House for Mr Biswas* (*House*) within the canon of the Great Tradition is not unproblematic, for its *difference* as Commonwealth or Caribbean literature must initially be recognized. It is only, however, on condition that it transcends its 'narrow', 'parochial', colonial concerns and achieves 'universality' that it gains admittance into the pantheon. Once it is appropriated as a good object, however, its status in turn signifies the liberalism of the Great Tradition and the pre-eminence of the Anglo-American literary institution. Universality is achieved by introducing a split in the text such that the signification of the colonial *content* is set as *fact* against a retrospective literary or *fictional value* which is represented in the progress of the narrative, its ability to transcend and resolve the colonial contradictions of cultural heterogeneity, racial mixedness, historical and social anomie.

This split is visible in the very language of Landeg White's assessment,[41] the fullest to date. He commends the solidity and comprehensiveness of Naipaul's evocation of 'a whole history (which) has passed before our eyes'. Naipaul, he writes approvingly, *notes* economic change, *records* changes in characters, *chronicles* the loss of India and the Creolization of the Hindu Community: he *attends* to the smallest *detail* of background, unobtrusively, accurately, and then we see the *island as a whole*. The *fixity* of the colonial, its reality is grasped *wholly* in the eye of the viewer; its discourse is descriptive, anatomical, enumerative. Its vocabulary is engaged, as Said says of the discourse of Orientalism, 'in the particularizing and dividing of things into manageable parts'.[42] But change, growth, choice, will and resolve, these are the terms – ethical and formal – which mark the progress of narrative, and give fiction its value and resolution. This is achieved, according to White, through the *metaphor* of the House which is the cumulative centre of the novel, the perfect symbolic identification between inner and outer. The value of the narrative then lies in the ability of this metaphorization to heal the break between the descriptive and the evaluative, colonial content and literary value, signifier and signified. *A House for Mr Biswas* then becomes the first of Naipaul's novels to reach confidently *beyond* Trinidad...writes White, 'it is a novel dealing with human problems of universal application, drawing on a mass of local detail to make itself credible.'[42]

To 'metaphorize' the production of meaning is to introduce a principle of equivalence whereby the work of the narrative – the transformation of differential narrative and ideological codes into the textual system and mode of address – is concealed within a set of categories of closure and resolution, such as 'character', or 'mimetic irony'. That these are also substitutions which introduce a specific *cultural* cohesiveness is clear: behind 'character' stands the Western liberal humanist individual; behind the realist irony, a European philosophical tradition of ethical realism. Stephen Heath is surely right when he identifies this direction of the narrative subject as a conversion of desire into affectivity, its purpose is to hold 'the process of production, the enunciation, onto the product, the enoncé, *without any gap or loss*, in a simple identity in meaning and subject.'[44]

To demonstrate thematically how *House* resists its appropriation into the Great Tradition of literary Realism would not be difficult. It would be possible to see the tropes of the text as metonymy and repetition instead of metaphor, and its mode of address as the 'uncanny' rather than irony. For the text abounds with references to loss, circularity and the demoniacal. This process begins with Mr Biswas's primal loss of a finger, his birth which accidentally or prophetically causes the death of his father; it proceeds with the repeated and uncanny gains and losses of a series of homes. This is accompanied by the constant loss of his paternal and professional position; the sad story ends, ambivalently, with the gain of a deeply faulted home where he feels entirely cheated by the loss of his son Anand who has gone abroad and refuses to write. His death is lost in tiny print at the end of a newspaper page, whereas he expected it to feature in banner headlines. Each turn of fate or plot is initially seen as the promise, in Biswas's words, of 'a real life that was to begin soon and elsewhere'. He defers all his

pleasure in life until that day when anything could happen, but
each time the future comes 'it was a blackness, a void like those
in dreams into which past and tomorrow, next week and next
year he was falling.' If the real is always elsewhere, its loss is
never explained other than as the pursuit by a demonic
power – either the blackness outside him that forever drags
him back to the place that had 'already been hollowed out for
him'; or the recurrent pain of the encysted ulcer, the wound
inside, which accompanies anger and langour. And finally,
almost in the centre of the novel, there is the spectacle of
Biswas's madness when he is haunted by the repetitive chaos
and cacophony of 'words', sliding, shifting, terrorizing, and the
continual fear for his 'fleshy parts' – a disjunction between the
word and the flesh so complete that he says 'I am not whole'.

If this theme of castration and loss produces an alternative reading, its collusion in a successive schema makes it
merely another form of mimetic reading. The disturbance in
narrative enunciation that I want to draw attention to will not
be contained within a realist problematic. It is the process by
which narrative authority and control is lost, precisely because
the very objective of narrative – its plenitude, its signification
of a unitary real – is jeopardized in the articulation of the
scenarios of colonial fantasy. These are the 'amazing scenes' of
colonial desire: the day-dreams, within which Biswas is
repeatedly narrativized – as observer, as actor, as writer, as
Samuel Smiles and the Scarlet Pimpernel, as *padre* and
padrone – and each time, uncannily, the fantasy is interrupted
or left incomplete ....

Narrative control has initially to be maintained *between* two
discourses: one, the discourse of Hinduism, the main signifier
of which is the republic of Hanuman House (The Tulsis); the
other, the discourse of individual romance – that's to say,
'Biswas'. Playing over the Tulsis is the divinely guaranteed sign
of Hanuman – and the closed narrative of Hindu mythology
and astrology. Its mode of address is the fabular and the
mock epic; its trope is metaphor and its linguistic register
is the spoken word or prophecy – inflections, implications,
innuendos – but always within the world of close correspondences guaranteed by destiny and divine intentionality.
Its class location is the rural or provincial Indian petty

bourgeoisie, protecting their fragmented, traditional, migrant culture in the face of a growing Caribbean Creolization. This ascriptive realm is also called the world of 'women', where there are only congealed nameless collectivities and statuses, such as the Hindu joint family confers. Its political register is a law of benevolent despotism, not above perpetuating trace elements of a tradition of indentured labour. It is a discourse that denies the positive force of individual will and action, plots a form of temporality that is anecdotal, incidental, picaresque and, from Biswas's view, lacks the full-blooded, multi-layered narrative of romance.

However attractive it may be for the omniscient narrative metalanguage to ally with this *histoire*, its complete erasure of the marks of enunciation in myth and fable cannot reasonably allow a beginning, a proper novelistic narrational initiation. It is for this reason that the narrative continually has to perspectivize the stability of the Hindu discourse through the movement of the other discourse of romance and phantasy which is the individualist progress of Biswas, described in the text as the desire to 'paddle your own canoe'.

The narrative of 'Biswas' and the discourse of 'character' satisfy those ideological and formal demands of realist narrative that in displacing the ascriptive totalitarian discourse of Hanuman House foregrounds the values of individualism, progressivism, and the autonomy of character. Its trope is metonymy, its sign is the written word. It is the discourse of *colonial promise*: of the familialization of relations in a Western sense – the repeated desire for the independent Home, the nuclear family – and the familiarization of the signs of the Western literary tradition – Dickens, Shakespeare, Marie Corelli. Its political register is a tropical liberalism, set against the oligarchy of the 'Om', but caught deeply in the imaginary of late Victorian moralism, its Smilesean self-help.

To the extent to which stasis and romance are in a dynamic relation, the narrative can play one discourse off against another in the manner of classical realism, generating irony and humour, conjuring up the *comédie humaine*. But the driving desire of 'Biswas' conceals a much graver subject: the subject of madness, illness and loss; the repetition of failure and the deferral of desire; the trauma of being always inscribed between the unwritten – Biswas's unfinished narcissistic fables; and the endlessly re-written – the beginning of the novel re-writes the end and in that sense it never really begins or ends. It is here that the fantasy of the text lies; a fantasy that is resistant to the tension releases of humour, and so to the structural resolutions of comedy.

For as Freud reminds us, the uncanny ambivalence of fantasy comes from its mixed nature.[45] It is a problematic scenario in which both the pre-conscious imaginary day-dream and the unconscious structure of primal fantasy both play their parts in ever-changing ratios and roles. The important distinction between them, relevant to fictional discourse, is that the imaginary scenario of the day-dream is basically played out in terms of the first-person who is then the 'author' of the fantasy. The structure of primal fantasy, however, is characterized by the absence of subjectivization; and subject's presence in the scene may split, shift, slide, move from the first to the third person, be the actor and observer all at once. It is with this in mind that Freud always held the model of fantasy to be the reverie, that form of novelette, both stereotyped and infinitely variable, which the subject composes and relates to himself in a waking state.[46] The problem that this raises for narrative is not that of an opposition between different forms or moods of narration. It poses a troubling question to the whole project of narrative intention and control as we encounter it in realist texts, and suggests that they may be decentred and subverted from within.

To the extent to which the narrative omniscience can assimilate the fantasy at the level of its *imaginary* ingredient – that is, to the extent that it is structured in the first person – it can resolve its disturbance in terms of irony and comedy. But there is always the threat of the figuring of 'desire' in the *structure* of fantasy, in the literally end-less repetition of Biswas's fantasies. It is not so much the circulation of the same signifiers as the fear of repetition itself which disturbs the narrative. For it faces the traditions of realist discourse with a spectacle of loss and failure unparalleled in its social and generic history. For what the repetitive scenes of fantasy pose, in shifting and unsettling the otherwise unitary space of narrative enunciation, is the impending crisis in a myth of subjectivity founded on the assumption of 'identity', and in a myth of narrative based on linear progression and closure. In the spectacular failure of Biswas's desire to be both Father and Author, in those repeated incompletions, is based the whole problem of 'beginning' in two obvious, familiar senses. The structural crisis of the staging of the subject in fantasy questions both myths of origination on the grounds of colonial desire.

To the myth of the holy, nuclear family as the site of the authoritative marking of the subject's 'identity' and entry into the social sphere as an Individual, colonial fantasy faces the spectacle of other bodies, marked racially or tribally. Colonial fantasy raises questions about the link between self-consciousness and moral conduct which has become the Western norm for the individuation of the 'person' and the basis of its social designation – what Hirst and Woolley have recently termed the 'consciencization' of the Western subject that extends its influence to Althusser's concept of interpellation.[47]

To the myth of realist narrative – its grand syntagms and sequentiality, its pleasure, irony, comedy, characters and consolations, its historic utterances and easy identifications between I and you – colonial fantasy presents scenarios that make problematic both Authority and Intention. It registers a crisis in the assumption of the narrative priority of the 'first person' and the *natural* ascendancy of the First World. And this colonial fantasy – this specific historical formation of the 'subject' – demands another kind of reading, another gaze. Foucault has described it well:

A glance that distinguishes, separates and disperses, that is capable of liberating divergence and marginal elements – the kind of dissociating view that is capable of decomposing itself, capable of shattering the unity of man's being through which it was thought that he could extend his sovereignty to the events of the past.[48]

In shattering the mirror of representation, and its range of Western bourgeois social and psychic 'identifications', the spectacle of colonial fantasy sets itself up as an uncanny 'double'. Its terrifying figures – savages, grotesques, mimic men – reveal things so profoundly familiar to the West that it cannot bear to remember them. It is in that sense, and for that very reason, that 'The horror! the horror!' said in the heart of darkness itself, and the 'Ou-boum' of the empty Marabar caves will continue to terrify and confound us, for they address that 'other scene' within ourselves that continually divides us against ourselves and others.

NOTES

* Written in mid-1980, this essay tries to bring together diverse critical practices to demonstrate the limits of certain forms of representationalism. Its original aim was to raise questions about the colonial text – that specific articulation of cultural and racial difference within the colonial and post-colonial context. I wanted to draw attention to a theoretically underdeveloped area and to argue for a consideration of the ideological and textual practices of colonialism within recent theoretical developments. The colonial text functions, in this essay, more by implication and example than as a substantial, theoretical category. For developments in that direction see my 'On Colonial Discourse' to be published in the collected papers of the Sociology of Literature Conference 1982, University of Essex.

1 E. Said, *Beginnings* (Baltimore : London: Johns Hopkins University Press, 1978) pp. 76–7.

2 B. Bergonzi, *The Situation of the Novel* (Harmondsworth: Pelican, 1972), p. 42.

3 F. R. Leavis, *D. H. Lawrence Novelist* (London: Chatto & Windus, 1955). See especially 'Lawrence and Tradition'.

4 Iris Murdoch quoted in Bergonzi, *op. cit.* pp. 57–60.

5 W. J. Harvey, *Character and the Novel* (London: Chatto & Windus, 1965), chapters, 5 & 6.

6 W. Booth, *The Rhetoric of Fiction* (Chicago & London: University of Chicago Press, 1967), pp. 297–8.

7 Said, *op. cit.* p. 82.

8 Wilson Harris, *Tradition, The Writer and Society* (London: New Beacon Publications, 1973).

9 V. S. Naipaul, 'Jasmine', *Times Literary Supplement*, 4 June, 1964.

10 Iris Murdoch, 'The Sublime and the Beautiful, *Yale Review*, Vol. XLIX, p. 271.

11 R. W. Sander, 'The Thirties and Forties', in *West Indian Literature*, ed. B. King (London: Macmillan 1979), pp. 50–1.

12 A Giddens, *Central Problems in Social Theory* (London: Macmillan, 1979), p. 201.

13 Leavis, *op. cit.* p. 135.

14 M. Foucault, *The Archaeology of Knowledge* (London: Tavistock Publications, 1972), p. 12.

15 'Nationalist criticism': i.e. that written from a Third World perspective,

anti-colonialist and anti-racist, demanding that discriminatory stereotypes should be identified, and so replaced with authentic images of
Black consciousness.

16   P. Hirst, 'Althusser's Theory of Ideology', *Economy and Society*, Vol. V,
     No. 4, 1976, pp. 408–11.
17   Derrida quoted in M. Cousins, 'The Logic of Deconstruction', *Oxford
     Literary Review*, Vol. 3, No. 2, p. 72.
18   P. Macherey, *A Theory of Literary Production* (London: Routledge &
     Kegan Paul, 1978), p. 18.
19   L. Althusser and E. Balibar, *Reading Capital* (London: New Left
     Books, 1975), p. 313.
20   K. Ramchand, 'Concern for Criticism', *Caribbean Quarterly*, Vol 16,
     No. 2, June 1970, pp. 51–60.
21   R. Scruton, *Art and Imagination* (London: Methuen, 1974), pp. 248–9.
22   Macherey, *op. cit.*, p. 16.
23   F. Mulhern, *The Moment of 'Scrutiny'* (London: New Left Books,
     1979), p. 117.
24   T. Eagleton, *Criticism and Ideology* (London: New Left Books 1976),
     p. 164.
25   T. Abbott, 'Theory of Authority in Politics and Cinema', *Screen*
     Vol. 20, No. 2, p. 16.
26   For last three references, see Mulhern, *op. cit.*, especially chapter two,
     section four, pp. 115–78.
27   Chinna Achebe, 'Colonialist Criticism', in *Morning Yet on Creation Day*
     (London: Heinemann, 1975), p. 9.
28   S. Neale, 'The Same Old Story: Stereotypes and Differences', *Screen
     Education*: Nos. 32/33.
29   P. Macherey, 'On Literature or an Ideological Form', *Oxford Literary
     Review*, Vol. 3., No. 1, p. 7.
30   L. Althusser, *Lenin and Philosophy* (London: New Left Books, 1971),
     pp. 150–2. His structuralism requires the designation of ideology-in-
     general as an immanent function, a 'history-less' model, acting as basis
     for predicting specific ideological practices.
31   H. Mitterand, 'Colonial Discourse in *Journey to the End of the Night*, *Sub-
     Stance*, 15, 1976.
32   *ibid.*, p. 30.
33   *ibid.*, p. 28.
34   Althusser and Balibar, *op. cit.*, p. 319. Especially: 'The economic base
     '*determines*' ('in the last instance') *which* element is to be dominant in a
     social formation. But the dominant element is not fixed for all time; it
     varies according to the overdetermination of the contradictions and their
     uneven development'.
35   T. Bennett, *Formalism and Marxism* (London: Metheun, 1979).
36   Eagleton, *op. cit.*, p. 75.
37   *ibid.*, p. 28.
38   Mitterand, *op. cit.*, p. 24.
39   See F. Jameson, *The Political Unconscious* (London: Metheun, 1981)
     which appeared after this chapter was written.

40 C. MacCabe, 'Discourse, Cinema and Politics', *Screen*, Vol. 19, No. 4, p. 35.
41 L. White, *V. S. Naipaul* (London: Macmillan, 1975).
42 E. Said, *Orientalism* (London: Routledge & Kegan Paul, 1980), p. 72.
43 White, *op. cit.*, p. 126.
44 S. Heath, '*Touch of Evil*: Film and system', Part II, *Screen*, Vol. 16, No. 2., p. 108.
45 See J. Laplanche and J-B Pontalis, 'Fantasy and the Origins of Sexuality', *International Journal of Psychoanalysis*, Vol. 49, 1968, pp. 1–17.
46 ibid., p. 13.
47 P. Hirst and P. Woolley, *Social Relations and Human Attributes* (London: Tavistock Publications, 1982), chapter seven.
48 M. Foucault, *Language, Counter-Memory, Practice* (Oxford: Blackwell, 1977), p. 153.

4 Bakhtin, Sociolinguistics and Deconstruction

Allon White

In this essay I want to show that Bakhtin produced a theory of literature which encompassed and pushed beyond the present opposition between structural and sociolinguistic views of literary language. Moreover, since literary structuralism and deconstruction are ultimately linked to the same debate, I believe Bakhtin's theory simultaneously encompassed and pushed beyond them too. By 'pushed beyond', I mean that Bakhtin's work prefigured both structuralist and deconstructionist views of the language of literature, but crucially placed them both in a sociolinguistic framework which thereby makes them responsive to an historical and thoroughly social comprehension of literature. In other words, Bakhtin's theory of language can *give an account* of the split between structural and functional linguistics which is something neither tendency can do within its own terms.

For Bakhtin, language is conceived neither as a closed system of self-identical norms nor as a subjectively expressive medium, but as the concrete and ceaseless flow of *utterance* produced in dialogues between speakers in specific social and historical contexts. Throughout all his writing it is this emphasis on the centrality of dialogue, the dialectics of utterance, which grounds his ideas. His linguistic project set out to avoid abstract objectivism and individualistic subjectivism by centring its attention upon dialogic interaction.

Dialogue foregrounds speech diversity. Decades before they became of importance in sociolinguistics the concepts of *sociolect* and *register* were used by Bakhtin to explore the *heteroglossia* of social formations made manifest in discourse. Bakhtin writes:

At any given moment of its historical existence language is heteroglot from top to bottom: it represents the co-existence of socio-ideological con-tradictions between the present and the past, between different epochs of the past, between different socio-ideological groups in the present, between tendencies, schools, circles and so forth all given in bodily form.[1]

Heteroglossia is Bakhtin's key term for describing the complex stratification of language into genre, register, sociolect, dialect and the mutual interanimation of these forms. In 'Discourse in the Novel' he gives his most extended and detailed outline of the various elements which make up heteroglossia; it is clear that it covers a wide range of linguistic forms. Language is stratified according to social activity. Bakhtin does not use the term register, which was unavailable to him, but says:

There is interwoven with . . . generic stratification of language a *professional* stratification of language, in the broad sense of the term 'professional', the language of the lawyer, the doctor, the businessman, the politician, the public education teacher an so forth, and these sometimes coincide with, and sometimes depart from, the stratification into generes.[2]

Bakhtin considers the formal linguistic markers of register indissociable from the intentional dimension of its meaning. To study only the formal linguistic features of different registers without understanding how they appropriate, possess and dispossess language of specific concrete meanings, is to produce a mere catalogue of dead forms. Every register is typification, a style, the bearer of specific sociocultural inten-tions; at the same time register is the bearer of self-referential identity which we recognize as such. Registers cannot help advertising themselves. We recognize them as pertaining to certain groups and certain social activities, hence as the registration of historical and social distinctions – not least power relations and hierarchies. Registers are thus not only a form of stratification, they are simultaneously language-images of stratification.

Furthermore, each social group or class stands in a different relation to the abstract system of the speech community in which it finds itself. Sociolects refer to the differential posses-sion and concretizing of that system by different social groups defined by age, gender, economic position, kinship, relation and so forth. Bakhtin has a much more conflict-centred view of sociolect than most linguists. Not only does he emphasize the way differences between the forms used to convey meaning identify and differentiate social groups, he sees sociolects as constantly struggling to attract words and linguistic forms into their own orbit, in order to reinflect them for their own use. Words are inflected by a certain sociolect so as to impose upon them 'specific semantic nuances and specific axiological overtones, thus (the sociolect) can create slogan-words, curse-words, praise-words and so forth.'[3] M. A. K. Halliday and Roger Fowler (the latter explicitly drawing on Bakhtin) have developed sociolinguistic analyses of groups in an antagonistic relation to the dominant culture; deviant sub-cultures, 'thieves, junkies, sexual, "perverts", convicts, political terrorists, street vandals', groups which systematically invert, negate and relexicalize the norm language. It is this area of linguistic combat, the ideological interanimation between unmerged voices, which focuses *dialogism*. For Bakhtin, heteroglossia is not simply a range of sociolinguistic variation nor a kind of horizontal spread of dispersed speech forms: because languages are socially unequal, heteroglossia implies dialogic interaction in which the prestige languages try to extend their control and subordinated languages try to avoid, negotiate or subvert that control. 'Language is not a neutral medium that passes freely and easily into the private property of the speaker's intentions: ... Expropriating it, forcing it to submit to one's own intentions and accents, is a difficult and complicated process.'[4]

'The word in language is half someone else's.'[5] Language, intention and ideology are inextricable for Bakhtin, and correspondingly, his concept of intention is a thoroughly linguistic one which involves a *directedness* towards objects and addressees, but always in a linguistic environment saturated with, and overlaid by, the intentions of others:

But no living word relates to its object in *singular* way: between the word and its object, between the word and the speaking subject, there exists an elastic environment of other alien words about the same object, the same theme, and this is an environment that is often difficult to penetrate. It is precisely in the process of living interaction with this specific environment that the word may be individualized and given stylistic shape.[6]

This agonistic conception of the word struggling to achieve its intention amidst a throng of alien words is recalled in the work of Harold Bloom. Indeed, the *Anxiety of Influence* can be seen from this perspective as a precious and somewhat neuraesthenic version of the same idea. Bloom's 'strong poems' are those which succeed in the agonistic struggle against the alien word. How close Bloom is to Bakhtin when the latter writes:

The word, breaking through to its own meaning and its own expression across an environment full of alien words and variously evaluating accents, harmonizing with some of the elements in this environment and striking a dissonance with others, is able, in this dialogizing process, to shape its own stylistic profile and tone.[7].

Bakhtin and Bloom share a sense of the resistance put up by language against intention, as well as a sharp awareness of the consequent pattern within "thousands of living dialogic threads' woven by consciousness around a given object. But whereas Bloom's heroes are romantic individualists, enlivened and ennervated by the pathos of solitary poetic combat, haunted by the need for strength (there is something enigmatically boyish about this desire for 'strongness' in Bloom), Bakhtin on the other hand generalizes the phenomenon into a broad sociological conception of language. *All* discourse, for Bakhtin, 'lives on the boundary between its own context and another, alien context.'[8] Each and every time it is uttered, a word is recontextualized, pulled in a slightly different direction, imbued with a different inflection:

The word, directed towards its object, enters a dialogically agitated and tension-filled environment of alien words, value judgements and accents, weaves in and out of complex inter-relationships, merges with some, recoils from others, intersects with a third group: all this may crucially shape discourse, may complicate its expression and influence its entire stylistic profile.[9]

What is striking about this passage is not so much its anticipation of a Derridean void inside discourse, carried here in Bakhtin's use of 'alien words', 'trace' and 'recoil', but its remarkable sense of heterogeneity as the living condition of language. Bakhtin uses a variety of rather vague metaphorical terms to grasp this quality of difference which words take on – 'taste', 'profile', 'accent', 'inflection' – all suggesting something subtle and intimate in the difference made to the word in new contexts. This kind of meaning-variation is not normally addressed by formal semantics or sociolinguistics; it is somewhat literary in feeling. This is because, for Bakhtin, even individual words have 'style'. Like Vossler, Bakhtin believes in the precedence of style over grammer; that verbal forms generated in social interaction can later solidify into accepted grammatical norms. His linguistics therefore follows Vossler in this one respect that his studies on language stand on the boundary between stylistics and linguistics. He has a keen ear for what he terms the 'timbre' and the 'overtones' of words, and his insistence upon the 'multiaccentuality' of signs leads naturally to an interest in *the way words present themselves as representing*, their style of presence and address. Bakhtin richly develops the idea of dialogic interaction between 'high' and 'low' forms of language and it is this which prevents the concept of heteroglossia from degenerating into a mixed bag of sociolinguistic variables. Although separate aspects of heteroglossia (genre, register, sociolect, dialect, intertextuality, addressee-anticipation) can all be found under different names in current sociolinguistics, Bakhtin mobilizes them within a social dialectics of contention and negociation. Heteroglossia not only foregrounds the words of people normally excluded from the realms of the 'norm' and the 'standard', it also relativizes the norm itself, subverting its claim to universalism. I think Bakhtin pushes the implications of this to such a point that it becomes a radical critique, not only of 'high' language, but of any theory which tries to generalize and universalize on the basis of that high language, like, say, Transformational Grammar. It is this reason that leads me to suggest that an understanding of heteroglossia may lead one to avoid not only the extravagance of most popular forms of deconstruction but also the restrictions of traditional structuralism.

Let me recall that in 1967 Uriel Weinreich, one of the founders of modern sociolinguistics and the teacher and mentor of William Labov, wrote:

The facts of heterogeneity have not so far jibed well with the structural approach to language .... The solution ... lies in the direction of breaking down the identification of structuredness with homogeneity.[10]

It is precisely this project – breaking down the identification of structuredness with homogeneity – which plays such an important part in Bakhtin. In his work heterogeneity is positive, productive and enriching. He witnesses the perpetual unfolding of social heteroglossia surrounding objects, 'the Tower-of-Babel mixing of languages that goes on around any object; the dialectics of the object are interwoven with the social dialogue surrounding it.'[11] Not only is the word born in a dialogue with the alien words that already inhere in the object; it is born expecting an *answer*, 'every word is directed towards an answer and cannot escape the profound influence of the answering word that it anticipates.'[12] This is a new form of internal dialogism determined by its orientation towards the addressee. It is worth quoting Bakhtin in full:

> The listener and his response are regularly taken into account when it comes to everyday dialogue and rhetoric, but every other sort of discourse as well is oriented towards an understanding that is 'responsive' – although this orientation is not particularized in an independent act and is not compositionally marked . . . now this contradictory environment of alien words is present to the speaker not in the object, but rather in the consciousness of the listner, as his apperceptive background, pregnant with responses and objections . . . .
>
> Therefore his orientation towards the listener is an orientation toward a specific conceptual horizon, toward the specific world of the listener; it introduces totally new elements into his discourse; it is in this way, after all, that various different points of view, conceptual horizons, systems for providing expressive accents, various social 'languages' come to interact with one another. The speaker strives to get a reading on his own word . . . .[13]

This line of dialogism is rhetorical. It is the distinctive form imparted to an utterance when it shapes itself to penetrate as deeply as possible the imagined resistance of its addressee. A kind of reader-oriented self-consciousness, it can be compared to the effect created in discourse by the 'implicit reader' spoken of by Wolfgang Iser. Every utterance is for or to someone, even if s/he is not actually present, and the dialogic anticipation of response is always already inscribed in language as it is spoken. This does not necessarily imply subterfuge. It means, however, that words will be inflected in a slightly new or different way, nuanced to gain power for themselves. As the addressee changes, so do they. Again this is by no means a purely subjective matter: the word is projected toward an alien conceptual horizon which is ideologically illuminated. Bakhtin thus anticipated much of the current German thinking about reception and there are various points at which reception theory and dialogism may be connected up; however that cannot be covered here. What I wish to emphasize is that dialogism is oriented in two directions at once, toward the object (theme) and toward the addressee, both exerting active pressure on the profile and formation of the word.

Let me recall Ulrich Weinreich's exhortation to break down the habitual identification of structuredness with homogeneity. Bakhtin has a strong sense of structure – indeed we should expect as much from a thinker whose work was so closely intertwined with that of the Formalists in the 1920s. In 'Forms of Time and of the Chronotope in the Novel', he explores a wide range of scene and narrative structures in fiction from the Ancient Greeks to Flaubert. But he always considered plot in the novel to be the articulation of different language-images or verbal-ideological discourses. 'In a word', he says, 'the novelistic plot serves to represent speaking persons and their ideological worlds.'[14]

But unlike the early Propp, or many modern structuralists, Bakhtin never envisages structure as transcendental. The authority of structure (political, narrative and syntactic) is socially constructed and historically changing. It is only in societies isolated from significant linguistic diversity that structures of narrative (underpinned by a unified, homogeneous and therefore 'absolute' language) appear to have complete authority – the authority, precisely, of *myth*. For Bakhtin, there is a decisive moment in the life of a speech community when it encounters powerful language other than its own. Suddenly, everything changes under the pressure of this newfound 'polyglossia', 'the simultaneous presence of two or more (national) languages interacting within a single cultural system.'[15] This moment of polyglossia relativizes the 'host' language and displaces it, opening out a distance between language and reality in such a way as to bring both into view for the first time.

After all, it is possible to objectivize one's own particular language, its internal form, the peculiarities of its world view, its specific linguistic habitus, only in the light of another language belonging to someone else, which is

almost as much 'one's own' as one's 'native language'... where languages
and cultures interanimate each other, language became something entirely
different, its very nature changes: in place of a single, unitary sealed-off
Ptolemaic world of language, there appeared the open Galilean world of
many languages, mutually animating each other.[16]

This movement, in a given speech community, from monoglossia to polyglossia, is of extraordinary significance. Two
myths perish simultaneously: 'the myth of a language that
presumes to be the only language, and the myth of a language
that presumes to be completely unified.'[17] Certain traditional
genres such as myth, epic, and tragedy are the products of a
centralizing tendency in language, a monoglossic absolutism.
This is why structuralism works so well for these genres: sealed
off from heteroglossia, they are immune from an intertextual
interference. Nothing can intervene across their endless cycles
of telling and retelling, production and consumption, to
alter the strong regularities which have solidified into their
sequence of articulation. They are the narrative equivalent of
what Marx called 'simple reproduction' in the economic
sphere. That is, a kind of discursive economy which cannot
expand its base because it has not developed a division of
(linguistic) labour to any significant extent. This static cycle of
simple reproduction leads to the constant repetition of a
pattern of self-identical norms, which of course is precisely
what a system or structure consists of. Structuralism tends to
look towards monoglossia to provision its best research. By
contrast, polyglossia begins to free consciousness from the
tyranny of its own language and its own myth of language.
Languages gradually become visible as different, they emerge
as 'language images' which can be represented, set over against
one another, tested and contested. The novel, for Bakhtin, is a
more extensive genre than normally conceived and is born
from this interanimation of language-images. His most cogent
definition of the novel describes it as 'a diversity of social
speech types (sometimes even a diversity of languages) and a
diversity of individual voices, artistically organized'.[18] The
Roman Empire and the Renaissance were both, according to
Bakhtin, periods of marked polyglossia, and in both periods
novelistic genres emerged as a result. Menippean Satire, Ovid's
Metamorphosis, Apuleius's *Golden Ass* are the novelistic fictions

which emerge from ancient Rome, a culture which, Bakhtin says:

> at the outset was characterized by tri-lingualism – Greek, Oscan and Roman. Lower Italy was the home of a specific kind of hybrid culture and hybrid literary forms. The rise of Roman literature is connected in a fundamental way with this trilingual cultural home; this literature was born in the interanimation of three languages – one that was indigenously its own, and two that were other but that were experienced as indigenous.[19]

'Oscan' is important to Bakhtin's argument about both Roman and Renaissance literature. It was from the Oscans that the Romans derived a kind of crude farce called Atellanae, which *The Dictionary of Greek and Roman Geography* defines as resembling

> the performances of Pulcinello, still so popular at Naples and its neighbourhood. When they were transplanted to Rome they were naturally rendered into Latin; but though Strabo is probably mistaken in speaking of the Fabulae Atellanae of his day as still performed at Rome in Oscan, it is very natural to suppose that they were still so exhibited in Campania so long as the Oscan language continued in common use in that country.[20]

The Atellanae provide fascinating evidence for Bakhtin's persistent linking of carnival farce, novelistic form and polyglossia, and it is food for thought that the Atellanae, instrumental in the dialogizing of the literature of ancient Rome, may also have been instrumental (in the transformed guise of Neapolitan folk comedy) in dialogizing Renaissance literature in the way that Bakhtin suggests in *Rabelais and His World.*

Trained in classical philology, Bakhtin is acutely attentive to this hybridization – the influencing and mixing of distinct language-strains. In the Renaissance he sees the birth of modern narratives like *Don Quixote, Gargantua* and *Pantagruel* as crucially determined by an active polyglossia, a dialogic interaction between 'high' classical languages (chivalric romance, sermon, homily, idealist philosophies) and 'low' vernaculars (anecdotes, street-songs, folk-sayings, the languages of the street, the square, the marketplace and the carnival). It is this dialogic relation between high and low languages which became the foundation of his brilliant study of *Rabelais and His World*, in which he shows carnival languages of the common people 'playing up' against the tragic pathos and high seriousness of the dominant artistic, moral and political discourses of the period. In this view the 'earthy' folk word – scatalogical, irreverent, humorous and contradictory – becomes both a critique of, and corrective to, the lie of pathos. The lofty word of authority is 'brought down a peg or two'. In polyglossia the focus of interest for Bakhtin is not merely the interanimation of 'equal' languages, but the interanimation of 'high' with 'low', the conflicts engendered when the dominant, centralizing and unifying language of a hegemonic group is contested by the 'low' language of subordinated classes.

In the modern novel Bakhtin's notion of polyglossia is of decisive importance. Julia Kristeva, together with writers of the once radical *Tel Quel* group in France, have emphasized the polyphonic qualities of major modernist fictions. The hybridization of voices in *Ulysses* and *Finnegans Wake*, the parodying and deflation of the language of authority by 'low' languages, is a fundamental feature of Joyce's work. The Catholic Mass, the Lord's Prayer, the 'high' languages of aesthetics, philosophy and politics, find themselves pulverized by 'common' forms of language – the language of the pub, the gutter press, the brothel, of Dublin working-class life, the market place and the bedroom. Blocks and fragments of language interanimate one another, recontextualizing familiar class, gender and racial styles so that each is reinflected, made-strange or even made questionable by the mobility of context. Official and authoritative languages are plagued by parodic echoes and jokey versions of their sacred words. Even the counterpoint of Stephen Dedalus and Leopold Bloom can be seen, not only as a Don Quixote/Sancho Panza double act, but as a dialogic play of high against low. Stephen's priggish intellectualism collides with Bloom's ingenuous obsession with body and bowels; again and again throughout the day, spiritual intensity is discomfited by the material world of the 'bodily lower strata', of buttocks, belly and feet.

Both *Ulysses* and *Finnegans Wake* are thoroughly carnivalesque in Bakhtin's sense. The opening lines of *Ulysses*, in which 'Stately, plump Buck Mulligan' travesties the Mass, inaugurates a dialogic interplay which will be amplified throughout the text into a total polyphony:

He held the bowl aloft and intoned:
– *Introibo ad altare Dei.*
Halted, he peered down the dark winding stairs and called up coarsely:
– Come up, Kinch. Come up, you fearful jesuit.[21]

In discussing medieval literature Bakhtin underlines the central role of 'degradation' through comic parody or semi-parody of Church Latin forms. 'Cyprian's supper' (*coena Cypriani*) was a peculiar festive travesty of the entire Scriptures; in *Rabelais and His World* Bakhtin remarks that

the influence of the carnival spirit was irresistible: it made a man renounce his official state as monk, cleric, scholar, and perceive the world in its laughing aspect . . . . *Monkish pranks* (*Joca monacorum*) was the title of one of the most popular medieval comic pieces.[22]

It is striking that one of the great works of modern literature should open with hybrid linguistic form, a monkish prank on the part of the irreverent iconoclast Mulligan at the expense of the 'fearful jesuit' Dedalus which, by parodying the Latin Mass, replays the early Renaissance student combat between high language (Latin, the Church) and the vulgate.

It is not my purpose here to apply Bakhtin's ideas in any sustained way to particular novels. A full Bakhtinian analysis of *Ulysses* would be an extraordinarily fruitful enterprise. It is worth nothing, however, that Joyce is almost alone in earlier modern fiction in rejecting the 'lie of tragic pathos' through polyglossia and thus, whilst *he* can be seen as a true inheritor of the carnivalesque spirit, there are many modern writers who recuperate the use of polyglossia so as to reinforce the authority of 'high' languages. Often this is done through a kind of 'stalemating' of sociolects and registers, whereby the cacophony of voices indicates not a robust debunking of powerful groups but a chaos of competing voices, a dissonant chorus wailing within some twentieth-century necropolis.

Malcom Lowry's *Under the Volcano* appears to be a work of the modern carnivalesque. Not only does its story take place on the day of a great fiesta, a real Mexican carnival, the elements of which are woven into the content of the hero's life, but it is self-consciously polyphonic. English, Spanish, Aztec, French and German make up its active polyglossia, whilst the

inebriate, bar-room dialogues of its increasingly drunken
protagonist are played off against the authority of traditional
literature (Faust, Shakespeare, Romanticism, Conrad) and of
dominant discourses (diplomacy, geography, national history). But the fiesta is The Day of the Dead and the polyphony is
that of Babel. The Consul 'proudly insists' that the ruined
pyramid which dominates Cholula is the 'the original Tower of
Babel' and the novel spirals into a confusion of tongues, a tragic
chaos portending the Consul's incomprehension and death:

'My tongue is dry in my mouth for the want of *our* speech. If you let anything
happen to yourself you will be harming my flesh and mind. I am in your hands
now. Save – '
'Mexican works, England works, Mexican works, sure, French works. Why
speak English? Mine Mexican, Mexican United States he sees *Negros* – de
comprende – Detroit, Houston, Dallas . . . .
'¿Quiere usted la salvación de Méjico? ¿Quiere usted que Cristo sea nuestro
Rey?'
'No.'[23]

Here is an exemplary polyglossia, not only mobilizing
Yvonne's pleading – 'My tongue is dry in my mouth for the
want of *our* speech' – words written in a letter – in such a way
as to equate lost love with the alienation of speech; but also
invoking the cacophony of the bar (its Spanish radio programme, the Consul's drunken ramblings and the conversation
of the Mexican) as a metonymy of breakdown – the Consul's
and also the world's, for each is slithering to its own ravine, the
Consul to his grave and the world to the Second World War (it
is 1938). Here then, polyglossia is pressed back into the service
of romantic pathos, recuperated through its evocation of
alienated misunderstanding and irreducible foreignness. 'Our
Speech' has become lost in the clamour of heteroglossia, a sea
of tragic babble. *Under the Volcano* rejects any form of
salvation and the Consul's monosyllabic 'No' to the rhetorical
inquiry of the radio as to the desire for salvation (of Mexico, of
the soul) underwrites the form of the book as a whole. Often
highly comic in its parody of high language (I particularly
remember the Consul's drunken misreadings of Dr Vigil's
visiting card, turning his list of certificates, diplomas and
university qualifications into a bizarre enumeration of sexual
debility), the novel nevertheless operates overall to stay within

a religious and Faustian myth of a fall without resurrection. Its complex heteroglossia (to which I can do no more than gesture here) does not automatically produce a carnivalesque subversion of the old hierarchies.

A more complex case than either *Ulysses* or *Under the Volcano* is provided by the novels of Thomas Pynchon. Again, *The Crying of Lot 49*, *V* and *Gravity's Rainbow* appear to provide perfect examples of Bakhtin's thesis. The 'high' languages of modern America – technology, psychoanalysis, business, administration and military jargon – are 'carnivalized' by a set of rampant, irreverent, inebriate discourses from low life – from the locker-room, the sewers (in *V*), the jazz club and cabaret, New York Yiddish, student fraternities and GI slang. In *Gravity's Rainbow* history is referred to as a 'St Giles's Fair', and the symbolic pig, the carnival animal *par excellence*, wallows everywhere in Pynchon's writing as the foul-mouthed but irrepressible subvert of prissy WASP orderliness. Krinkles Porcino, 'Pig' Bodine, Porky Pig and others grunt their indulgent, sardonic disapproval of American corporate Enterprise. Dozens of different registers, dialects, sociolects and even national languages interanimate each other in Pynchon's work to provide a dazzling intertextuality of misquotation and bizarre dialogue. But Pynchon does not simply amalgamate or relativize a host of different language-forms. He produces a dialogic confrontation whereby power and authority are probed and ritually contested by these debunking vernaculars.

The result, however, is different both from the positive carnival of *Ulysses* and the romantic dissolution of *Under the Volcano*. Pynchon neutralizes the conflict of high and low language by framing it within narratives of enigma. He appears, again and again in his stories, to reject *both* the high and the low, setting them off against each other in hilarious scenes which unnervingly flip over into sinister intimations of death and apocalypse. *Gravity's Rainbow* is strangely like a *Ulysses* written by Lowry mixed into *Under the Volcano* written by Joyce: a feast of words is set against conspiracies of holocaust and war. At any second in the Byzantine plot a wisecrack may become a clue to violent political apocalypse, or the hieratic language of ALGOL become comic-book farce. Pynchon's heteroglossia occupies an ambiguous middle ground between those of the other two writers. His fascinated disgust at the carnivalesque decadence of his low discourses (the language of The Whole Sick Crew) is matched by his conspiracy view of the international corporate systems of capitalism. The heteroglossia becomes immobilized into a cold war without positive issue, absurd and terrifying at once.

Bakhtin is perfectly aware that the polar opposition between a sealed-off and impermeable monoglossia and a developing polyglossia is something of a fiction. Elsewhere he writes:

It is our conviction that there never was a single strictly straightforward genre, no single type of direct discourse – artistic, rhetorical, philosophical, religious, ordinary everyday – that did not have its own parodying and travestying double, its own comic-ironic *contre-partie*.[24]

What they represent, however, are two fundamental tendencies: monoglossia embodies the hegemonic force of a language established as 'the' language of the speech community, unified, centralized, authoritative, always *mythic* because unrelativized and unpunctured by travesty. Polyglossia embodies the forces of dispersal and differentiation, the reality of actual speech situations, their disjunctions and productive heterogeneity. The movement of a speech community from monoglossia to polyglossia may best be thought of as similar to the movement of a social formation from *simple reproduction* to *expanded reproduction*. This is not, of course, to posit any perfect 'fit' or homology à la Goldmann, between economic structure and linguistic development. But there is an obvious correlation between an increasing division of labour and a growth of new linguistic registers, the latter providing precisely a heteroglot potentiality for the development of intertextuality (and hence of 'novel' forms). Monoglossia and polyglossia are thus *tendencies* rather than strictly separable stages in the life of a speech community. Thus, even after a society has engaged with another language as a deeply important part of its own culture, monoglosia tends to reassert itself, one language attempts to gain hegemony, to incorporate the new.

Just as structuralism has an affinity for genres which pertain to monoglossia, deconstruction can be seen as an attempt to grasp the conflicting heterogeneities of language, rewriting its heteroglot difference as precisely the impossibility of a master-discourse, the impossibility of an invulnerable metalanguage.

This may seem an eccentric way to come at deconstruction, but when we realize that a fundamental form of dialogism exists between speaking and writing, then the project of a *grammatology* is revealed for what it is, a simple metaphysical inversion of the old hierarchy which gave ontological priority to speech over writing. In fact, the relation of written forms to spoken forms in any speech community is an historical question, one which Derrida fails to address because he has a purely *metaphysical* notion of heteroglossia insulated from the transformative and conflictual social arena of speech events.

As far as I understand it, deconstruction is an attack upon traditional tenets of Western philosophy carried out through a close critical unpicking of the language of some 'key' texts. Deconstruction shows that language does not simply 'come after' the concepts it is supposed to represent, like some kind of delayed supplement or exposition. For Derrida, language ensnares and defeats rationality, rendering some of its fundamental categories – origin, presence, meaning – perfectly useless. Derrida does this in three ways. Firstly, he pushes to breaking point Saussure's idea that a language is only constituted by differences without positive terms. Meaning resides in the pertinent distinctions made *between* signifiers in a system, not in the individual terms of the system. Thus, the meaning of any term employed in discourse is determined by its difference from a set of elements *not present* in that discourse. Its precondition for meaning then, is always absent, always elsewhere, like a horizon we can never reach. The moment of full meaning, the plenitude of presence, when the end of the chain of signification will be reached, never comes: full presence is endlessly deferred, it is always 'in *différance*'. Secondly, rational finality will always be frustrated because concepts never escape from metaphor, and syntax never escapes from rhetoric. However hard the thinker tries to produce a self-sustaining 'pure' reason, the thinking is always 'engrained' in metaphor and 'bedevilled' by rhetoric. Thirdly, however much we think we are thinking only with ideas, the actual phonetic and graphic material of language is constantly drifting our thought along currents of its own. The words we choose to express ourselves are influenced by the sounds or the shapes of the signifiers already produced. Everyone is familiar with that irritating habit words have of settling on the end of the pen so that they return again and again over a few pages. Likewise rhymes, rhythms, cadences, homonyms, assonance and alliteration all have their subtly determining effect upon what and how we write. What Mallarmé called 'la musique dans les lettres' is a prose as well as poetic phenomenon. The patterning and flux of phonic and graphic material cannot be discounted as a determiner of meaning in discourse.

These three points (albeit briefly and crudely sketched) seem not implausible. What is implausible is the exaggerated claim made for them by Deconstruction. Reading deconstructive criticism in both its French and American varieties one comes to believe that all discursive paths are dead ends or labyrinths which turn back upon themselves. Indeed the rhetorical figure for this is 'doubt', *aporia* (from the Greek meaning 'unpassable road') and *aporia* has become the transcendental signified of Deconstruction. With a mixture of playful mischief and pathos, the would-be Derrideans find that all traces of meaning lead to paradox, absence and doubt, which for them become the signifieds of the text. Deconstruction is a carnival of scepticism, demythologizing the pretentious claims of monoglossia, demystifying the complete, sovereign, philosophic word, yet hermetically sealed in a Saussurean problematic which fails to understand the positive, socially constitutive role of heteroglossia. It is true of course that in a famous essay founding grammatology, Derrida rigorously criticized Saussure. But the focus of his critique was the way Saussure subordinated 'writing' (in the large, Derridean sense) to speaking. Bakhtin's critique of Saussure (one of the linguists who produced an 'abstract objectivism') is more radical and far-reaching than Derrida's, despite the Nietzschean panache of the latter. For Bakhtin, language is also split, conflict-ridden, dispersed and drastically heterogeneous. But as well it is systematic, highly coded, patterned and regular. Both poles, the homogeneous and heterogeneous, operate to produce meaning, and from this dialectical perspective Bakhtin can analyse a whole range of speech events in their historical specificity, according to their social group, context and power relations. Only for those who identify language as such with

Saussurean *langue* does it appear paradoxical and impossible that dispersal, '*différance*', lacks, absence, traces and all the other modes of radical heterogeneity should be there at the heart of discourses which pretend to be complete. Much of the time, Deconstruction is rediscovering in texts, with a kind of bemused fascination, all the indices of heteroglossia which Saussure had excluded from consideration in his own model, by consigning them to the trashcan of 'parole'. To discover that rationality (the logic of the signified) may be subverted by writing itself (the logic of the signifier) seems to put the 'whole of the Western episteme' into jeopardy, but is in fact a fairly trivial business. This triviality is one of the reasons why Deconstruction has so quickly found that its natural métier is fairground nonsense and game-playing. When Derrida deliberately played the fool at Searle's expense in the *Glyph* exchange, ridiculing his name, punning, cracking jokes, changing masks like a comedian, he was doing nothing more than we should expect, he was fulfilling the natural role of Deconstruction as a carnivalization monoglossia. The *Glyph* essays of Derrida put me in mind of this passage from Bakhtin:

At the time when poetry (and we may add, philosophy) was accomplishing the task of cultural, national and political centralization of the verbal-ideological world in the higher official socio-ideological levels, on the lower levels, on the stages of local fairs and at buffoon spectacles, the heteroglossia of the clown sounded forth, ridiculing all 'languages' and dialects; there developed the literature ... where there was no language centre at all, where there was to be found a lively play with the 'languages' of poets, scholars, monks, knights and others, where all languages were masks and where no language could claim to be an authentic and incontestable face.[25]

This, surely, is the Deconstructionist project. Insisting upon a 'language with no centre at all', ridiculing all languages and dialects, Derrida constantly makes 'lively play' with the 'languages' of poets and scholars (monks, knights and others rather less often, I grant). Indeed, a key strategy of grammatology was to confound genres by cutting across the usual boundaries between poetry, literary criticism, philosophy and fiction, mocking the seriousness and haughty autonomy of each – 'the heteroglossia of the clown sounded forth'. Deconstruction is a compromised, idealist carnival so obsessed with rooting out metaphysical error that it remains enmeshed – if only by dependent negation – upon metaphysics itself. It sets out to carnivalize the pretentious academic word by destroying monoglossia from within – a project doomed because to remain within monoglossia is to retain a base in metaphysics rather than in social history. The luxury of 'endless deferral' is only available to those who play with themselves in the abstract idealist realm of 'langue'. The real social difference of hetero-glossia in fact puts a swift end to the unmotivated *'différance'* of Derridean discourse: Derridean *'différance'* evaporates once you move from 'langue' to 'parole', or from competence to performance. The trick of Deconstruction is to treat texts not as specific performances within a social discourse, but as abstract repertoires of competence. As soon as you do this, then all the terms of the repertoire become ambiguous and fall away from each other. They are no longer held together by the social motivations, functions and uses of the discourse, but fall back into their plurality of potential. By contrast, the dif-ferences which Bakhtin registers in heteroglossia encode real social differences. For him inequality of power and access are already inscribed in the way language shifts to resist, negotiate or accommodate a realm saturated with alien words, other people's words.

Bakhtin recognized that any abstract objectivist theory of language always went hand in hand with the language of the dominant social class. 'High' languages are imperialistic. They establish themselves as both 'standard' and prestige by a variety of methods, including 'objective' grammars, the pre-scription of norms, structural theories of language (and even deconstructive theories) insofar as all these systematically exclude the actual speech-use of the majority of people. All theories of *langue, deep structure, basic systemic sentences* and *différance* are metaphysical in that they are attempts to isolate a pure and unmotivated language anterior to the use of actual speech by social groups. But this abstract 'langue' is nothing other than the modern myth of a perfect monoglossia, universal and unitary only in the abstract. The principal social function served by these theories of language is to act as sophisticated agents of cultural unification and centralization. 'Langue', and all theories derived from it, are but the homogenizing power of myth over language, or of metaphysics over utterance. The only place where 'langue' and its deconstruction actually exist is in the (highly motivated) *utterances* of the professional linguist or philosopher, in the 'high' languages of academic culture.

Bakhtin's work seems to me to transcend both Deconstruction and Structuralism by revealing each to be a one-sided abstraction from the lived complexity of language. On the one hand, Structuralism, following Saussure, treats language as 'langue' by isolating unified structures within monoglossia. This works well for monoglossic societies, as the work of Vernant, Vidal-Nacquet and Detienne on Greek tragedy and myth has shown. Like Propp's work on folk-tale, and that of Alan Dundes and Levi-Strauss on myth, Structuralism (for reasons elaborated above) finds its 'good object' of study in monoglossia. But Structuralism notoriously failed to produce a significant and convincing theory of the novel, since it is, through and through, a heteroglot composition – a multiaccented, hybrid construction which requires both structuralist *and* sociolinguistic analysis. The novel *plays with the historical and social boundaries* of speech types, languages and belief systems, and is thus irreducible to the norms governing any one of them. It is, as Bakhtin notes, a 'militantly protean' form, always novel when it appears, feeding on its own variation and self-criticism. This places it beyond the reach of any theory like Structuralism which seeks *systematic* regularity as its exhaustive protocol.

On the other hand, Deconstruction abstracts only those aspects of language where intention and unity appear to falter. It is like a geological map of language which marks out the slippage, the fault-lines and the crevices, but omits all the strata and formations between them. Whereas Bakhtin sees both formations and their fractures as constitutive of style and meaning, the deconstructionist sees only the fault-lines; an impasse, a *non plus ultra*. Bakhtin's sociolinguistic knowledge gives him a more inclusive understanding of how discourse works than the Deconstructionists for whom – most of the time – discourse fails to work at all (it plays). Bakhtin writes:

It is precisely the diversity of speech, and not the unity of a normative shared language, that is the ground of a style .... Even in those places where the author's voice seems at first glance to be unitary and consistent, direct and immediately intentional, beneath that smooth single-languaged surface we can nevertheless uncover prose's three-dimensionality, its profound speech diversity, which enters the project of style and is its determining factor.[26]

This has something in common with the Deconstructive view, but it is informed by a broader sociological sense of discourse as a functioning ensemble, creating its identity (style) through an exploitation of language diversity. Thus, throughout Bakhtin's essays we encounter passages which seem impeccably 'structuralist' and elsewhere strikingly 'deconstructionist'. By centring his theoretical understanding of language upon dialogic utterance, he fuses the insights of both schools into a critical sociolinguistics of culture which supersedes both.

'Critical sociolinguistics of culture' was carefully chosen. I think it is clear how Bakhtin fulfils the dictum of Weinreich, already quoted, about breaking down the identification of structure with homogeneity. Bakhtin studied the historical mobility of discourses through the dynamic of language pulled in one direction by the structural unity of monoglossia, and in the other direction by heteroglot speech diversities of genre, register, dialect, sociolect, cohabitation and intertextuality. What puts him beyond most current sociolinguistics (however unsystematic his attention to the full range of speech variation) is that his work is critical as well as descriptive. He is aware, even when writing about something as apparently remote as Renaissance comedy, that speech diversity in class society indexes actual inequality. This is not meant in a Bernstein sense and has nothing to do with the quarrel about restricted and elaborated codes: there is nothing in Bakhtin to suggest he thought one language any better or worse than another. But he emphasizes that the centralizing and unifying of language is a crucial act of hegemony by a powerful social group.

Thus a unitary language gives expression to forces working towards concrete verbal and ideological unification and centralization, which develop in vital connection with the process of sociopolitical and cultural centralization.[27]

The brilliant stroke in Bakhtin – and what saves his work from falling into crude 'reflectionism' whereby language simply mirrors class – is in his dynamic model of language in which 'centripetal' forces seek to unify and homogenize it against 'centrifugal' forces which seek to pull it a apart. These opposed pressures or tendencies keep language mobile just as they are responsible for its transformations. What is more, any theory of unified language becomes itself a key agency in the struggle, and is itself one of the forces which serve to unify and centralize the verbal-ideological world. It is this informing sense of hegemonic struggle which makes Bakhtin a Kultur-kritiker as well as a descriptive sociolinguist. The key passage is worth quoting fully:

Aristotelian poetics, the poetics of Augustine, the poetics of the medieval Church, of 'the one language of truth', the Cartesian poetics of neoclassicism, the abstract grammatical universalism of Leibniz (the idea of 'universal grammar'), Humboldt's insistence on the concrete – all these, whatever their differences in nuance, give expression to the same centripetal forces in sociolinguistic and ideological life; they serve one and the same project of centralizing and unifying the European languages. The victory of one reigning language (dialect) over the others, the supplanting of languages, their enslavement, the process of illuminating them with the True Word, the incorporation of barbarians and lower social strata into a unitary language of culture and truth, the canonization of ideological systems ... all this determined the content and power of the category of 'unitary language' in linguistic and stylistic thought, and determined its creative, style-shaping role in the majority of the poetic genres that coalesced in the channel formed by those same centripetal forces of verbal-ideological life.[28]

Bakhtin reveals the intimate connection between theories based upon a unified conception of language and the development towards hegemony of that language itself. There is an especially snug 'fit' between linguistic theories of abstract objectivism and a process of sociopolitical and cultural centralization. Grammar, poetics and unitary language theory are modes whereby the prestige language simultaneously canonizes itself, regularizes and endorses its system and boundaries, makes itself teachable and assimilable in educational practice and above all 'naturalizes' itself over against all competing sociolects, dialects and registers.

Interestingly, Bakhtin's assertion is supported by Charles Ferguson's seminal 1959 article in *Word* in which he coined the term 'diglossia' (a preliminary version of Ferguson's study had

been entitled 'Classical or Colloquial, One Standard or
Two' – a title with a certain Bakhtinian ring about it). This
term 'diglossia' describes the situation of those speech communities in which two or more varieties of the same language
are used by the same speakers under different conditions. As
examples, he took Swiss German, Arabic, Modern Greek and
Haitian Creole, all four speech communities which operate
both with a 'superposed prestige' form of the language (H or
'high') and with regional dialects (L or 'low'). Ferguson writes.

In all the defining languages there is a strong tradition of grammatical study
of the H-form of the language. There are grammars, dictionaries, treatises on
pronunciation, style and so on. There is an established norm for pronunciation, grammar and vocabulary which allows variation only within
certain limits. The orthography is well established and has little variation. By
contrast, descriptive and normative studies of the L-form are either non-
existent or relatively recent and slight in quantity. Often they have been
carried out first or chiefly by scholars outside the speech community and are
written in other languages.[29]

This perfectly confirms Bakhtin's own work. But Ferguson's
work – and indeed much of the sociolinguistic research on
diglossia since 1959 – is content to register and describe the
inter-relation between prestige forms and 'low' forms. Indeed,
Deuchar and Martin-Jones (in a paper presented to the
Sociolinguistics Symposium at Sheffield in March 1982) remark that:

It is not clear to what extent variation theory (the dominant approach of
current sociolinguistics) constitutes a theory, since so much attention is
devoted in this approach to the description of the facts of linguistic variation
with relatively little reference to explanation.[30]

They also remark, acerbically and with perfect justification,
that 'those who describe themselves as sociolinguists do not
appear to have a social theory.'[31] Bakhtin, however, pursues
the political and cultural point made in passing in the
quotation given above. The H-form becomes the prestige or
standard in a variety of ways which are all linked to the socio-
economic and political power of a given group or class. The
specific H-form is constituted as unitary through the agencies
of scholars, lexicographers, grammarians and literary critics,

thus becoming a centripetal force of language in a political process of centralization and incorporation.

Much of Bakhtin's work can be read as a brilliant, lightly disguised polemic against the process of centralization and State domination going on in Russia during the period of Stalinism. By championing the heteroglossia of the 'folk' against the imposed authority of monoglossia, he was implicitly criticizing from a populist perspective the 'dismal sacred word' of ruthless State centralization. But Bakhtin's penetrating comprehension of hegemonic violence and popular forms of resistance to incorporation in the realm of discourse speaks directly to us, too. The question of heteroglossia, correctly addressed, focuses analysis on the political realities informing all levels of cultural production, from the sophistication of transformational grammar down to dirty jokes. Without ever diminishing the Utopian ideals of play and pleasure which Deconstruction embodies, Bakhtin nevertheless shows up, through and through, the ludic narcissism at the heart of the Deconstructionist project. Even more, he reveals the naive complicity Deconstruction may have with social control and domination, and the consequent role that dialogic resistance must play to disrupt this.

NOTES

1   M. Bakhtin, *The Dialogic Imagination*, ed. M. Holquist, trans. by C. Emerson and M. Holquist (Austin: University of Texas, 1981), p. 291.
2   *Ibid.*, p. 289.
3   *Ibid.*, p. 290.
4   *Ibid.*, p. 294.
5   *Ibid.*, p. 293.
6   *Ibid.*, p. 276.
7   *Ibid.*, p. 277.
8   *Ibid.*, p. 284.
9   *Ibid.*, p. 276.
10 U. Weinreich, W. Labov and M. Herzog, 'Empirical Foundations for a theory of language change', in W. P. Lehmann and Y. Malkiel (eds.), *Directions for Historical Linguistics* (Austin: University of Texas, 1968), p. 100.
11 Bakhtin, *op. cit.*, p. 278.
12 *Ibid.*, p. 280.
13 *Ibid.*, pp. 280–2.

14 *Ibid.*, p. 365.
15 *Ibid.*, p. 431n.
16 *Ibid.*, pp. 62–5.
17 *Ibid.*, p. 68.
18 *Ibid.*, p. 262.
19 *Ibid.*, p. 63.
20 *The Dictionary of Greek and Roman Geography*, edited by W. Smith (London: Murray, 1856), Vol. I, p. 253.
21 J. Joyce, *Ulysses* (Harmondsworth; Penguin, 1969), p. 9.
22 M. Bakhtin, *Rabelais and his World*, translated by H. Iswolsky (Massachusetts; M.I.T., 1968), pp. 13 & 85.
23 M. Lowry, *Under the Volcano* (Harmondsworth; Penguin, 1976), p. 367.
24 Bakhtin, *The Dialogic Imagination*, op. cit., p. 53.
25 *Ibid.*, pp. 272–3.
26 *Ibid.*, pp. 308 & 315.
27 *Ibid.*, p. 271.
28 *Ibid.*, p. 271.
29 C. Ferguson, 'Diglossia', in *Word* 15, (1959), pp. 325–40.
30 M. Deuchar and M. Martin-Jones, 'Linguistic Research in Majority and Minority Communities. Goals and Methods', Paper presented at the Sociolinguistics Symposium, Sheffield, March/April 1982 (Xerox), p. 4.
31 Deuchar and Martin-Jones, *op. cit.*, p. 7.

5 Autonomy Theory: Ortega, Roger Fry, Virginia Woolf

Frank Gloversmith

The embarrassed and contradictory nature of theories of the autonomy of the artwork show up very clearly indeed in the brilliant essays of José Ortega. Summing up the achievements of fifty years of modernist movements, with ambivalence and some sharp irony, Ortega indicates its main principles. They comprise certain 'tendencies': '(1) to dehumanize art; (2) to avoid living forms; (3) to see to it that the work of art is nothing but a work of art; (4) to consider art as play and nothing else; (5) to be essentially ironical; (6) to beware of sham; (7) to regard art as a thing of no transcending consequence'.[1] So modern art produces 'ultra-objects' – painting a cone instead of the mountain – which stimulate aesthetic pleasure in 'the triumph over human matter'. Such a stylization, a dehumanization, correctly avoids the sentimental confusion of life and art endemic in popular work. Yet this admirably antipopular 'artistic' art marks' a maximum aberration in the history of taste', and may stem from a sense of art as an inferior thing. Simultaneously, this deformation of reality, this shattering of human substance gives life to the patterns, the concepts, the abstract ideas by which we humanize the world. The art is (correctly) lean and angular in giving visible form to our mental constructions – Nietzsche's 'fictions' – rendering them pure and transparent. We look at truth in seeing their essential unreality; the painter has painted ideas (pp. 19 & 38).

On the one side, art is ironic, self-deprecating, youthfully engaging, playful, relishing its antagonism to traditional styles, treating everything as reducible to subject-matter, a mere starting point. On the other side, it avoids sentimental

147

humanitarianism – 'Tears and laughter are, aesthetically, frauds' (p. 27) – and in turning its back, with loathing, on 'living forms or forms of living beings', suddenly shows our reality as sham, deconstructing our comfortable myths. This scandal is achieved only through the paradoxical practice of modernists to whom art is probably of little consequence, and who despise traditional concern with human problems, human dignity, truths, justifications. Ortega himself sums up the tradition which modernists implicitly assault – in their enthusiasm for the remote, the prehistoric, the primitive, and in their stylistic 'higher algebra of metaphors':

Art was important for two reasons: on account of its subjects which dealt with the profoundest problems of humanity, and on account of its own significance as a human pursuit from which the species derived its justification and dignity. (p. 50).

In the nineteenth century, art had been expected to take upon itself the salvation of mankind; and Ortega's regret for the passing of that moment touches all he says about the paradoxical achievements of modernism with ironic reservation, as it also prompts his closing insistence that modernism of this sort must be superseded. Though he notionally represents the changes in art as historically conditioned, Ortega tends to see the present as a deviation, however necessary. The weight is behind the traditional conception of art, and it is a philosophical role that he suggests.

Yet Ortega's second, equally weighted concept is of art as a pursuit having its 'own significance'. In this approach we can see the ground of his sympathy with all the antitraditional elements that give modernism its idiosyncratic nature. its algebraic, abstract, metaphoric, antihumanist and formalistic styles. Art is not and cannot be bound to the mimetic, the naturalistic, the representational: its horizons must, by definition, be other than those of 'lived' reality and the perception of that reality. Here, in the juxtaposition of two major principles for art (of all times and places), Ortega articulates the paradoxes (which often collapse into contradictions) which press in on twentieth-century formulations of the autonomy of art. The paradoxes play between art's concern with fundamental human problems, and its existence as free play of the spirit; between art as philosophical, even redemptive, and art as 'artistic', formalistic, stylized, indifferent to human or living forms. It is, for Ortega, both concerned with 'the inherent nature of things', and so mimetic of reality; and indifferent to these, open to a visual (or written) algebra of metaphors, to surrealism, to 'infrarealism' (pp. 35–6). That Ortega so often, almost manneristically, apologizes for prejudice, and abruptly alters the topic, seems to signal his sense that the aberration or anarchy are genuine manifestation of the integrity of art, its inalienable right to assert its autonomy.

The concept of autonomy has been produced in so wide a range of complex theoretical definitions, and for so varied a range of ideological purposes, that its own apparent clear contours have been eroded. It becomes confusedly rich, open, and plural, yet relativized, almost self-deconstructing; its critical history finally suggests ways of questioning the whole notion in aesthetic composition of the 'extrinsic' and the 'intrinsic'. To go on from Ortega's commentary on modern art in general to his scrutiny of the novel in particular – written concurrently[2] – is to sense acutely the sharp compulsions which give their energy to an aesthetics. They often point back to commitments and passions linked to analogous systems of definition, to an ethic, a metaphysics, a politics, or a history. So, in brief, behind Ortega's definitions of (commendably) antipopular, stylized, 'dehumanized' art is his division of society into two groups: artists (which includes those who understand favourably); and others, 'the hostile majority'. A tiny élite faces (and defies) 'the shapeless mass'. The work of art is a social agent. it 'segregates two different castes of men' (p. 5) Its inaccessibility is not inadvertent, but operational, being the very form of the test. The 'autonomy' of the art links directly to an 'autonomous' élite. The large-scale contrast of nineteenth- and twentieth-century concepts of art turn out to exemplify a socio-political history of culture, a story of degeneration of values directly connected with the advent of mass-democracies. Ortega's other work, such as *The Modern Theme* (1931) and *The Revolt of the Masses* (1932), provides ample supporting instances.

The modestly titled *Notes on the Novel*[2] seem to resist any resituating of the aesthetic concepts inside other systems of thought, or their unpacking to reveal ideological ('non-aesthetic') perspectives. Ortega develops a clearer, unambivalent account of aesthetic antonomy in his definition of the literary genre:

> A literary genre means a certain stock of possibilities... its resources are definitely limited. It is erroneous to think of the novel... the modern novel in particular... as of an endless field capable of rendering ever new forms. Rather it may be compared to a vast but finite quarry. But present-day writings face the fact that only narrow and concealed veins are left them. (p. 58).

This a precise version of art's autonomy: a literary genre is represented as a vast but finite repetoire, a 'given' supply of material. At an advanced point in its unfolding – since it is received and used, not developed or radically altered – its dwindling resources can be reviewed. The metaphors of a quarry and of a zoological species (with Darwinian chronology and entropy, an eventual 'wastage') naturalize the definition, attributing aesthetic phenomena to some immanent ahistorical Idealist realm. Perhaps already the empirical/Idealist coupling behind the 'neutral' definition signals an aesthetic that accommodates ideas of the transcendent, the visionary, the mysterious givenness and 'thereness' of meanings. Ortega abruptly discounts the artist's authority, in his attack on talent, inspiration and the innovatory force of genius. He respects and admires Cervantes, Stendhal, Dostoevsky, Dickens, and Joyce: but each is nothing, an abstraction, 'a woodsman in the Sahara desert', unless the 'independently' given material of his favoured genre is already available (p. 58) The immense riches of the aesthetic practice of fiction are absolutely autonomous, since their provision and 'authorization' are matters for contemplation, not speculation or interrogation. The concept of a 'pure' autonomy in aesthetics turns out to be anything but transparent: the more refined the definition aims to be, the more opaque and richly loaded with connotations it becomes.

The suggestiveness of Ortega's discussion of the novel genre is again in the way that he keeps antithetical ideas juxtaposed with one another, until the parallel developments suddenly overlap. (They are presented, of course, as complementary, not antithetical: they are made contradictory only by the absoluteness of the definition of autonomy.) For example, the fixed resources of the genre consist of a number of possible themes or subjects: innovation is the moving on to a 'novel' theme – one not replicated elsewhere, and so increasingly unusual, to defeat habituation, the complications of changing taste and fresh expectations, and to counteract the inevitable weakening of the form. A law of diminishing returns ensures this decline of the novel; at the same time by the same rule, the pioneers and the classical models inevitably 'drown in the reader's boredom'. Having given definitive priority to an essentialized subject/theme principle, which precedes any possible single representation in writing, the historically accumulated instances all disintegrate, drown, disappear. Ortega's principle of entropy involves simultaneously the self-erasure of critical evaluation: the objects of appraisal have dwindled in power simply with the passing of time, displaced or effaced as the genre develops, ineluctably exhausting itself (p. 60).

Unconvincing and unconvinced on the nature and the fate of the special stock of themes and subjects available for the genre, Ortega turns writers' attention to 'the exquisite quality of the *other* elements that compose the body of a novel'. The most important by far is form, 'the true substance of art'. What 'form' comprises is what to readers ('the uninitiated') seems abstract, accidental and extrinsic: 'the structure of the novel as such'. Ortega tenders several ways of defining this essential formal principle, which clearly is difficult to fit in with his concept of the autonomous genre and its enumerable features: 'A work of art lives on its form, not on its material; the essential grace it emanates springs from its structure, from its organism' (p. 75). Too much stress on the subject, by poet, painter, or critic is taken as a sign of the Philistine. His argument is now reversed: the defining characteristic of the genre is its working with a minimum of action or subject-matter. The genre is 'diffuse', non-dramatic; Proust's work, brilliantly exemplifying this sluggish quality, falls short of giving even the minimum. 'With a pinch of drama – really, we should have been satisfied with almost nothing – the work would have been perfect.' Again, with the rich, dense, turbulent movement of Dostoevsky's novels, readers are caught by 'a curious optical delusion'. For, like Proust and Stendhal, Dostoevsky is a sublime craftsman, a great technical innovator: the structural purity emerges from, makes its effects beyond, the mere action, plot and human adventure. The elemental passions, the frenzied exchanges, the dash and colour of the events, the fascinating characters: these merely compose the surface of Dostoevsky's fiction. But his power and his 'realism' are little to do with all this: 'The so-called dramatic interest has no aesthetic value, but forms a mechanical necessity.' (p. 80).

With this startling turnabout,Ortega is defining the specificity of the novel as structural, as quintessentially formal: while insisting that the plot material, action and emotion are secondary, contingent, an interest to be kept to a minimum. The aesthetic quality of fiction is only discernible by the reader's resistance to the surge of emotion and action. The critical reader cannot be immersed in persons and events: Dostoevsky's 'realism' is in his compelling the reader to reflect, to consider how to deal with them. The working of form is precisely in disengaging us from 'vital emotion', from our usual interest in action. Form induces contemplation, distantiation: great novels, like great French drama, stimulate 'ethical contemplation'. The mechanical element, 'aesthetically dead weight', is the dramatic interest, satisfying only that form of consciousness which art intrinsically aims to transcend: 'Art is an enjoyment of contemplation'. regrettably, elements from the realm of action, 'interests, sentiments, compulsions, affective preferences', are re-admitted as indispensable to the working of the higher faculties, above all to the aesthetic consciousness (pp. 80–7).

Ortega's alternative specification of the aesthetic autonomy of the novel quite rapidly reveals elements of a psychology of perception, an ethic and a philosophy. The account of the genesis, structure and functioning of art, incorporates attitudes and evaluations which reach well outside what he normally includes in the aesthetic. The most tendentiously prescriptive strictures are to do with the superiority of the contemplative over the active principle. From a (rather artificial) point about the individual mind, Ortega implicitly describes social phenomena and practice. Predictably, the detached, disinterested intellectual contemplates the blind action of others, 'induced to take sides', stumbling frenetically through 'interests, senti-ments, compulsions, affective preferences'. So the description of the internal organization of fiction, of the structural relations of its elements, becomes a figure of how perception of 'the form of life' can produce, on the one hand, the greatest art, because, on the other, it bestows on the percipient 'a theoretical sanctification and an untransferable mission of wisdom'. What began as a definition of the subtlety of form in a literary genre turns out to define the subtlety of being of 'certain types of existence' (p. 86). (Questions of autonomy in art seem in-eluctably to incorporate rationalizations of élitism.)

Ortega's argument tacks about once more. Firstly, the autonomy of the genre is related to an exhaustible stock of the themes and subjects, which the artist draws upon, but which cannot be added to or radically altered. (Privileging content, the theory can relegate genuine innovation to the margins, describing it as 'craft' 'technique', 'formal variation'.) Secondly, form, as an essentialized structural effect, is profer-red as the specific aesthetic determinant of the novel genre. This means that themes and subjects are now infrastructural, vital only in a minimal way, and all too likely to create a dramatic opacity which hinders response to the formal grace. The third major definition of the autonomy of the novel is perhaps the most radical, and the more comprehensive in its bringing together the previously separated principles of form and content. The novel, Ortega asserts, offers a total world, one of its own, completely unlike that of its presenter and its readers. The principle of aesthetic distinctness now is designated not as subject or as structure, but as 'imperviousness'.

Imperviousness is but the special form taken on in the novel by the generic imperative of art: to be without transcending consequence ... By virtue of a purely aesthetic necessity ... it must possess the power of forming a precinct, hermetically closed to all actual reality. (pp. 93–4).

(A quite intriguing intermittence is so often seen in discussions like this of Ortega's, an over-valuation of art alternating with an under-estimation.) So the novel is a world, an alternative, eccentric world, a 'provincial life'. But this is not a warrant to write more *Middlemarch* fictions, not a validation of either Hardyesque regionalism or documentary fiction. The 'province' is non-locatable, non-geographical, unrelated to daily living: it is 'the inner realm' of the novel, which the author creates only by cutting off the reader's real horizon, and imprisoning her or him in the aesthetic 'village'. The novelist's success is masked by the reader's forgetting altogether that 'an extramural world' exists (pp. 87–90).

Each novel is idiosyncratically autonomous: no 'province' or 'inner realm' can replicate any other (fictive) realm. Good novels are therefore unique: what makes them instances of a genre is their mode of being, their form, their presentation of an imaginary life unrelateable to living. This is an account of the novel as an aesthetic monad, a pure entity, an ultimate ontological unit. It involves Ortega in critical contradictions which stem from the fraught, paradoxical constraints hedging in the concept of 'automony' in aesthetics. At one moment, the novel is its own world, self-referential and self-validating, because it is contracted, limited, everything in it foreshortened and reduced on precisely the same scale. (The reader is an Alice-in-Wonderland, not a Gulliver.) At another moment, the world of the novel is as extensive as the extramural world, and covers it at all points. The substantiality of fiction is brought back: its density, opacity, its web of circumstances and endless wealth of detail. The 'infrastructure' (which could blot out the grace of form) is now the play of the artist's wide knowledge: 'He carries the furnishings of a whole world on his back . . . . He must produce *ex abundantia*.' This prolixity, minuteness and lavishness produce a material infinity, so that all the other facts are potentially present. The real words is displaced entirely by being presented all over again (pp. 97–8).

Obviously, a fictive world which is unrelateable to the actual world is a massively tendentious concept which annuls itself as soon as it is formulated. Ortega inevitably offers quite other concepts, of 'alternative' worlds, since even the simplest mock-world is contoured and deeply scored by responses to actual experience. Gradually, Ortega's 'province' of the imaginary, the hermetic 'village' of narrative, lets in forms and movement from the extramural existence: 'unquestionably true-to-life elements' and realistic effects. But their customary entailments and connotations are shorn away:

Within the novel almost anything fits: science, religion, sociology, aesthetic criticism – if only it is ultimately derealized and confined within the inner world of the novel: i.e. if it remains without actual and effective validity (p. 103).

The anxiously asserted reservations are part of a casuistry finally worked out in Ortega's discussion of fictive characters and novelistic psychology. The argument has exactly the same pattern as that about the presentation of ideas, places and things. To be consistent, Ortega has to attribute to characters in the novel's imaginary 'province' the same existential privilege: they are alternative beings, not transcriptions of human characters. They please and delight because they are 'possible' – not because they are realistic, or even indications of human potentiality. The novelist, in creating them, constructs an 'imaginary psychology', parallel to, but completely distinct from, any actual, scientific psychology. (This is an area for which Ortega shows great interest and respect.) The motives, thoughts, responses and passions of fictional figures are as hermetically sealed off from actual behaviour as the 'inner realm' is from the reader's world (pp. 99–100).

The same leakage occurs, as it has to: Ortega allows a bonus, once the 'imaginary psychology' has been properly set in action. 'Psychological interpretation of actual social types and environments can provide an additional piquancy.' (But any interpolation from the quotidian world was said to collapse the hermetic fiction.) A series of remarks has suggested that modern writing has shifted the emphasis from plot to character, from actions to persons. Using a contrast between French and Spanish theatre, Ortega opposes 'an art of figures' in modernism to the earlier 'art of adventures'. This is the key to the novel's distinctively 'sluggish' form – 'paralytic' is the (positive) term for Proust's mastery of diffuse, 'atmospheric' representation:

We want the novelist to linger and to grant us good long looks at his personages, their being, and their environment till we have had our fill and feel that they are close friends whom we know thoroughly in all the wealth of their lives.... The essence of the (modern) novel lies... in the personages' pure living, in their being and being thus, above all, in the ensuing milieu (pp. 61, 66).

The reminder of Salinger's Holden Caulfield – characters in books taken as familiar friends – shows how the 'imaginary psychology' of figures in an hermetically sealed-off aesthetic realm has been hard to sustain. Ortega's appreciative responses to characterization do not really differ from those he usually dismisses as uninitiated. Like many avid readers, he speaks affectionately of his sharing characters' lives with them, immersed in their atmosphere, in their time and place. This prompts the usual tribute to the novelist's instinctive under-standing of the human heart and mind: 'The great novelist, contemptuous of the surface features of his personages, dives down into their souls and returns, clutching in his hand the deep-sea pearl' (p. 98). The advocates of the disdained 'coarse reasoning' of realism often say just that.

So, with indirection, but with remarkable force, people, places and things re-occupy the provinces of the novel. What can only enter if it wears hermetically-sealed clothing is the idea, the belief. Political, ideological, symbolical or satirical intentions kill off the novel the moment they appear. Attention and interest collapse 'when the author forces us to face the acute problem of our own political or metaphysical destiny'. For Ortega the term 'historical novel' is an oxymoron: mixing fact and fiction, the imaginary and the historical, 'leads to their mutual annihilation'. (Yet his preferred authors, Stendhal and Dickens, compose historical narratives.) Social, moral, politi-cal themes are non-artistic: 'A poet's politics rarely attain to more than an ingenuous inept gesture' (p. 94). Dostoevsky is exempted, though religious and political ideas are part of his characters' frenetic passions. Such ideas, passions and com-mitments are properly assimilated in his work, transformed, and so do not occur as 'operative agencies'. Where they are insistent and active in fiction, then the art is annulled: 'The novel (as art) cannot propagate philosophical, political, so-ciological, or moral ideas: it can be nothing beyond a novel' (p. 94).

This circular and self-validating assertion is reiterated endlessly by the early Modernists in Europe, and by New Critics in America; it focuses a position which can be ideologically filled out in a number of (related) ways. Used slackly sometimes by Ortega, it implies the triviality of fiction, a 'frail floating globe' if the reader is reminded at all of 'the absolute realm' of actual living. Used rigorously, it claims parity for fiction with science, history and philosophy. The poet-novelist has the 'possibility of constructing human souls...he carries the furnishings of a whole world on his back'. Ortega's reconciling principle for these incompatibles is one which compounds the problem: magic. The imaginary life where, incommunicado, the reader is the centre of a universe, is created by hypnosis, by a 'glorious and unique magic'. Hypnotic compulsion by a 'divine somnambulist' makes us identify the hermetic, synthetic world with our own (pp. 94–5). But Ortega's desperate jokiness or charm won't do to lead into a problem, and out again, if it is the pseudo-problem of ideas in fiction. It does not charm Ortega himself: the dispassionate intelligence stays active even in the shadowless dreamworld. After magical immersion, when he is recollecting the novel, 'all sorts of vital repercussions' occur. 'The symbolical meaning of *Don Quixote* is not contained within the novel, we construct it from without.' Again, the handy-dandy: fiction has such meaning, but not while it actually engages us. There is a pause, a gap, an intermittence: the frenetic action and the pure, insistent presence of the characters have to withdraw. Then, after the pause, 'the novel will furnish the strongest intellectual emotions.'

What Ortega is doing, rather than describing structural autonomy or genre specificity, is recommending a way of reading. This cross-over explains the vacillation and confusions in his account: the topic, hardly kept in control, is belief and commitment. So the insistence on autonomy – in subject, thematic development, form and structure – is an insistence on curtailing the action in art of ideas and ideology. The sustained ideological inflection of the concept of autonomy itself is clear in what it suppresses. 'Action' is equated with adventure and conflict, without its thematic significance; 'character' is defined as pure presence, without its motives, thoughts, or even its formation through action. Ideas and ideology are freely admitted, with the stultifying proviso that they are 'derealized', that they remain 'without actual and effective validity'. These can only be recommendations on how to resist the passionate persuasiveness (to which he clearly responds) of Cervantes,

Stendhal, Dickens, Dostoevsky, Proust, and Joyce. The ideological force of their drama must be controlled by breaking it down into discrete components: action (splendidly enjoyable, but inferior) – or representation of characters (pure presences, knowable individuals). Any 'alien elements' – politics, morality, sociology – must be seen as alien, and anaesthetized; or, at best, entertained as provisional, as hypotheses, dissolvable in the atmosphere of 'the novel as such'. All the ambivalent allusions to hypnosis, somnambulism, dreaming and magic are admonitions, checks against letting ideas in art have some consequentiality outside the art. Their undeniable and vigorous activity in the artwork has to be literally (i.e. anachronistically) charmed away, enchanted, experienced as though the effect of a spell. Metamorphosed in this way, the delights and the intensities of art seem to be dispersable by the rational intelligence. This literal and metaphorical mystification is the desperate warding-off of the disturbing presence in art of impassioned ideas, rational force, of reflection about feelings and actions. Ortega's responsiveness to the inextricable interplay of art and life – 'outer'/'inner', 'extrinsic'/'intrinsic', 'world' of fiction/'world' of readers and writers – is quite clear in this whimsical rationalization, as it is in all his pervasive ambiguities and paradoxes.

Over the first quarter of the twentieth century Roger Fry was producing a philosophy of art and an aesthetic theory as comprehensive as those of Ortega, and far more assured in formulation (*Vision and Design*, 1920; *Transformations*, 1926).[3] In galleries, showrooms, studios, craft workshops, in his writing and in discussions, Fry ceaselessly interpreted the modern movements. He found in them, particularly the Post-Impressionists, the language of the spirit, a fundamental vision that informed the other arts – music, architecture, poetry and drama. The perception of 'Significant Form' – never a matter of optical pleasure, of any evident patterns or harmonies – is the work of the aesthetic sense.[4] This, for Fry, in its unique mode of functioning, endows the contemplated object with the grace of autonomous being, since the response is never a matter of sensation, nor response to objects as such. Fry suggests, for instance, that sensations prompted by colours are in turn overridden by emotions aroused by relations between colours.

(These emotions are looping back directly to the idea or vision which prompted the artist initially to compose such a juxtaposition of colours.) Cézanne is the type of the true artist in that his works are discoveries of an 'underlying structural unity which answers a profound demand of the spirit'.[5]

Fry's account of the features which Ortega ambivalently designates as the dehumanization of art is rigorously single-minded, affirmative, idealistic: he makes aesthetic activity and response the fundamental form of human perception. Ortega's inconsistencies reveal his taste for dramatic activity and for passionate characters, for the psychologically intriguing. For Roger Fry, any representation of persons and events is subject to art's transformations, as are objects and sensations: they facilitate plastic and spatial expression. However emotionally intense, whatever the nature of the dramatic or psychological appeal, situations, actions and personages take other significations in their being represented. Poignancy, curiosity, direct emotion, if present at all, fall away; and other relations, 'plasticity', the correspondences of form persist 'as a more permanent motive force', as the spiritual function displaces the emotional, the psychological and the ethical. The aesthetic experience is *sui generis*, intellectually self-validating, clarifying to the consciousness everything that the artwork has brought into attention.[6] As Fry wrote to Virginia Woolf, strong dramatic action tended to diminish the pleasure of perceiving the inevitability of an unfolding sequence, the curve of crescendo and diminuendo. Added to this Ortegan paradox on the nature of intensity in art – a preference for the 'sluggish' modes – is the insistence on the hermetic and the monadic: 'The purpose of literature is creating structures which will have for us the feeling of reality: these structures are selfcontained, self-sufficing, and not to be valued by their reference to what lies outside'.

Woolf's close intellectual relation with Fry (whose biography she was to write[6]) was part of their intimate friendship. His conception of the novel as 'a single perfectly organic aesthetic whole', and his readiness to centre this within the comprehensive theory of Significant Form and the nature of perception itself gave Woolf the confidence to convert it all to her own artistic purposes. There certainly seems a fuller, closer

relation to Fry's aesthetic in general than to the theory or
practice of any comparable modern novelist. Many of these
distinctive notions are discussed in the translation by Fry of the
French writer Charles Mauron's *The Nature of Beauty in Art
and Literature*. Printed by the Woolfs' Hogarth Press (1927)
alongside Fry's essays – especially *Transformations* (1926) – it
echoes his notions of the way art may be damaged by dramatic
intensity, and by concern with mere manners and morals. The
writer must cultivate detachment from instinctive life: the key
to form and structure must be the Post-Impressionist discovery
of the fundamental mode of art.

For literature, we should transpose the idea of volumes from the domain of
space to the domain of spirit, and conceive the literary artist as creating
'psychological volumes'. This enables us for the first time dimly to grasp what
it is of which the relations are felt by us when we apprehend aesthetically a
work of literature.[7]

These concepts of Mauron's, and their extension in Fry's
discussions, are probably more directly useful in elucidating
Woolf's formal experiments than the theories of Joyce and
Henry James, or the fictions of Conrad or Lawrence.

Roger Fry's ease in moving so freely from one form of
art to another, along with his linking his theorizing with
practice and production, gave him a special exemplary authority. He draws together so many new and difficult ideas, and
he gives a more comprehensive and sharply focused account of
principles dispersed over so many areas: art and culture
criticism (Clive Bell); philosophy (G. E. Moore, J.
McTaggart); literature, psychology, and the novel (Charles
Mauron); Socialism and politics (Leonard Woolf, J. M.
Keynes). He brings together in a radically new synthesis the
whole group's concepts about 'vision' and 'design', over-
lapping and interpenetrating ideas which reflect an idiosyncratic mental climate and the associated experiments in art and
in living. The synthesis is offered as the modern mind's answer
to the absence of purpose in nature, to intractable matter, to
the essential conditions so inimical to mind itself, to consciousness and sensibility. (Virginia Woolf has an image of the world
as vast blocks of matter, and human consciousness as patches
of light upon them.) Significant Form cannot be objectively

incarnated in existents, but it registers their redemption, as art and as perception, by human consciousness. Imaginative life, as McTaggart insisted, had a faculty of direct perception which superseded that involved in time-bound, experiential perception. For McTaggart, its quintessential form was the conscious perceiving of one self by another. For Fry, the modes of this perception were conditioned by the given physicality of life, qualities of rhythm, gesture, mass, relations in space, dissociable from social and historical time, which McTaggart simply declared as illusory.[8]

A fundamental postulate of all these interrelated speculations was McTaggart's axiom: the universe comprises only discrete selves, each constituted by its perceptions, each of which has the quality of being an emotion. Love itself is defined as the direct perception of another self. (The philosophical theory, with its subsequent reformulations by such followers as G. E. Moore, runs a very high risk of representing consciousness as a collective solipsism, as Merleau-Ponty argues.) The terms 'love' and 'emotion' are clearly taking on a distinctive sense. in Fry's definition, we both feel an emotion and we watch the emotion. This self-reflexive element is the vital, differentiating factor, setting such emotions apart from the feelings of ordinary life. Yet these emotions are free of self-indulgence, since they compose the 'intense disinterested contemplation' of the imagination. Its self-presence, its self-transparancy is the quality which enables its penetration into such self-presence in another, the regard defined as love. Such a regard is acquired by Peter Walsh at the close of *Mrs Dalloway*, and suggests precisely Lily's understanding of Mrs Ramsay (*TL*), as it defines Bernard's insight into all the others around him, in *The Waves*.

McTaggart, Fry's lifelong friend, was tutor to G. E. Moore, whose *Principia Ethica* (1903) gave this cluster of ideas and values its most accessible formulations.[9] Both philosophers disclaim interest in the spiritual and the mystical, or in theistic systems; yet both have absolute and objectivist theories of a strongly metaphysical colouring. G. E. Moore's immediate appropriation as a 'philosophy' and as a guide to civilized living was a consequence of this controlled ambivalence. The nature of the 'Good' is directly knowable, perceivable, independent of dogma and unanalyzable: it is a given, an entity, a perceptual real. In its incarnating the true and the beautiful, it sets the ultimate human goals, and, refining human awareness of these, reconstitutes them as 'states-of-mind'. These mental entities have the status, the given, objective quality, of the perceived, irreducible 'goods' which give them their form and their being. As without, so within: the duality is that of a philosophy which unites a metaphysic and a psychology, and subtends or entails the conception of sensibility as the agent of all order. Perception itself is here both aesthetic in its registration of the indefinable givens – the good, the true, the beautiful – and in its composition of ordered consciousness, the states-of-mind. These are non-utilitarian, intransitive and self-validating. Human awareness fulfils itself, is most richly true to itself, in its attainment of such equipoise: the state-of-mind which is its own reward.

Roger Fry's commentary on Raphael's *Transfiguration* (in his 1920 'Retrospect') characteristically unifies many of these notions, and characteristically transposes readily into a theory of literary form. The distinct sections of this painting, upper and lower, convey to the believer, like Goethe, a single, highly complex message, a unified 'dramatic story'. Such content is irrelevant to the non-believer:

Such a spectator will be likely to be immensely excited by the extraordinary power of coordination of many complex masses in a single inevitable whole, by the delicate equilibrium of many directions of line. He will at once feel that the two parts are coordinated by a quite peculiar power of grasping the possible correlations.[10]

The perception is deeply moving and exhilarating, but the 'emotions' are not Goethe's – the believer's – emotions, nor are they the usual emotions of other situations. Fry later suggests that Goethe's moral, philosophical reflections are a misdescription of his actual response. 'Goethe was deeply moved by the marvellous discovery of design, whereby the upper and lower parts cohere in a single whole.' From this assumption, Fry has necessarily to conclude that such 'significant form' was Raphael's own apprehension and artistic aim.

That apprehension was of a special and peculiar kind and implied a certain detachment... It implies the effort to bend to our emotional understanding, by means of his passionate conviction some intractable material which is alien to our spirit.[11]

This mode of analytic interpretation sets Fry well apart from Clive Bell, whose narrow insistence on Significant Form precluded any founding emotions or passionate convictions, detached or mediated. (Fry, much later, was to realize the fuller implications of these differences.) The Raphael-criticism brings together the artist's emotions, his apprehension of their basic coordination of forms perceived in the 'intractable material' of life; and his projection of designs, complex and abstract, which re-create, in detachment, his passionate conviction and original feeling. This works out a theory of art's genesis, form and reception, of its attainment of impersonality, which was to be so definitively expressed in T. S. Eliot's concept of the Objective Correlative.

Fry's account of the nature of form and of the perception of aesthetic structure, both here and in the Mauron translation, gives direct indications about Woolf's experimental writing. The sections of Raphael's canvas are Mauron's 'psychological volumes': power above, impotence below; compassion, suffering; sustenance, need. For a novel like *Mrs Dalloway*, these contrasts are of life and death, sanity and insanity, according to her Diary (June, 1923). 'The design is so queer and so masterful. I'm always having to wrench my substance to fit it. The design is certainly original and interests me hugely.'[12] This innovatory and transindividual narrative psychology implies the deliberate subordination of the individual figures: 'Characters are to be merely views: personality must be avoided at all costs' (*W.D.*, September, 1923). The intended narrative juxtapositions involve patterning and studied, extensive design. There are no locally intense emotional contrasts of the kind Woolf deplored in the Edwardian realists. The reductive interpretation of the Septimus figure as Clarissa's evil double, the dark antithesis to her social brilliance, ignores both the writer's purposes and the text's achievement. Clarissa and Septimus, as she insisted in the American preface, are one character: they oppose the seeming order and rationality of other characters, of their society and of human existence itself.

The emotions of the book have their ground in these large contrastive rhythms, not in any specifics of personal interaction, or of dramatic tension, emotional crises and their resolutions. The montage of separated sequences, focusing on two figures unknown to each other, effects its extraordinary conjunction only as the writing closes. Clarissa, hiding her displeasure about Bradshaw's vulgarity, suddenly reflects on what has been told of Septimus's suicide. the narrative then identifies the two figures, and, retroactively, establishes that the form of one experience provided a complex understanding to enrich the complementary experience. This subtle psychological patterning is intelligible only within the totality of the text; it is not internalized as a personal insight or revelation for any single protagonist.[13]

The other novels extend this peculiarly intense concern with form. They attract the critical label, 'experimental', long after comparable works have lost it. (Geoffrey Hartman, 1961, applied the term to almost all her writing.) With or without critical unease, the term does register a sense of the unusual ways that these novels correlate feeling and form, emotions and structure. With Fry and Mauron in mind, besides her own considerable reflections on theory, it is easier to see the irrelevance of deciding whether Clarissa is a scatter-brained hostess or a refined consciousness, or the heroine of a psychic melodrama. The narrative mode, initiated with *Jacob's Room* (1922), is one which works self-reflexively, emphasizing its design as a way of extruding and detaching the emotions. As with Fry's account of how emotions in art differ radically from immediate feelings, so with Woolf's representation of them. The reader is meant to observe the emotion, to reflect at a distance, to go beyond it. What is immediately perceived or experienced is transient: what is caught in art's designs is not so vulnerable. Although Jacob's ideas, thoughts and feelings are not evident, and cannot perhaps be known, the formal patterns that encircle this silence and absense are there to render the poignancy and the human mystery. The composition of the aesthetic structures, with their subtle interconnections and coherence, is the deeply ironic means to indicate disconnection, incoherence, loss.[14]

There is a paradoxical interplay of structure and feeling, of life's emotions and those intrinsic to aesthetic form. The elegant construction of *To the Lighthouse* shows this in its complex counterpointing. The final section, after a mid-section from which all the participants of Part I have been withdrawn, seems to complete the original interrupted action. But many figures are not restored: the mid-section covers a decade of disappearance, change, loss, destruction. The 'completion' of the journey represents both fulfilment and a commemoration of loss; the central figure, Mrs Ramsay, is the major absence. At the moment when all the movements in the book suggest renewal of purpose, restoration and continuity, they are also suggesting their diminution, their fragility, perhaps their impossibility. It is a sophisticated variation of the formal catachresis in *Mrs Dalloway*, the conjunctural device of fusing Clarissa's progress towards affirmation with Septimus's degeneration and self-destruction. So Mrs Ramsay's dedication to affirmation, participation, continuity – the communal 'journey' – is realizable only after her death, perhaps only because of her absence. What Part III so markedly adds is emphasis on the ordering of art and its registration of other kinds of feeling. Lily's painting is not only in the book, but *is* the book, its stylized mirror-image, abstracting its form in all senses of the word. Moreover, the meticulous parallels between stages of the boat's journey and moments in the painting foreground the narrative strategies and formal patterning. It is, again, an ambivalent closure: the aesthetic emotions, so sharply extruded, witness their own inadequacy in the narrative's attempt to give 'significant form' to a recognition of what it can no longer directly represent. The pleasures, the exhilaration, the poignancy which the self-conscious designs should evoke by their distancing of dramatic emotion are rendered unsatisfactory precisely to the degree that they recall that plenitude. Lily's cry of anguish at Mrs Ramsay's absence makes her canvas (as she knows) a triviality.[15]

Woolf's self-scrutiny during the composition of this novel confirms both the intensely theoretical nature of the experiments and her awareness of the risks. The narrative montage, the structural patterning, the autonomous design are rigorously controlled: 'I feel as if it fetched its circle pretty completely this time.' But she realizes the cost of this scholastic rigour and formal constraint, as she puzzles about the closing section. She is aware of cornering herself with problems which have become only technical in kind. She confusedly permutates the options while wrily commenting on their collective unsatisfactoriness (*W.D.*, 5th September 1926). What she longs to achieve is a simultaneity of endings, not their schematic interlinking – a desire that is deeply revelatory in its intriguing blend of contradictions. With the previous novel, the climactic correlation of the two components had caused her to expect misunderstanding, and it prompted Strachey's criticism that it arbitrarily imputed significance disproportionate to what Clarissa herself represented (*W.D.*, 18 June 1925). The extensiveness of Part III, 'The Lighthouse', is her representation of the necessary emergence of aesthetic perceptivity and its distinctive, expressive modes, from the experiences, the situations, and the existential constraints of Parts I and II. One section gives the tensions, the miscognitions, the discontinuities of living; the following section gives these a grounding in the forms of the natural universe. The final section extrapolates into a perfected, absolute mode, that of aesthetic perceptivity, the finer values at play in the initial situation. These were focused in the intuitive, creative consciousness of the central figure, Mrs Ramsay, and everywhere present in the texture of the narrative itself. The stay against human and natural disorder is the unifying force of the creative sensibility, especially in its fashioning the impersonal order of art.

Woolf insists that this is the nature and purpose of her work: Lily Briscoe's function is to provide the position of intelligibility within the text, as her canvas is its emblematic summary. The sequence of the Ramsays' reading together, crucially placed at the close of Part I, is almost pedagogic, an incorporated guide on how to read this narrative. It directly transposes the kind of critical commentary offered in Fry's 'reading' of the Raphael canvas. Mr Ramsay's simple enjoyment of Scott's novel, his immersion in its characters' joys and sorrows, is replaced by a subtler response. He begins to think of the totality, to analyse and to compare its parts, to contrast it with his own philosophical writing. He begins, in fact, to respond to the novel as Mrs Ramsay is responding to the poems, particularly the Shakespeare sonnet. He therefore discards the dramatic emotions, and comes to perceive the general, abstract relations in the narrative, patterns and designs which are the essence of Scott's narrative. Though his procedures are more intellectual than Mrs Ramsay's intuitive receptivity, he progresses towards that intransitive mode. Significantly (for Woolf's purposes) he is reading again on the boat-trip, prior to his achieving something of his wife's capacity to communicate, understand, to bring others together in sympathy. But this 'moment', like Mrs Ramsay's many 'moments', including her reading of the sonnet, is held within a stylized, closely patterned sequence. By this stage of the narrative's complex movements, dramatic emotions have been transposed, distanced, re-interpreted.

Woolf's theory of reading, and the distinctive notions about narrative form that it relates to, marks much of her prolific literary journalism.[16] Though so much of this writing is belletristic, meant for the civilized 'Common Reader', it also contained a precise bold and radical conception of the novel.

Think away the surface animation, the likeness to life, and there remains, to provide a deeper pleasure, an exquisite discrimination of human values. Dismiss this too ... [in favour of] the more abstract art. It is possible to enjoy it, as one enjoys poetry, for itself, and not as a link which carries story.[17]

Few, perhaps none, of Jane Austen's readers will be persuaded to jettison quite so much, or know how to peel off so many layers, to reach the 'itself' of the narrative prose. This is the Roger Fry-Mauron aesthetic autonomy in its sharpest form: even when dramatic emotions and action are a work's most obvious features, they are critically discountable:

The meaning of a book, which lies so often apart from what happens and what is said, and consists rather in some connection which things in themselves different have had for the writer, is necessarily hard to grasp.[18]

Poet-novelists – here, the Brontës – must be intolerant of the restrictions of prose, which is intrinsically confined to 'the accepted order of things'. Major writers reveal their greatness in directing an 'untamed ferocity' against such order, creating a new language and new forms to do so. The Brontës demonstrate one way, as each author becomes 'an other self...almost impersonal in an intense individuality'. An alternative way, seen in Meredith and Turgenev, is the patterning of lyrical images: such designs work 'to crush the truth out in a series of metaphors or a string of epigrams with as little resort to dull fact as may be'. The bad writer, like Gissing or any of the Edwardians, has to describe tables, chairs, cups – 'this appalling narrative business of the realist: getting on from lunch to dinner' (*W.D.*, p. 138.) The authentic novelist, like Meredith, will evoke it all by 'a ring on the finger and a plume passing the window'; in Turgenev, lyricism transfigures the commonplace: 'a tap drips and a nightingale sings'. Yet this displacement of the substantial, the apparent and the factual by the incidental and the marginal gives perceptual reality its irrefutable, overwhelming presence:

There is staring us full in the face nothing but a large earthenware pot.... By reiterating that nothing but a plain earthenware pot stands in the foreground, Defoe persuades us to see...the solitudes of the human soul. He has subdued every other element to his design; he has roped the whole universe into harmony.[19]

This converts its text – Defoe's *Robinson Crusoe* – from a straightforward relation of practical adventures, in a language heavy with factuality and description of objects and places, into a Symbolist prose-poem. The same compulsion offers us Jane Austen's texts as prose-poems which secrete a quintessential mode of perception, a formal structuring which concerns the universe, not the parsonage (*C.E.*, I, p. 141). Woolf's theoreticism is obvious in all these instances, which openly discount the established critical accounts of nineteenth-century fiction, and revaluate the major authors, from Defoe, Austen, Scott, the Brontës, to Meredith, ranking them as poet-novelists. They are set in place as predecessors of Turgenev, Dostoevsky and Proust. The strained interpretations and almost comic misreadings are less important than their obvious workshop function for Woolf's own practice. Each substantial narrative (including the Russian and European texts) is a quarry from which Woolf cut out an inner form, a crystalline novel-poem:

And then, there it was, suddenly entire shaped in her hands, beautiful and reasonable, clear and complete, the essence sucked out of life and held rounded here – the sonnet. (*T.L.*, p. 139)

The positives that emerge from these critical explorations are components of her distinctive definition of the autonomous fiction, the lyrical novel. The negatives are the critical assaults which effect a radical deconstruction of traditional novel form. As with Fry's ambivalence about the art and the beliefs of Raphael, so with Woolf's duality in assessing the representative works of Austen and Scott. From one view, with some keen envy, she realizes that the fullness and confidence of their narratives have their support in a community of shared social, moral and philosophical beliefs.

In both there is the same natural conviction that life is of a certain quality.... They know the relation of human beings toward each other and towards the universe. (*C.E.*, II, p. 159)

From another standpoint, she is driven to deny that beliefs and values can so support the artist: their presence in the densities of narrative only block the perception of the inner and abstract forms. So, Fry suggests, both Raphael and his ideal viewer, Goethe, mistakenly attribute to their religious convictions those perceptions which are universal, abstract and which spring from the aesthetic sense. They misdescribe, as meaning, subject and value, what is fundamentally a registration of form, of timeless relations of spirit. So readers, critics and traditional novelists themselves, all mystify these formal relations and structures in their concern with fact, appearances, social values and conventions.

The pointed and rather disdainful comments on 'the Edwardian bullies' – Arnold Bennett, H. G. Wells, John Galsworthy – spring from the same unease and distrust. She relays Fry's dismissive remarks on artists' jejune obsession with photographic representation and 'trivial verisimilitude', applying them to her contemporaries' 'materialism' – meaning their debilitating realism:

Whether we call it life or spirit, truth or reality, this, the essential thing, has moved off or on, and refuses to be contained any longer in such ill-fitting vestments as we provide.[20]

The polemical pieces increasingly represent her own criticism and fiction as exemplary of literary modernism, speaking for the revolutionary vanguard: *Modern Fiction* (1919), *Mr Bennett and Mrs Brown* (1924), *The Narrow Bridge of Art* (1927). Their sense of historical change authorizes this rejection of art that refuses to surrender outworn values, defunct meanings, sterile conventions. Though here, as with Scott and Austen, the interrelations of art, belief and the historical moment are simplified, Woolf displays shrewd insights into the complexities of style and literary form. The problems in artistic expression go well beyond definition in terms which are only artistic. Life, spirit, truth, reality: these universal concepts crop us throughout the polemics, as they do in her characters' thoughts. Woolf's own sense of their content is very much that of her own circle, naturally enough. Her philosophical supports are there in McTaggart, Moore, Fry, Charles Mauron; and they provide the base for her strictures on her older contemporaries. The novelist's task is anything but light; to see human beings not only in relation to one another, but in relation to the nature of reality as the modern mind now conceived it:

Life is a luminous halo, a semi-transparent envelope surrounding us from the beginning of consciousness to the end. Is it not the task of the novelist to convey this varying, this unknown and uncircumscribed spirit . . . with as little of the alien and external as possible?[20]

The elusive nature of the aberrant, complex consciousness is a notation from Freud, whose translations were being published by the Woolfs; the predominant images of mind and reality are transposed from Clive Bell's and Fry's own appraisals of modern art. Post-Impressionism was the historic marker of the change in human nature and its understanding of itself which rendered established art and attitudes irrelevant. The 'reality' of the Edwardians was inverted, it had become the alien, the external.

Inside the generalities, the sweeping phrases, the pronouncements and the fiats, the particular contradictions are very revealing. The plenitude of early novels is consonant with the richness and complexity of social values, attitudes, beliefs and behaviour. The narratives are grounded in their historical moment: the themes, the problems and the resolutions have a social authenticity. Part of the scornful dismissal of the Edwardians is that they write as if such authentication remained unchanged: they are obtuse to the major shifts in socio-historical realities. But the substantiality of a Scott or Austen is also dismissed as alien and external: their strength is that they wrote poem-novels, formally compact. The Bennett and Wells fictions are not given such a re-assessment, though even a Defoe can qualify. The updating of Austen, her installation as a modern lyrical novelist, is part of a need to provide Woolf's experimental forms with some support in the past. But it is also a sign of a deep unease about the consequences of accepting that any considerable narrative art can substantially incorporate social actions, beliefs, problems, practices, the stuff of daily living. Woolf strongly desires to formulate a comprehensive theory of narrative in which the concept of the aesthetic will necessarily, intrinsically, exclude socio-historical material. The nervous, arrogant remarks about the carefully labelled 'Edwardians', and about 'ordinary everyday waking Arnold Bennett life', betray her sense of their nearness. Their concern with social problems, with class and money, with injustice, conflict and the possibilities of change, these all remain demanding and relevant, even if their artistic style and structures are old-fashioned.

Woolf impatiently reiterates her polemical slogan, 'Life tells no stories'. Popular novelists, in their bogus claims to follow tradition, seemed to do nothing else. Like E. M. Forster, she felt that all storytelling pandered to an atavistic sense. To carry on such narration in the 1910s and 1920s was anachronistic, since it ignored the nature and the recognitions of contemporary sensibility. The rigidities of fictive plotting precluded any awareness of contingency, indeterminacy, discontinuity, the elusive spirit of reality.

If a writer were a free man, and not a slave, if he could write what he chose, not what he must, if he could base his work upon his own feeling, and not upon convention, there would be no plot, no comedy, no tragedy, no love interest or catastrophe in the accepted style.[20]

(One free gesture would have been to alter the gender of all the pronouns here.) Woolf's minimal regard for received plot-forms, for the genre-conventions, themes, patterns of development, is very effectively demonstrated in her fiction. The term 'narrative' seems hardly to apply to her books, which strip action down to a few incidents, an even plane of meeting, drifting apart, being together at a meal or a party. The rhetorical emphasis of 'No plot, no comedy...' is programmatically realized. These dispersed, low-key and 'sluggish' developments are not alternatives or variants of any other familiar narrative structures.

A novel, Woolf acidly exclaimed, was something she hoped not to be accused of any more – thinking of *Jacob's Room* as having reached, if not crossed, that shadow-line:

The approach will be entirely different. no scaffolding; scarcely a brick to be seen; all crepuscular, but the heart, the passion, humour, everything as bright as fire in the mist. (*W.D.*, p. 31)

The experimental fiction is a rebuttal of realism, whose unquestioning 'materialism' overloads the novel with fact, appearances, stolid characterization and labyrinthine plots. The answering structure can only be evoked in images, sensory, tactile, predominantly visual and painterly. The forms of modern perceptual reality are only to be alluded to obliquely, tentatively, impressionistically. So the critical terms must surrender claims to solidity, to conceptual definitiveness. Like the writing itself, they must take meaning from metaphor, from figurativeness, and evoke order and structure by poetic conceit. The Post-Impressionist critical terminology was a crucial source of such concepts: luminosity, transparency, halo, mist, the crepuscular. Like 'Pointillism' and 'Impressionism', they may be indeterminate, loose, conceptually amorphous. But they mapped out Woolf's directions which, innovatory as they were, did not coincide with those of early Modernism – James, Conrad – or of later Modernism – Joyce, Lawrence, Stein.

The lyrical novel was Woolf's carefully crafted, scrupulously considered form, subjected to experiment and supported by critical research. The theoretical terms were part of the provisionality, and the experimental pieces and the novels themselves were always controlled by the theory. For Woolf, the fiction confirmed the original conceptions. They brought together her sense that form itself is a perception of relations independent of detail and appearance; that a writer's vision suffuses the whole writing with a fierce yet impersonal presence; and that imagery, metaphor and symbol can unify the composition. Her fundamental project, which made explanations so difficult, was to refashion the medium itself, to reshape its every detail. The restrictions of realistic plot were only a signal of the inadequacy of prose itself. The lyrical novel is to be the novel-poem, not only closely structured like a sonnet, but using its rhythms, its phrasing, its patterns, its density of language. Woolf's theory assumes a total distinction between prose and poetry; and, very selectively, considers lyrical intensity to be the quintessential quality of poetry itself. She was not concerned to make fiction less prosaic, nor to add metaphoric patterns or symbolic focus to a basically expressive narrative language. The fiction is to be a poem, not to be just poetic. The experiment is extreme, like the theory; the ambition and the accomplishment are audacious.

Woolf's astounding attempt was to make everything structural, to make each and every word contribute to the form – perhaps only feasible, if even then, in a sonnet or a brief lyric. This is her form of what she sensed in the poetic language of the Brontës, 'an untamed ferocity perpetually at war with the accepted order or things.' Her key-term for this is, aptly enough, 'saturation': it comprises word-choice, fluent phrasing, echoic sentences, a patterning of syntax, a rhythmic disposition of longer paragraphs, a repetition of key-words, the use of images and literary allusion. The whole passage of Clarissa's sewing by the window is set out by Sean O'Faolain as vers libre: 'Quiet descended on her, calm, content . . . listens to the passing bee' (*M.D.*, pp. 44–5, see O'Faolain, 1956.[21]) This is just as easily seen in the section in which Septimus responds to the livingness of the trees (*M.D.*, p. 26). (The whole of Septimus's reveries, without verbal changes, has been incorporated in an English version of *Noh* drama, *The Green Park*,

Richard   Taylor,   1981.[22])   Even   the   attempt   at   a
Bennett – Galsworthy type of writing, *The Years* (1937), is
unable to shake off this kind of movement:

> The quick northern river come down from the moors;
> It was never smooth and green,
> Never deep and placid like southern rivers.
> It raced; it hurried.
> It splayed itself, red, yellow and clear brown,
> Over the pebbles on the bed....
> She watched it eddy round the arches;
> She watched it make diamonds and sharp arrow streaks
> Over the stones.[23]

The final novel, *Between the Acts* (1941), originally included
poems in metre; and throughout the book, Isabella's inner-
monologue ('musing', 'humming', 'muttering') is represented
by this lyrical notation:

> Dispersed are we. The wave is broken.
> Left us stranded, high and dry. Single,
> separate on the shingle. Broken is the
> three-fold ply.... Now I follow....·To what
> dark centre of the unvisited earth, or wind –
> brushed forest, shall we go now? Or spin
> from star to star and dance in the maze of
> the moon? Or?...[24]

Nothing suggests that this is satiric in intent, and certainly not
that it makes fun of Woolf's own style, as she had so extensively
developed it throughout *The Waves*. Other figures in the book,
like Bart and his sister Mrs Swithin, speak to each other
exclusively through quotations, poetic allusions and verbal
jingles.

   Two writers were singled out as her models for lyrical prose:
Sterne and De Quincey. The lines from Sterne are pleasant,
fluent, visually fresh, musical; Woolf clearly aims at such
effects. Discussing De Quincey, she concludes that a writer is
poetic in 'gathering up and putting together these echoes and
fragments', to 'arrive at the true nature of an experience'. This
sums up her strategy for getting rid of the realistic novel's
massive narrative blocks: the marginal and contingent details,
in their textural density, will create a finer sense of perceptual

reality. The 'central things', the major truths about living must submit 'to beautification in language' (*W.D.*, p. 63). She faces the difficulty of doing without the major structural patterns, the narrative strategies, the usual modes of action and characterization. She acutely senses the danger of making her language both too fluid and too atomized, verbally fragmented: 'One must write from deep feeling .... And do I? Or do I fabricate with words, loving them as I do?' (*W.D.*, p. 63). This 'pendulum' principle, swinging from 'the generalization of romantic poetry' to particularization, was also a procedure that risked colouring everything with the writer's own perceptions. She felt the accuracy of Fry's warning that she was overdoing the prose-lyric vein: 'I poetise my inanimate scenes; stress my personality; don't let the meaning emerge from the matière.' But her determination to convert the novel into completely expressive prose remained throughout. The selected guardians – Sterne, Peacock, De Quincey, Proust – made her feel that good novelists are poets insofar as they write 'for the sake of the beauty of the sentence, and not for the sake of its use' Her revision of *The Waves* is directed by this thought: 'to break up, dig deep, make prose move as prose has never moved before: from the chuckle, the babble, to the rhapsody' (*W.D.*, p. 162).

Most criticism has shown positive appreciation of Woolf's search for alternative large-scale modes to give the novels a clear structure. The verbal music prompted E. M. Forster's description of her form as characteristically that of the sonata, instancing the three movements of *To the Lighthouse*. This analogy is pressed home by E. K. Brown,[25] analyzing the development and musical interweaving of themes: Part I hymns the splendour of life (with some actual chanting and singing by characters); Part II is a 'sombre lamentation'; Part III, a symphonic finale, blends the two earlier sections, and closes with 'great chorus'. The mixed configurations – sonata, symphony, hymns, chants, chords – like that of 'a formal dance' (J. Bennett)[25] – are so nebulous that they only emphasize the difficulty of discerning clear outlines. There are comparable drawbacks with many related suggestions: the three sections are the three lighthouse beams (Fleishman); the lighthouse is a multifaceted symbol (Tindall)[25]; each book is a web of interconnected images (Brower, Hartman)[25]. The unity and coherence is attributed to a network of motifs, metaphors and symbols, but these are often inseparable from the 'local texture' of reiterated figures. The discussion of full-scale patterning dissolves into analysis of 'verbal nuances', and finally into the reader's 'hazy, synaesthetic impression', as repetition becomes disintegrative and monotonous (Lodge)[25]. The critical goodwill in all these figurative labellings is in their wish to stress the forward impetus, the thrust and movement. The more convincing analyses show such impetus is present, not in separable features like images, but in the movement of the language itself. It has a simultaneous flow and acceleration, and a pausing rhythm (Hartman[25]). This has been brilliantly analysed (Mepham, 1976[26]) as a sustained stimulation of the reader's physical enactment of the text's 'bodily' action, its compelling – in enunciation, in breathing, in syntactical phrasing – a physical reception which determines the imaginative comprehension. But the force of this analysis is to show how thoroughly Woolf did saturate every minuscule part and item of her language. The extensive, complex elements are composed of innumerable units and functions. The holistic, unifying principles are abstract, metatextual: 'There are the oppositions between life and death, presence and absence, sterility and fertility... creating unity out of disorder'[26]

Woolf's own frequent use of visual and spatial figures to describe her methods and her forms only stresses how elusive the temporal rhythms are. The Fry – Mauron terminology of volumes and of montage is only the most obvious.[27] Discussions with the painter Jacques Raverat produce similar ideas: the novel as composition, as sketch, as concentric circles, as diagram.[28] She imagines a new novel: 'I shall have two different currents – the moth flying along; the flower upright in the centre.' This is part of her notebook musings when she stops 'to consider the whole effect'. Much of this is a principled resistance to the relentlessly chronological calibration of novelistic plot, with its keyboard precision and its alphabetic logic of conflict, crisis and resolution. The linearity of plot was one-directional, a railway-line, besides engendering much cumbersome description. Spatial metaphors suggested the multiplexity of experience, the simultaneity and co-existence of contrary impulses and ideas, the co-presence of past and present, of the personal and the impersonal. The most compelling of the explicit, large-scale figures are spatio-temporal, a complex imbrication of movement and arrest. So the lighthouse's altering beams of light and intervals of darkness; the triple motion of waves-gathering, equipoise, dispersal; the movements of the sun during a whole day, with the intermittence of darkness. There are long-term contrasts of outside motion and flux with inside stillness and harmony: city traffic against private rooms (*M.D., W.*); wind, storm, and sea, against quiet gatherings of friends (*T.L., W., Y.*).

Woolf's project was 'to tell all ... everything, everything', and to tell it in a 'playpoem', an 'Elegy', a 'novel about Nothing'. This apparently ineffable form and substance – 'everything I know' – has given literary criticism its two Woolfs: the Mystic and the Psychologist. The same elements in her writing illustrate each analysis: the connections between Septimus and Clarissa, and the closing metaphors about 'redemption'; Mrs Ramsay's becoming 'a wedge-shaped core of darkness', and her 'return' after death; the intuitive reading of one another's thoughts by a whole group in *The Waves*; the frequent occurrence of trance-like 'Moments'. So many points in the fictions are interpreted as images of transcendence, or as images of psychic penetration, even as both at once. Climaxes are very often in terms of rising or sinking, climbing or falling, ascending or descending. But they all seen to be held within one form or another of the narrative's unfailing activity: *looking*. The authentic self, the clear mind, is 'a central oyster of perceptiveness, an enormous eye'. The flux of life, boisterous or momentarily stilled, is watched from a window: Woolf herself (*R.O.O.*), the lady writer (*W.*), Elizabeth on a bus (*M.D.*), Mrs Ramsay; or dangerously thrilling, surveyed from the roadside: Woolf again ('Street Haunting'[29]), Clarissa, and Eleanor (*Y.*). The regard of many separate figures may focus on an external point: a car, a plane (*M.D.*); the lighthouse; the sea (*T.L.W.*). Or the regard of all will turn to one person, present or absent: (Clarissa, Mrs Ramsay, Jacob, Percival (*W.*).

For the eye has this strange property: it rests only on beauty; like a butterfly it seeks colour and basks in warmth .... The eye is sportive and generous; it creates, it adorns; it enhances.[29]

This concept of the *regard* is the prime token of Woolf's 'everything', her psychology and philosophy, the 'silence' that the playpoem is to articulate. Perception and the perceptual reality are the ubiquitous, singular and obsessive concerns, determining every level of the writing. They are humanly inextricable, mutually defining: the flux of being and the flow of awareness produce and sustain each other. The beauty is there for the eye to rest on; but it, in turn, only exists by creating and enhancing:

Examine for a moment an ordinary mind on an ordinary day. The mind receives a myriad impressions – trivial, fantastic, evanescent, or engraved with the sharpness of steel. From all sides they come, an incessant shower of innumerable atoms; and as they fall, as they shape themselves into the life of Monday or Tuesday, the accent falls differently.[30]

This radical relocation of the novelist's interest, 'an ordinary mind on an ordinary day', affects every feature of the representation. The uninterrupted flow of awareness must prompt an uninterrupted flow of words to ensure the motions of the real:

An immense profusion of sensations, images, sentiments, memories, impulses, little larval actions that no inner language can convey, that jostle one another one the threshold of consciousness, gather together in compact groups, loom up all of a sudden, then immediately fall apart, combine otherwise and reappear in new forms.

Nathalie Sarraute,[31] in describing this identity in Woolf's writing of the form and the content, precisely defines its distinctive processual nature. The narrative 'propones' – Sarraute's term – opens laterally, incorporates a circularity, while it never interrupts it own forward motion. Sarraute's neologism for this form, 'tropism', distinguishes its aims from the 'inner language' of modern psychologistic writing, since it essentially binds outer and inner. It catches the conflicting, shifting contingencies which conform briefly, to be replaced by the next conformation. (One concealed metaphor in Sarraute's account is Woolf's own favourite symbolic emblem, that of waves). Intermittency, the disintegration into the random, is that feature of the perceived and of the perception that insistently prompts the human ordering, just as it insistently threatens it.

The abstract motions of the narrative, linking its multiplying tropisms, are those of the aesthetic theories which Woolf developed from Fry, Mauron and G. E. Moore. The abstraction includes what is comprehended as 'seeing', for 'the central oyster of perceptiveness, an enormous eye', is the aesthetic sensibility. It is that other sense of 'vision', that rapt intransitive attention which intuitively grasps harmony and relations. What a character here sees is little or nothing to do with the optical:

> The carriages, motor-cars, omnibuses, vans, sandwhich men...some aeroplane overhead was what she loved; life; London; this moment of June...(*M.D.*)

> It was odd, she thought, how if one was alone, one leant to things, inanimate things: trees, streams, flowers; felt they expressed one; felt they became one. (*T.L.*)

> Snow falling – a sunflower with a crack in it; the yellow omnibus trotting along the Bayswater Road ...(*Y.*)

> Then (as I was walking in Russell Square last night) I see the mountains in the sky; the great clouds; and the moon which is risen over Persia. I have a great and astonishing sense of something there which is 'it'. (*W.D.*)

> The idea of some continuous stream, not solely of human thought, but of the ship, the night ... all flowing together: intersected by the arrival of the bright moths. A man and a woman are sitting at the table talking. (*W.D.*)

Each 'moment' is the realization of a unity, an interconnection between all things; the perceiver's 'state of mind' is the rapt intransitive attention of the aesthetic sensibility. The harmony is in the relation itself, the design as index of all design, of universal coherence. The implications are mystical only insofar as Woolf has made a total and absolute value, a textual metaphysic, of the psychology of perception and the theory of aesthetic feeling developed by Fry and Moore. So the individual components are fortuitously specific, their particularity swept into a patterning which is non-specific, abstract, Idealist. The omnibuses and vans are interchangeable with the trees and streams, and these again with the clouds or the moths. Essentially, the units dissolve in the flux, outer and inner: there is an equalization of everything 'seen'. The omnibus, the snow, London, life, are essentially just as abstract and just as particular as one another. The perception of their relations overrides their differentiation: abstract or

concrete, outer or inner, each component has an identical status
and function. The perceiver, whether an internal character, or an
actual person (Woolf in Russell Square), or the novelist (Woolf
planning *The Moths*) 'is aware of "life itself"; of the atmosphere
of the table rather than of the table; of the silence rather than of
the sound.' (Woolf's comment on the writing she most learnt
from, that of Dorothy Richardson.)[32]

'Her discoveries are concerned with states of being and not
with states of doing': what is singled out in Richardson is also
clearly Woolf's own project. The 'trophies brought to the
surface', which other writers have 'guiltily suppressed' are those
which Sarraute describes. Despite the Freudian hints, the
retrievals are not from the deep unconscious, the regions of
libidinal or visceral response. Joyce's explorations were
profoundly shocking to her: 'The pages reeled with indecency
.... This goes back to a pre-historic world' (*W.D.*, p. 343). 'How
distressing, how egotistic, insistent, raw, striking, and ultimately
nauseating' (*W.D.*, p. 54). The intensities of the moment of
perception have no deep, tentacular roots, no reaching after the
inarticulable and pre-reflective grounds of unmediated
experience. That they can seem so, as for instance with Mrs
Ramsay's becoming 'a wedge-shaped core of darkness', is an
effect of their being context-free. Just as the components of the
moment are interchangeably physical objects, places, ideas,
whose differential qualities are pared away; just so the state of
mind is unmotivated, disjoined from any immediate causal
ground. But Mrs Ramsay attains no private psychic revelation;
the reader is given no subtle personal psychological insights.
This moment is like many others, not only her own, but those of
other characters, in this and in other novels by Woolf.

The crucial turns and narrative climaxes are the representations of states-of-mind, impersonal and interchangeable in their
contouring. They are not specific or restricted to the context, not
given dramatic motivation. The state-of-mind is not definable as
the consequence of sense response, since the objects and places
are not given full-bodied sensuous identity. Neither is it built up
from thought processes, from mental response to the pro-
vacation of action and immediate pressures. Woolf's characters,
as thinking and feeling subjects, are not versions of the
relativized consciousnesses of modernistic fiction. The trans-

individual awareness that connects all the figures in *The Waves*, or relates Clarissa, Walsh and Septimus in *Mrs Dalloway*, is necessarily contrary to such psychological differentiation. What each figure may attain is an access to a perceptual real which could not be self-identical if it varied from one sensibility to another. The perceptual real, caught by the contingent, transitory moment, is the persisting horizon of the narrative itself. The narrative is a continuous representation and dramatic enactment of a mode of consciousness which is only inter-mittently co-incident with that of internal figures. The preferred consciousness will reflect this narrative mode, and be attributed with the same power to build fictions of unity. Clarissa and Mrs Ramsay set out to bring together the others who are scattered and isolated: this social harmonizing will be a party, a luncheon, a holiday group, a reunion of friends, even match-making for the young. Each is a form of the creative moment, a shared state of being, an aesthetic patterning of human relationship:

This, that, and the other; herself and Charles Tansley and the breaking wave; Mrs Ramsay bringing tham together; Mrs Ramsay saying 'Life stand still here'; Mrs Ramsay making of the moment something permanent (as in another sphere Lily herself tried to make of the moment something permanent). (*T.L.*, p. 183)

The blunt reminder in parenthesis is superfluous, since all the texts are constructed on these parallels between various forms of aesthetic sensibility. The society hostess, the mother, the painter, poet or writer: each manifest its predominance, its definitive human centrality.

It is this would-be absoluteness, this dogmatic com-prehensiveness, which fractures the narratives and which makes them much richer texts than they would have been, had they mainly illustrated the theoretical notions from which Woolf begins. The aesthetic sensibility, whether intuitively receptive or actively creating harmony, is tested by the autonomy of the 'moment'. As a moment of ordered perception, it readily falls back into the assembled constituents: if the trees can be yellow omnibuses, then no ordering or selection has been achieved. As Katherine Mansfield remarked: 'Everything being of equal importance, it is impossible that everything should not be of equal unimportance'. Again, if the trees are there insofar as 'they express one' – Clarissa, Septimus, Mrs Ramsay, Susan (in *The Waves*[33]) – then no relation or connection is really being made outside the perceiving ego. Clarissa's apocalyptic realization of her final identity with Septimus is literally that: a relation to a version of her self. The climactic evening party, to which the whole narrative leads, is effectively not shown in itself. That parallel sequence, the Ramsays' dinner-party, is an intriguingly complex instance of the extended 'moment', and its self-deconstruction. The disparates are said to be reconciled, and social communion rendered as poetry and music, or even as a transcendent, sacred communion. Yet Woolf's own language insists on the scene as visually, graphically rendered, on the deliberate, individual ordering by one character, and on the way everything is 'composed'. The poignancy is in the rendering of the fragility, in the separateness of Mrs Ramsay's view, and in the disintegration of the scene as she leaves:

She waited a moment longer in a scene which was vanishing even as she looked ... it had become, she knew, giving one last look at it over her shoulder, already the past.

The exhilaration of a Clarissa, the affirmations of a Mrs Ramsay, the ecstatic perceptions of a Jinny, a Bernard or a Rhoda (*W*) share a high-pitched breathlessness which hardly restrains its anxieties and hysteria. The states-of-mind and states-of-being, even if they are shareable, admit their impotence 'against that fluidity out there' (*T.L.*, p. 112).

This fracturing of the autonomy of the individual state-of-mind and of the communal state-of-being is given other contradictory and sombre forms. Clarissa's buoyancy and self-discipline, her defiant affirmations of significant order have an inner contouring of depression, disintegration of the self, and explicit traumatic intuitions of absurdity and incoherence. Existence is simultaneously the one (Clarissa) and the other (Septimus): they are not contrasts, alternatives, or mutually exclusive. The 'madness', as E. M. Forster noted, is always lucidly, rationally presented. The teasing ambivalence is in the way that the discourse of 'madness' is an extreme extension of Clarissa's (and the narrative's) mode of awareness. Septimus is locked in an infinity of moments, condemned to an endless hyper-awareness. This is touched on for all the figures in *The*

Waves, and given a singularly intense form in the presentation of Rhoda. The narrative seems to include representations of the destructive cost of its own values, especially its distinctive mode of consciousness. This is one of the troubled impulses which inform the extended mid-section of *To the Lighthouse*, 'Time Passes'. This 'narrates the production of a discourse of madness'.[34] It is, paradoxically, an aesthetic ordering, by Woolf, of the destructiveness consequent on the attempt to comprehend (i.e. to aesthetically order) the flux of perceptual reality. Time, place, person are annihilated: the lyrical, rhythmic language is to image that annulment. It strives to represent an unmediated, inhuman reality; and obscurely admits what it would strenuously deny, that it is self-mirroring. The aesthetic sensibility here faces that chosen definition of itself, and its consequent disintegration. The bad infinity cannot be authenticated as an objective, non-human flux. To attempt to authenticate it is only to point within, to describe the perceiver's chosen form of perception.

Woolf was always keenly aware of the related problems of authority, narrative control and personal inflections in prose. She detested the masculine re-iteration of 'I . . . I . . . I' in fiction, and felt that to 'lyricize the argument' would help avoid this. Reading Joyce and Richardson brought out strongly the way that any notation of consciousness set traps for the 'damned egotistical self'. The rejection of plot and the strategies of realism increased the dangers of her fluency: 'I have come to a crisis in the matter of style: it is now so fluent and fluid that it runs through the mind like water . . . . Shall I now check and consolidate?' (*W.D.*, p. 136). The piquancy is that her major concern is the fluency of the sensibility: to set this at a distance would be to question, to qualify, to ironize. This is the source of the narrative checks and consolidations in the richly diverse characterization and language of James, Conrad and Joyce. Consciousness is conditioned, individualized, located by contrasts in their fictions. Woolf represents consciousness as unconditioned and trans-individual: and the authentication for its being so must inevitably be her own consciousness, the sensibility that saturates the text. The cross-play of contrasting minds is the source of tension and drama in any modern fiction which has undercut the predominance of outer

action. But the centres of consciousness that encircle Woolf's
major figures only endorse the sensibility there represented.
The contrast is with the obtuse, the impercipient, the buffoons
of sensibility: Bradshaw, Holmes, Kilman; Tansley, Mr
Ramsay (in Part I). They cannot be seen from the inside:
Woolf's historiography of the consciousness sets them at the
borders of nullity. The perception of a Walsh, a Tansley, even
of a Mr Ramsay, is corrected or 'redeemed' by its reverential
assumption of the state-of-being incarnated in a Clarissa or in a
Mrs Ramsay. Any irony in the text about the protagonists,
explicit or unwitting, is about their incidental, diversionary
preoccupations, mannerisms, personal behaviour. This is the
dross that clogs the sensibility, the hindrances to the intuitive
imagination. The six characters in *The Waves*, totally free of
any irony, are never seen in any relation to that level of
mundane involvement. Sensibility making total claims for
itself cannot test them by ironic self-scrutiny, without modifying radically its fundamental assumptions: 'When I write I am
merely a sensibility. Sometimes I like being Virginia, but only
when I'm scattered, and various and gregarious.'

   The history of the various versions of *The Moths* and its
modulation into *The Waves*,[35] confirms the accuracy of this
rueful, ambivalent self-assessment. When the reviewers praised
the novel's characters, she was genuinely puzzled, noting rather
proudly that she meant to have none (*W.D.*, p. 171). The
ambiguities and the confusions about her own presence in the
texts are reiterated throughout the *Diary*. 'Who thinks it? And
am I outside the thinker?' She worried that the books were
'essays about myself', while developing a theory which could
only maximize that possibility. *Jacob's Room* provides instances, with its mini-essays about the mystery of personality,
about perception, about the difficulty of writing fiction. The
writer's appearance is meant to dramatize the difficulty of
analysing or understanding character, a demonstration of
Jacob's otherness and distance from the author. But her
presence replaces his, blocks his becoming either mysterious or
knowable. The more pervasive, less obvious presence, which
perhaps marks all her novels, is in the close control of the
representation. The sequences are manneristically patterned,
the dialogue edited, the scenes restrained, the action mini-

malized. There is an arbitrariness which binds everything in to the author's originating conceptions about character, about action and about their representation. There is an open, ingenuous formulation of how this art of fiction involves the attribution to characters of qualities, intentions, and meanings which are validated only by their intrinsic interest:

> But something is always compelling one to hang vibrating...endowing Jacob Flanders with all sorts of qualities he had not at all...what remains is mostly a matter of guess work....

This power of fictive attribution is approvingly given to internal characters in other novels: Peter Walsh, Mrs Ramsay, Bernard. It is the whole point of *An Unwritten Novel* (1920). The *Diary* has many such reveries and speculations: 'Street Haunting' demonstrates some of them. Most significantly, the whole argument of 'Mr Bennett and Mrs Brown', a major illustration of her theory, depends on whose 'attribution' of qualities to 'Mrs Brown' – i.e. people, experience, life – is most convincing. The styles of the various attributions, of course, are in turn attributed by the winner herself, Virginia Woolf.

'Who thinks it? And am I outside the speaker?' Placing herself in view, directly in *Jacob's Room*, indirectly through Lily, Bernard, or Miss La Trobe, did not ensure her being outside the speaking. The 'speaking' of the texts became increasingly idiosyncratic, multi-layered, ambivalent in its origins and its narrative dispositions. Echoing her questioning, John Mepham asks 'Who speaks in *To the Lighthouse*?' He brilliantly analyses the subtle modulations from the fictional subjects to the narration's own contribution. As Auerbach indicates,[36] Woolf represents herself as 'someone who doubts, wonders, hesitates', so that the fictive voice and the narrative voice are hardly distinguishable. This indeterminacy of attribution is used by Woolf 'to provide extra dimensions of meaning and association on behalf of the subject'. This is the author's addition of cross-reference, allusion and imagery which the internal figure 'would recognize as expressive of the force and content of his (or her) experience'.[37] This single source of authentication, the character 'itself', was Woolf's allegedly final authority in *Jacob's Room*. That Jacob or any other figure is part of the whole narration's flow of language is vital, however obvious, in this search for meaning's origins. That personality is mysterious, that identity is dislimned, is the founding perception of exactly this sort of narrative language. It is not a perception by the characters, but a conception about identity, which the figures serve to illustrate and embody. The slippage between fictive voice and narrative voice clearly works both ways: Woolf's mode of perception extends into that of the characters. The local strategies to keep the division flexible are the signals that it is there, and that it is being traversed. A minor example is the umbrella pronoun 'One', which blurs and fuses the attitudes of character and of narrator, and often implicates the reader.

The rhetoric of the lyrical novel is not in the command of the characters: its generality and its structural function has to subsume their individuality. The metaphoric level, with its patterned systems of imagery and allusion, has formal functions that belong in most fiction to the plot. This innovatory displacement, at the centre of Woolf's experimentalism, was consciously at the expense of interest in characterization. The multidimensional playpoem moves on a vertical axis, a rhetorical, stylistic, verbal interaction. It discards the linear axis, the metonymic and syntagmatic procedures of expository narrative. What the characters say is of little or no importance, against how the saying is part of the totalizing, non-individual movements of the language. The voice of the narration is composed by any and all other voices of characters, whose names are often irrelevant. Any page of *The Waves* can be quoted without names as an instance of the saturated texture and poetic movement that Woolf wanted. Such choric writing marks significant moments in all the novels, even in the would-be factual *The Years* (e.g. the conversation between Sarah and North, 'Present Day'). The intonations that bind the separate utterances together are almost always in the spectrum from the poignancy of recollection, the commemorative, to the plangently elegiac:

'Well, we must wait for the future to show,'
'It's almost too dark to see.'
'One can hardly tell which is the sea and which is the land.'
'Do we leave the light burning?...
One by one the lamps were all extinguished. ('Times Passes', *TL*)

The Waves is the most intensive and most extensive exploitation of every element contributing to the poem-novel. It elegantly displays how 'lyricizing the argument' makes the writing choric in every part. The 'argument' has disappeared, and the formality of the profuse figurative, rhythmic language has to provide its own contours and dramatic punctuation, its origins and its closures. The checks and consolidation of character and action have been abandoned. Language itself has to provide the objectification, the impersonality, the rein against the 'damned egotistical self'. But language is no more autonomous for these purposes than the states-of-mind which it is to express and to connect by its rhythms. This order of impersonality is not sealed into language as such, and certainly is not hermetically enclosed in imagery and metaphor. Woolf is obsessively concerned with style in language, which can only mean the decisions and choices she makes, explicitly or implicitly. The retreat to a hypothetical absolute position which language stripped of 'personality' should have is illusory, like 'omniscient perspective' attributed to metaphoric patterning in the lyrical novel. (Itself a pseudo-genre: cf. R. Freedman.)[38]

The distinctively individual, even idiosyncratic, deployment of language, verbally and structurally, is enthusiastically appraised by Woolf's critics. The further assumption is that the metaphoric profusion brings impersonal, objective reference through the archetypal force of its patterns: sun, sea, light and dark, day and night, the seasons, gestation, the life span, the flux of nature or of human consciousness. Again, however, these can only be present in specific conceptions and formulations. Their presence in the flow of language that composes the prose-poem here carries, necessarily, many traces of their earlier formulations. These are, by Woolf's studied choices, increasingly confined to their use in earlier English verse. (She has an indifference, even a strong aversion, to modern poetry.) Her prose, then, has its affiliations not with other prose, and not with traditional fiction – except when she interprets particular instances as lyrical novels. The language is 'poeticized', but, again, in relation to a specific interpretative conception of poetic tradition. This singles out the quintessentially melodic, the rhythmic and the free-flowing, the insistently metaphoric, the sensuously impressionistic, the verbally 'orchestrated'. It ignores the play of ideas in verse, the referential, the non-evocative relational elements, the dramatic representations of conflict with the self or with the world. This highly selective definiton of the poetic comes from a search for the resonance and vibrancy of words disjoined from specific contexts, persons, perceptions, or dramatic situations. The 'poetic' is shorthand for reflection and reverie circling around abstractions labelled 'life', 'Time', 'Death', extrapolated from literary sources, and set out as the mythic forms which control the rhythms of the aesthetic sensibility.

A characteristically revealing note on the genesis and the intention of her writing is apropos of the mid-section of *To the Lighthouse* (*W.D.*, p. 92). She remarks that it is incredibly abstract, 'all eyeless and featureless with nothing to cling to'. At the same instant, she is struck by her exhilarated fluency, a rushing and 'scattering' of language: 'Why am I so flown and apparently free to do exactly what I like?' Not only are scene and characters removed, there is to be no narrator or implied author. This withdrawal of agency or focus is the enabling of the poetic narrative itself, the occasion for the voice of language to speak. But the annulment or death of this author allows the release of other authors. The style which aims at writing degree zero lets in all the other styles, and the passage is a pastiche of a whole range of idioms and tones. They include the Biblical, the prophetic, the elegiac, the stoically philosophical, the grotesquely comic, the visionary and apocalyptic. Specific borrowings might be traced to the Authorized Version, seventeenth-century baroque prose, Pater, Arnold, Dickens and Hardy. The images indeed have 'nothing to cling to', no house, no people, no situation. The voices become a medley of disparate voices whose only combinatory source has to be this narrator. Otherwise the words fall back into the myriad of atomistic sensations which present themselves for unification, for lyrical 'orchestration', by one voice. Woolf has to mediate, she cannot disappear behind language; she remains as a separate, authenticating presence, all the more pervasively because she has deconstructed the alternative mediations. The flux here is a stream of consciousness, but not that of a 'nature' or of the language: 'It is finally the emancipated associative flow of the novelist herself'.[39]

A variation of this inference about narrative form and its authority, the sense of 'Who speaks?' in this writing, produces the related suggestions that the one developed character is the androgynous mind (Hartman, 1975); or the feminine sensibility (Spivak, 1980). Both ideas, much discussed by feminists, have considerable support in Woolf's own criticism. They restore the possibility that the autonomy of the lyrical novel could dramatize the distance between the fictive voice (singular or composite) and the narrative voice. But their consonance, their interweaving, and their ultimate singleness are evinced in the peculiar form that Woolf gives to the internal monologues. The 'moments' and states-of-mind are always expressed as interior monologues; and the whole of *The Waves* consists of interrelated lyrical soliloquies. However, they have been edited, effectively shorn of all the features associated with theatrical soliloquy, or the complementary dramatic monologue. Whatever the variations, these traditional forms are utterances in which the speaker shows a sense of being situated. There is a sense of provocation, of opposition, of likely (or silently voiced) answers, which are anticipated, summed up, reflected on. They are theatrical or 'dramatic' in that they are located, with promptings and aftermath implied in the tense movements of the self-explanation and self-scrutiny. The soliloquy or monologue is an actual or mental withdrawal, but the thinker wants to act out all the implications of the actuality that informs the reflections. He addresses himself, and addresses others, temporarily absent; the soliloquizing is functional, directed, purposive.

The soliloquy or interior monologue in Woolf's fiction often signals its not being directed or purposively addressed. The ruefully reiterated 'But to whom?' is disingenuous when it is not self-pitying. The language of the soliloquizer is not meant to communicate, to answer, to impinge. It is an intransitive address, a verbal composition, a metaphoric transcript of an elusive, self-validating intuition. Its separateness, its privacy, its radical otherness is precisely what the whole force of the writing privileges and authenticates. That fictive characters or the narrative's voice should attribute pathos or pain to this isolatedness is confused and confusing, even if this inflection is more valid than the first kind. This larger, encircling evaluation is, however, not allowed to bring this clash into the movements of the text. The lyrical fluency of expression is itself the obsessive iteration of continuity and undividedness. This continuum of words has a marked unity of tone, and is itself an extended monologue. It preserves its essential qualities by erasing dialogue, by suppressing possible answers, by curtailing its origin and provocation. The absence of direct verbal exchange is not a neutral obverse of the concern with mental or psychological interiors. The remarkably extensive use of indirect speech, the voice of the narrative filtering all other voices, is not another experimental feature, a value-free technique. Its obsessiveness bothered the novelist: 'I think I can spin out all their entrails this way; but it is hopelessly undramatic. It is all in *oratio obliqua*. Not quite all; for I have a few direct sentences' (On *To the Lighthouse*, *W.D.*, p. 102). Yet it is the *oratio obliqua* which gives the narratives their density, their pace and tone, their peculiar atmosphere and pitch, and provides the complex modes of control which impose form on the material. It is yet one more manifestation of the penetration into all the voices of the inflections of the narrative voice. The linguistic register is changed, not from one character to the next, nor from one kind of scene to another, but within the sentence. A rhetoric is provided which is meant to articulate impressions, thoughts and perceptions which are unrecognized by the fictive subject. The narrative 'lends' its voice: but the voice it suppresses, however it might have fumbled its expression, cannot be heard. This stylistic variation of *erlebte rede*, then, may be seen as an ascription to nearly all the represented characters of fundamentally false consciousness.

The most obvious suppression of other discourse is seen in the peripheral *dramatis personae*. They are the gardeners, miners, cooks and cleaners, the street-singers and women with shopping bags. They are the 'base-born', the 'illiterate and underbred', the 'veriest frumps', seen in a mass – 'the mothers of Pimlico give suck to their young' – and as subhuman, animal-like – 'crawling', with 'stumps' for legs. (The delicately minded, old-fashioned, upper-middle class periphrases signify the social origin of the suppression.) More significantly, there is omission of the complementary voice in the 'dialogue' of friends, lover, married couples. Richard Dalloway never speaks, yet is a paragon; the conversation of Clarissa and her passionate admirer Peter Walsh is transmogrified into a cluster of mock-heroic images; the marriage of true minds, the Ramsays', is distinguished by silences, when the indirect, smouldering resentments have been first released. The same pattern is used for Giles and Isa, the central married couple in *Between the Acts*. The validity of relationships is rarely expressed and rarely tested in the form of dramatic dialogue. Exchange, connection and confrontation are summarized by indirect report.

The clearest and most damaging suppression of dialogue is the denial of a voice to those agents in the action whose values and consciousness are antithetical to those of the protagonist. These are the buffoons who lack sensibility: but since their own discourse is not given, the ascription is self-confirming and shows up as allegation. Holmes, Bradshaw, Mrs Bradshaw, Whitbread, through omission, become caricatures; they do not exist on Clarissa's own plane. Equally with Tansley (*T.L.*) and Laycock (*Y.*) or Mrs Manresa (*B.A.*): their attitudes and behaviour are already interpreted, and this bias turns out to be the attributed 'humour' of the character. The sketchily presented Whitbread is constituted only from the idea that authority at its least unacceptable is bland, pompous, pedantic and self-satisfied. Bradshaw is similarly composed, but from a bitter hatred of arrogant authority, of its mindless, destructive imposition of order. The representation combines a quadrupled indirection with the fracturing of the narrative control. There are wild, savagely sarcastic passages on 'Proportion' and 'Conversion', an allegory of diabolism, which are unattributed and unascribable to any textual voice. The reader's sense that this might be 'the most uncharming human being' – Lily's thought about Tansley, but it could be about Bradshaw or Doris Kilman – is not inferable from any instance of behaviour. The fiercely negative sentiments are so riddled with anxiety that they must stifle this hateful opposing voice, must perpetrate the same offence. This bizarre distortion of feeling, since it is approvingly installed in Clarissa's attitudes, refers the reader very directly back to Woolf as person, not as narrator or as implicit author, but simply as the explicit, judging writer. (The same disruption occurs often in the work of E. M. Forster.)

There is evident in all these texts a full-scale 'dialogue' between male and female, masculine and feminine. Their bold and damagingly simple lines have often been tabulated: Intellect/Intuition, Fact/Vision, Words/Silence, Society/Solitude, Clock-time/Duration in consciousness, Realism/Impressionism. *To the Lighthouse* has the clearest, most complete enactment of the antithesis. Its clarity and strength, however, do not consist in its giving equal presence to the complementary or adversative types of consciousness.[40] Mr Ramsay's inflexibly linear mind, immersed in externalities, is perceived through the intuitive feminine consciousness, which pervades all the writing, though it centres itself in Mrs Ramsay. The masculine mode of a Bradshaw is here temperately imaged, indulged with wry mock-heroic imagery which denies him any direct voice or presence. He is only immediate when he contemplates the wonder of Mrs Ramsay's being. The tilt in presentation, the uncontested nature of Mrs Ramsay's 'triumphs' and 'trophies', means that the narrative's own ultimate values are less securely dramatized. The intuitive and visionary sensibility is attributed to the 'feminine' mode of consciousness, in turn identified with that of the artist. Lily, the painter/writer, may be internal, and her 'canvas' finally disposable. But the text itself, which validates their shared sensibility, demonstrates its aesthetic mode, again without proving it in confrontation with the antagonistic 'masculine' mode. The ultimate appeal is to the aesthetic visionary mode, this novel itself, which is the controlled comprehension of all else.

The masculine/feminine polarity crosses gender lines: despite her name, Kilman, this character is evoked as 'masculine' in her wilfulness. Jacob and Septimus, destroyed by the men's world, are 'feminine' in temperament; as are all the artists and writers, like Bernard, Neville and Louis – three of the four clustered together in *The Waves*. This polarity of principles, taken as ironized by Woolf, and resolved (as 'androgyny') or superseded, is itself part of a larger dialogue. It is part of the narrative politics in which the displacement of realism is part of the re-ordering of experience by her own aesthetic forms: 'If Woolf moves away from facts and crises it is because she denies the claim of such ordering to be all-inclusive' (Beer, 1979[41]). The railway-line of Ramsay's logical progress is that of realistic narrative, of male ideology and philosophy, and the brutal, destructive hegemonic social order. The lateral, associative movement of Woolf's writing then symbolizes the receptivity to other possibilities and movements, alternative modes of social living. This intentionality may well be perceived; but the caricatural onslaught and the suppression of the masculine voices are not only tactical, a means of temporarily suspending their authority. As the uncontrolled feeling indicates, there is a fundamental ambiguity, a hyper-defensiveness about the writing whenever the Bradshaw-mentality is arraigned. The affected serenity of the witty allegorical conceits – Proportion, Conversion, the Seven Deadly Sins in a mackintosh (Kilman) – barely holds back a hatred for all interest in social ordering. This has been often mystified as a distaste for 'the idea of Society as such'. It is much more obviously an over-anxious dislike of commitment, analysis, social change. It contains a vigorous rejection of the society in transition which she was observing, England between the wars. Her kind of 'openness' to possible alternatives in social living, in the mid-1930s, is demonstrated very explicitly in *The Years*. The separate self, the centre, is the only location for change. Two of its proponents are given climactic, disruptive diatribes whose convolutions of ambiguous, unmotivated feeling refer straight back to the writer herself. All the bitterness of the earlier 'exposures' of commitment is intensified in an unbalanced commentary on manifestoes, social concern, political activism (*Y.*, p. 325). The 'young man' – Leacock or Laycock – is given no speech: he is a textual space for this unlocated, unprovoked animus. The sad offence that is here to be inferred was in Doris Kilman's case a wish for other modes of social living, other ways of thinking, feeling, behaving. Kilman wants her own vocation, and wants to convince others about change. She must be a feminist, and the text darkly hints, probably a lesbian. But like the vituperated, silent male target here, she has to be convicted of the politics of envy. Social change and political commitment are only symptoms of the persistence of the deadly sins.

This imbalance and negativity of feeling is there in the overall structure of the books that confront the present as historical time. In *The Years*, Peggy's metaphysical ennui and North's onslaught on political activism are the contours of the whole section, 'Present Day'. The parallel closing section of *Between the Acts* echoes the sense of the present as vacillating, unsatisfactory. Both narratives elegiacally commemmorate the past, despite the intention to show its dead hand in the earlier novel. History and its processes are domesticated, privatized, and deconstructed into successive, atomistic 'moments'. In the last book, each age is encapsulated, by pastiche and light parody, as an aesthetic moment, abstracted, self-contained. The continuity between these moments is purely verbal, and tradition is intensely aestheticized. The chronology is lifted out of actual historical time, into the non-specific phases of biological and evolutionary development. The pageant's history is, through the literary and the evolutionary filters, twice-removed from socio-political conflict or motivation, and from the causal-transformative mode of actual change. The present becomes a memory or a re-living of the past, and both dimensions, present and past, are not temporally rooted or specific.

This evacuating of the historical moment repeats what happens with each individual moment, that of the intuitive consciousness. Like the Ramsays' dinner-party communion among the disparate individuals, the moment elides into the past as it is registered – or because it is registered. Self-reflection and disintegration of what is observed coincide, often unwittingly, and at all levels. The myriad of sensuous impressions that are the spontaneous material of life itself, because of refraction through the prism of consciousness, break immediate sensation into its random components. Sensation itself, as a powerful unity, suffers dispersal, as the theory of unification through sensibility runs into its opposite. The impulse or apprehension cannot be sustained, unified with others, composing a fresh emotion or response towards the outside. There is a withdrawal, an evasion of immediacy and spontaneity: the composition of a moment halts the forward thrust: 'Life stand still here!' The aesthetic alternative, making a work of art of the primary response, is intrinsically retrospective. What is occluded is openness, immersion, anticipation.

A favourite fantasy of Woolf's was that she would write a novel with all the fact on one page, and all the fiction on the facing page. *The Waves* came fairly close to realizing that project: 'I shall do away with exact time and place.... My theory being that the actual event practically does not exist – nor time either' (*W.D.*, pp. 105 & 142). Behind the philosophical pretentiousness there is a complicated cluster of rejections, personal and social, which are triggered by tension, conflict, and confrontation. Terms like 'event', 'time', 'proportion', 'conversion' give a dignity and distance to responses which are far less measured and objectified. The hypostatizing of an aesthetic plane of 'event' and 'time', safely within the ambience of individual consciousness, complete the whole rationalization. Circumspectly absorbed by 'feminine' comprehension, the 'masculine' can be safely attributed with all the sources of disturbance impingeing on awareness. The demand of the other can be treated as alien, uncivilized, a threat to the self's centre. The 'other', however, includes the self's emotions, desires, needs for connection. Seen as a threat to civility and equilibrium, such emotions are frenetically acted through in Clarissa's other self. Septimus vicariously acts out the nightmares of emotion, loss, destructive passions. The aesthetic sensibility, like Lily's and Mrs Ramsay's, must preserve its identity by refusing the turbulence of acceding to emotional tensions. Lily's 'creativeness', her visionary sense, depend on stamping out her sexual response to Tansley, and on suppressing her insistently erotic awareness of Paul Rayley. The cost of individual, emotional autonomy is to kill off the 'masculine' other which is within.

The suppression of the masculine discourse has more complicated motives than a principled opposition to an oppressive social ordering. But it is not a question of attributing it to personal, temperamental or embarrassingly intimate sources. The exclusion of emotions, which return in arbitrarily placed images of violence and eroticism, is a blanketing of ordinary daily living. The imaginary left-hand page of *The Waves* is inscribed with the six characters' daily lives-their work, their family origins, their relationships, their love-affairs and marriages, their interests and their behaviour. These are all the locations of conflict, tension, emotional interaction. The playpoem, the lyrical novel itself, represents their search for the perfected realm of perception, self-awareness, the unviolated sensibility. Here there is and must be total silence about work, family, daily behaviour. They pursue the good, the true, the beautiful, living itself apprehended as Significant Form. This pursuit pays its reluctant tributes to the value of what it must ignore, mostly in its agonizing sense of loss, isolation, anxiety and impotence. Their paradoxical defiance consists in seeing all these as signals of their especial distinction. But the crucial symbolic focus of the book, the ritual meetings to mark Percival's departure, then his early death, and later to com-memorate his life, are the most ambivalent sequences in the whole of Woolf's writing. For Percival is no thinker, writer, or seeker after Platonic ideals. He never speaks, his consciousness cannot be entered: he has the unity and singleness of being that is marked by spontaneity in action. The characters' sad cere-monials are their shared longing to know and to be Percival, to live the life that has been silently signalling from the imaginary other pages.

NOTES

1   José Ortega y Gasset, *The Dehumanization of Art* (New Jersey: Princeton University Press, 1968), p. 14. All subsequent references are to this edition.
2   Ortega, *Notes on the Novel, op. cit.*, pp. 57–103.
3   Roger Fry, *Vision and Design* (London: Chatto & Windus, 1920; Harmondsworth: Pelican Books, 1937, repr. 1961).
    Transformations (London: Chatto & Windus, 1926)
4   Fry, *Vision and Design*, esp. pp. 22–39 & pp. 222–37.
5   R. Fry, *Cézanne* (London: Hogarth Press, 1927); *Vision and Design*, pp. 202–9.
6   R. Fry, letter to Robert Bridges, Jan 23rd, 1924; quoted V. Woolf *Roger Fry: A Biography* (London Hogarth Press, 1940), pp. 229–30.
7   Charles Mauron, *The Nature of Beauty in Art and Literature*, trans. Roger Fry (London: Hogarth Press, 1927).

8   J. M. E. McTaggart, *The Nature of Existence*, 2 Vols., (Cambridge University Press, 1927).

9   G. E. Moore, *Principia Ethica* (Cambridge University Press, 1903).

10 R. Fry, *Vision and Design*, p. 233.

11 *Ibid.*, p. 236.

12 Virginia Woolf, ed. Leonard Woolf, *A Writer's Diary*, (London: Hogarth Press, 1953); repr. Triad/Panther, 1978 Abbr. *W.D.*

13 V. Woolf, *Mrs Dalloway* (London: Hogarth Press, 1925); repr. Penguin 1954. Abbr. *M.D.*

14 V. Woolf, *Jacob's Room* (London: Hogarth Press, 1922); repr. Penguin, 1965. Abbr. *J.R.*

15 V. Woolf, *To The Lighthouse* (London: Hogarth Press, 1927); repr. Penguin, 1964. Abbr. *T.L.*

16 V. Woolf *Collected Essays*, ed. L. Woolf, 4 Vols. (London: Chatto & Windus, 1966–7). Abbr. *C.E.*

17 *C.E.* I, p. 148.

18 *loc. cit.*, p. 185.

19 *loc. cit.*, pp. 72–5.

20 'Modern Fiction' [*M.F.*], *C.E.* II.

21 Sean O'Faolain, *The Vanishing Hero* (New York: Universal Library, 1956).

22 R. Taylor, 'The Green Park', in *Komparatische Hefte* (W. Germany: University of Bayreuth, 1981).

23 *The Years* (London: Hogarth Press, 1937); repr. Penguin, 1968, Abbr. *Y.*

24 *Between the Acts* (London: Hogarth Press 1941); repr. Penguin 1953, pp. 70–1. Abbr. *B.A.*

25 J. Bennett, *Virginia Woolf* (Cambridge University Press, 1945).
    R. A. Brower, *The Fields of Light* (Oxford University Press, 1962).
    E. K. Brown, *Rythm in the Novel* (Toronto University Press, 1949).
    A. Fleishman, *Fiction and the Ways of Knowing* (Austin: University of Texas Press, 1978).
    G. Hartman, *Beyond Formalism* (New Haven: Yale University Press, 1970).
    D. Lodge, *The Modes of Modern Writing* (London: Arnold, 1977).
    W. Y. Tindall, *The Literary Symbol* (Bloomington: Indiana University Press, 1955).

26 John Mepham, 'Figures of Desire: Narration and Fiction in *To the Lighthouse*' in ed. G. Josipovici, *The Modern English Novel* (London: Open Books, 1976), pp. 149–85.

27 Tindall, *op. cit.* pp. 205ff.

28 Quentin Bell, *Virginia Woolf: A Biography*, 2 vols, (London: Hogarth Press, 1972) pp. 106–7.

29 V. Woolf, 'Street Haunting', *C.E.* IV.

30 *M.F., C.E.* II.

31 Nathalie Sarraute, *Tropisms (1939) & The Age of Suspicion (1956)* (London: John Calder, 1963).

32 V. Woolf, ed. M. Barrett, *Women & Writing* (London: Women's Press, 1979) pp. 188–92.

33   *The Waves* (London: Hogarth Press, 1931); repr. Penguin 1951. Abbr. *W*.

34   G. C. Spivak, 'Unmaking and Making in *To The Lighthouse*' in eds. S.
     McConnell-Ginet, R. Barker, N. Furman, *Women and Language in
     Literature and Society*, (New York: Praeger, 1980), pp. 310–27.

35   J. I. M. Stewart, 'Notes for a Study of *The Waves*', ed. B. Benedikz, in
     On the Novel (London: Dent, 1971).

36   E. Auerbach, trans. W. Trask, *Mimesis* (New Jersey: Princeton Univer-
     sity Press, 1953). repr. New York: Doubleday Anchor, 1957.

37   Mepham, *loc. cit.*

38   R. Freedman, *The Lyrical Novel* (New Jersey; Princeton Press, 1963).

39   M. Bradbury, *Possibilities* (Oxford University Press, 1973).

40   cf. Auerbach, op. cit.

41   G. Beer, 'Beyond Determinism: George Eliot and Virginia Woolf', in ed.
     M. Jacobus, *Women Writing and Writing about Women* (London: Croom
     Helm, 1979).

6   Contexts of Reading: The Reception of D. H. Lawrence's *The Rainbow* and *Women in Love*

Alistair Davies

The Cambridge critic F. R. Leavis has, for many, provided in his *D. H. Lawrence: Novelist* (1955) the definitive readings of Lawrence's *The Rainbow* and *Women in Love*.[1] According to Leavis, Lawrence presented in *The Rainbow* a broad but intimate social history of England at the crucial points of its transformation from an agricultural into an industrial society. He described this process from firsthand experience, and as he described, he also enumerated the losses, in community, in human relationships, in contact with Nature, which the change entailed. Indeed, for Leavis, it is as a recorder of the social and cultural traditions, of the modes of life, of a certain non-conformist civilization in English history, at the moment when industrial England interpenetrated and destroyed the old, agricultural England, that Lawrence has most value. In the modern period, Lawrence was, Leavis argued, 'as a recorder of essential English history ... a great successor to George Eliot' (p. 107). *The Rainbow* was in the tradition of *Middlemarch* and might have been written:

to show what, in the concrete, a living tradition is, and what it is to be brought up in the environment of one. (As to whether the tradition qualifies as 'central' I will not argue; I am content with recording it to have been that in the environment of which George Eliot, too. was brought up.) We are made to see how, amid the pieties and continuities of life at the Marsh, the spiritual achievements of a mature civilization ... are transmitted. (p. 105).

Lawrence, however, did not simply memorialize the non-conformist tradition out of which he (and George Eliot) had come. He showed, through the history of three generations of the

Brangwen family, that the tradition was not only a shaping and sustaining power, but that its pieties and sanctions remained, even in the contemporary world, a living presence. Ursula's quest for spiritual fulfilment was in no essential measure different from that of her predecessors. The new kind of civilization which had obliterated the world of Marsh Farm had not obliterated its spiritual heritage, its particular sacredness of vision. It was this vision which Lawrence had preserved and transmitted through his 'marvellous invention of form' which rendered 'the continuity and rhythm of life' (p. 144). If the final section of the novel dealing with Ursula often seemed tentative, if her final prophetic passages were 'wholly unprepared and unsupported' (p. 142), the achievement of Lawrence's novel as a whole was undiminished. He had described, and, more importantly, had enacted 'the transmission of the spiritual heritage in an actual society' (p. 145).

Women in Love, Leavis continued, was a more complex work, in terms of its fictional technique and of its social vision. There were 'new things to be done in fiction, conceived as a wholly serious art, and it was for his particular genius to do them' (p. 147). Lawrence created here a panoramic novel of Edwardian and Georgian England before the sickness which he diagnosed within it had precipitated the country into the destruction of the First World War. 'After reading *Women in Love*, we do feel', Leavis asserted, 'that we have "touched the whole pulse of social England"' (p. 173). Lawrence's powers as a novelist lay in exploring the essential, or the inner spiritual history of England, and he presented with brilliant insight the brutality and self-destructiveness of Gerald, the perversity of Gudrun, and the positive and creative drives of Ursula and of Birkin. Yet, if his diagnosis was first-rate, his solution to the problems diagnosed was less satisfactory. Ursula and Birkin may have discovered, as a couple, a realm of values and of being which allowed them to withdraw from the downward rush to destruction of the civilization around them, but their personal quest for salvation, a quest which led them to abandon England, was, Leavis acknowledged, perplexing and contradictory in a novelist so committed to social renewal. Lawrence perhaps had been defeated by the difficulty of life.

Leavis intended his study to champion Lawrence's peculiarly

English vision, his peculiarly English genius, and in this, he was brilliantly successful. With *D. H. Lawrence: Novelist*, he established Lawrence's reputation in English and American criticism as the foremost English novelist of the century. Moreover, he drew attention not only to Lawrence's merits as a novelist but also to his importance as a modern thinker. Lawrence, he argued, had analyzed the problems and the dilemmas of our present phase of civilization, when industrial society and industrial values were becoming paramount, with an insight which no other modern thinker possessed. Yet there was a paradox in Leavis's approach, for while he related Lawrence's work to a definite historical moment, he did not concern himself with the precise literary, social or political context in which the novels were written. He did not have, it is true, the advantage of the textual histories of *The Rainbow* and *Women in Love* which have been produced since his study was first published. We now know in detail, for example, not only how Lawrence reworked *The Rainbow* and *Women in Love* from an earlier work, "The Wedding Ring," but also exactly how he redrafted *The Rainbow*, after the outbreak of the First World War, giving (among other substantial changes) much greater prominence to Ursula's quest for freedom and independence. Even so, Leavis's disregard for the way in which the outbreak of the First World War might have affected Lawrence's reworking of *The Rainbow* and *Women in Love* is strange in a critic otherwise so conscious of the historical and social pressures upon Lawrence's writing.

It is a disregard which, in due course, led to a curious imperceptiveness in Leavis's reading. When Ursula, for instance, recovers from her illness, at the end of the *The Rainbow*, she insistently repeats: "I have no father nor mother nor lover, I have no allocated place in the world of things, I do not belong to Beldover nor to Nottingham nor to England nor to this world, they none of them exist, I am trammelled and entangled in them, but they are all unreal" (p. 492). These are hardly the words of a Dorothea Brooke, for Ursula does not believe that she should submit, as does George Eliot's heroine in *Middlemarch*, to the forms and limits of local and of national life, but seeks rather to find her identity by rejecting and transcending them. The contrast, indeed, is instructive: the importance of Ursula's quest lies precisely in her refusal to accept such forms and limits.

How are we, therefore, to understand her words—and the quest for freedom which, in the last and longest section of the novel, inspires them? They have profound implications for Ursula's private life; but they have no less profound implications for her (and for our) political life as well. It is impossible to ignore their subversive intent. We need, Lawrence suggests, if we are to become free, if we are to become truly ourselves, to reject all national values, all national perspectives and all those human ties which, under present conditions, uphold the nation-state. *The Rainbow* was not simply a novel rewritten during the First World War: it became, in the process, a novel about, and in opposition to, those forces which made war possible.

When the new universities were established in Great Britain in the 1960s, it was hoped, in the teaching and the study of literature, to extend the kind of reading, with its attentiveness to literary, social and historical influences, which Leavis had pioneered, but without the particular limits of his approach. The student of literature would read English literature *in context*, not simply of the English tradition but of the European tradition as well; he or she would examine not the general but the specific social, political and cultural context in which works had been written. I believe that the contextual methods developed in the new universities provide us with the most helpful and illuminating ways of reading and understanding literary works, and in the first part of the essay which follows, I want to undertake one such contextual reading by analyzing *The Rainbow* and *Women in Love* in the light of Romain Rolland's *Jean-Christophe* (1904–12). The ten volumes of *Jean-Christophe*, in which Rolland told the story of a man who triumphantly repudiated and transcended the limits of local and of national life, established its author, in the decade before the outbreak of the First World War, as the principal voice of non-violent and non-revolutionary opposition to European nationalism, European militarism and European imperialism. Lawrence, we are told by Helen Corke, read Rolland's chronicle in 1913. Did Lawrence not recall this work, as he presented, in the wartime version of *The Rainbow*, his account of a woman who similarly repudiated and sought to transcend the limits of local and of national life? Did he not echo, while he rewrote his novel during the War, Rolland's plea for internationalism, for the outright rejection of the values and institutions of the modern nation-state?

In *Jean-Christophe*, Rolland presented the life-story of a composer, Jean-Christophe Krafft, who overcame the particularities of his national origins – he was German by birth – to achieve, by the end of the novel, a kind of universal individualism, a moral citizenship of the world. Jean-Christophe (whose initials indicate that he is to be read as a modern Christ-figure) had become conscious, in a moment of mystical insight, of the 'life-stream' in which all beings had their existence: 'Through all these creatures from the smallest to the greatest flowed the same flood of life: and in it too he swam' (II, p. 46). He belonged, he understood, not to one time or to one place, but to the spirit of God which flowed through all Nature and through all Mankind. His story was salutary because he had broken through the old husk of the solitary ego, seeing thereby the unity of life and realizing the irrelevance of national differences. Accordingly, he undertook, as a musician, as a composer, to express his sense of the universality which he had glimpsed in his moment of rapture. It was the nature of true creativity – 'kraft' in German means 'strength' or 'power' – to issue in universal vision.

Yet, if Rolland was concerned to show Jean-Christophe's growth to Individuality and to universality, he was also concerned to reveal those forces which, in the contemporary world, prevented such authentic realization. The spirit of modern man, he argued, was trapped within the oppressive, militarist nation-state in which all men and women, in Western Europe and in Russia, were condemned to live. Such States, increasingly authoritarian and belligerent as the struggle for Empire intensified, had destroyed traditional liberties and threatened war. The golden age of liberty, he feared, would never be known again: 'The world was moving on to the age of strength, of health, of virile action, perhaps even of glory, but also of harsh authority and narrow order' (IV, p. 437). Yet, modern man, Rolland suggested, gave himself willingly to such a system because of his spiritual and psychological sickness. Men and women who had not realized themselves, who were still prey to the inner violence and self-destructiveness of the undeveloped spirit, found, in the ideals of an authoritarian, of a militarist, of an imperial State, that collective strength which they, as individuals, could not achieve. The cure for this lay in that journey toward self-realization, towards true individuality, which Jean-Christophe had completed, but it necessitated freeing the ego from the limits of time and of place, of opening up the ego to the mystery and wonder of the 'life-stream', of God Himself. Only then could the true self emerge, like a 'chrysalis issuing from its stifling sheath' (II, p. 46). The necessity for such rebirth was, however, urgent, for at the end of the chronicle, Jean-Christophe prophesied a future catastrophe for Europe arising from nationalism, from militarism and from the struggle for Empire. Europe, he stated, 'looked like a vast armed vigil' (IV, p. 504). It was necessary, if disaster were to be avoided, that men and women in the States of Europe underwent the kind of spiritual regeneration which Jean-Christophe had undergone.

From this brief account, it might seem that the links between Rolland's story of the life of the composer Jean-Christophe Krafft and Lawrence's story of the schoolteacher Ursula Brangwen are tenuous indeed; but when we examine the last sections of *The Rainbow*, it quickly becomes clear that Lawrence describes late Victorian and Edwardian England in terms which are remarkably similar to those employed by Rolland to describe the pre-War Europe of armed vigil. The England of Ursula's early adulthood is a world of jingoism, of imperialist war, of a new and sinister morality of the nation-state, all implicit, in Ursula's words, with 'a great sense of disaster impending' (p. 328). As the Boer War begins, and Anton Skrebensky, Ursula's lover, leaves for war, she 'knew the huge powers of the world rolling and crashing together, darkly, clumsily, stupidly, yet colossal, so that one was brushed along almost as dust . . .' She wanted 'so hard to rebel, to rage, to fight' (p. 326). But with what? Ursula's sense of helplessness was compounded by the fact that her friends and acquaintances had all seemed to have committed themselves, as had the men and women of *Jean-Christophe*, to the ideals of the nation-state. Anton Skrebensky, 'to his own intrinsic life . . . dead', had no qualms about fighting in Africa. He had quite literally dedicated himself to the State, to the army, as an instrument, as a tool:

Who was he, to hold important his personal connection? . . . He was just a brick in the whole great social fabric, the nation, the modern humanity. (p. 326).

Winifred Inger, Ursula's teacher, was committed to scientific socialism, with its own idealization of the powers of the State. Winifred and her radical friends, 'various women and men, educated, unsatisfied people' were, however, 'inwardly raging and mad' (p. 342). Ursula's Uncle Tom, the manager of one of the local colleries upon which England's political and industrial power was founded, had married Winifred, but his only mistress, we learn, was the machine. At the National School in which Ursula had her first teaching post, the teachers coerced the children 'into one disciplined, mechanical set, reducing the whole set to an automatic state of obedience' (p. 382). Even the college she later attended as a student had a sinister, coercive function, for it was simply 'a little, slovenly laboratory for the factory' (p. 435).

Ursula, understandably, feels crushed; understandably, she wishes to rebel. But what are to be her means? She significantly refuses the chances offered by the Suffragette Movement, for she does not want, she says, simply a mechanical freedom, a freedom within the existing nation-state. It is spiritual freedom she desires and spiritual health, for she believes that the commitment of her friends and acquaintances to the nation-state reveals their spiritual sickness, their submission to an external system which satisfies dimly understood needs either for power and significance, or for freedom from self-responsibility. It is, however, only when Anton Skrebensky returns from Africa, after several years of service, first in the Boer War and then in the administration of Empire, that Ursula finds the opportunity to express her spiritual rebellion, to begin her quest for spiritual freedom and spiritual health. Anton's newfound cynicism gives her the confidence to formulate her own dismissive thoughts. Civic ideals, she told herself, disguised the rage and the frenzy of the impotent and the unfulfilled:

'What are you, you pale citizens?' her face seemed to say, gleaming. 'You subdued beast in sheep's clothing, you primeval darkness falsified to a social mechanism.' (p. 448).

Ursula's renewed relationship with Anton, however, does not bring her freedom or health. A servant of Empire, finding in the bullying discharge of his duty the means to keep at bay his terrifying recognition of inner emptiness, Anton inescapably sets a limit to Ursula's quest for self-realization and for freedom. The very system Anton serves is the one which she must reject. She significantly feels her dissatisfaction with him most acutely when walking by the sea in Lincolnshire, where they holiday together before their proposed marriage. 'The salt, bitter passion of the sea, its indifference to the earth, its swinging, definite motion, its strength, its attack, and its salt burning, seemed to provoke her to a pitch of madness, tantalising her with vast suggestions of fulfilment' (p. 477). By comparison with the sea, with its 'vast suggestions of fulfilment', Anton seems puny and constricting. There was an essential element of 'reality' – evoked by the power and the motion of the sea – of which Anton had no knowledge and from which he would exclude her.

Accordingly, Ursula rejects Anton, and returns to her parents' home. It is a moment of defeat, for Ursula not only finds herself pregnant by Anton, but brings herself, on reflection, to write submissively to him asking '*no more than to rest in your shelter all my life*' (p. 485). Her energy, we are told in a suggestive image, was frozen, and her defeat, we can see, lies in the degree to which she denies within herself that sense of mystery, that sense of fulfilment which she had glimpsed while walking on the beach. Yet her defeat is not absolute. The remainder of the novel – with its account of her struggle with the horses amidst the blinding rain on the Common, with its account of her illness and miscarriage, with its account of her tenacious and willed recovery, in effect describes the processes by which that energy becomes unfrozen, by which Ursula is released from her old ego to a sense of true Individuality. On the heath, amidst the dissolving rain, she becomes conscious – as she had upon the beach – of the forces of life, and, as a result, she sheds the old ego which had tied her to family and to place, to lover and to nation-state:

I have no father nor mother nor lover, I have no allocated place in the world of things, I do not belong to Beldover nor to Nottingham nor to England nor to this world, they none of them exist, I am trammelled and entangled in them, but they are all unreal. I must break out of it, like a nut from its shell which is an unreality. (p. 492).

As Ursula rejects her allocated place in the world of things, as she frees herself from her entanglements in a world which is for her spiritually unreal, she achieves Individuality, and with that achievement, she comes, in her final prophetic vision, to an understanding of the universality of mankind, both in its present suffering and in its future glory.

The story of Ursula's spiritual revolt, of her struggle to free herself from the determinations of the nation-state, of her journey towards self-realization, provides the essential aspect of the last sections of *The Rainbow*. If Lawrence's criticisms of the world of the modern nation-state resemble those of Rolland, it is difficult not to find in Ursula's journey an image, a mirror of Jean-Christophe's own journey, his own creative response to and transcendence of the oppressive world of the nation-state. Even the language which Ursula employs to make sense of her own renewal and to foresee the renewal of all men and women echoes that of Jean-Christophe. Modern humanity, Jean-Christophe had seen after his moment of insight, was a 'preposterous mole-hill, an ant-like people', and he hoped that modern humanity could be brought to discard its husk, its shell (II, p. 47). Ursula, similarly, knew that 'the sordid people who crept hard-scaled and separate on the face of the world's corruption were living still', but she also hoped that they would cast off 'their horny covering of disintegration, that new, clean, naked bodies would issue to a new generation...' (p. 495).

Despite its often pessimistic analysis, *Jean-Christophe* had been an unashamedly optimistic work. Even with full presentiment of 'all Europe swept by flames', Rolland's intention had been to judge European society from a viewpoint which allowed individuals – admittedly 'great' individuals like Jean-Christophe – to understand, resist and finally transcend modern fatality. Christophe witnessed in France and in Germany the rise to power of the apologists of the new militarist nation-state. He saw in Paris a socialist party which, far from opposing, actually believed more fervently in the nation-state than had the conservatives. Even so, he still held to his vision of a new future, of a new dawn:

For the last hundred years all the nations had been transformed by their mutual intercourse and the immense contributions of all the brains of the universe. A new age is coming.... Society is on the point of springing into new vigour with new laws. (IV, p. 523).

This was the direction in which, Rolland suggested, the 'wave of today' was tending, and its direction could only be maintained by the courage and the efforts of a new, creative élite, the best brains of the universe, the constructors of the future, who had freed themselves from the constrictions of the nation-state. None of the present intellectual, political or cultural élites, Rolland feared, could provide the personnel for this new élite, for they were all, although in different ways, decadent. The political élite sought to overcome its sense of weakness through a belief in organization, while the cultural and intellectual élites eagerly yielded to the same sense of weakness by glorifying decline. The present *avant garde*, Jean-Christophe complained, was sterile and suffused with the 'odour of death': 'Sonorous words, ringing phrases, the metallic clang of ideas hurtling down the void, witticisms, minds haunted by sensuality, and senses numbed with thought.' It was all useless, he felt, 'save for the sport of egotism'. It led only to death (III, p. 81). Yet, amidst the decay of these circles, with their uncontained violence and spirit of barbarism, the creative example of Jean-Christophe – the great Individual who had transcended the destructiveness of his era – held out immense hope for the future.

When Lawrence wrote *Women in Love* in 1916, forming in his own words an organic artistic whole with *The Rainbow*,[5] the disaster which Rolland had feared had occurred. Europe was now at war. Lawrence, I believe, continued nevertheless to draw upon *Jean-Christophe*, for his novel not only presented a powerful satirical account of England's decadent intellectual, political and cultural circles in the manner of Rolland's novel, but also stressed that the future lay alone in the hands of those great individuals who might extricate themselves from the present destructive system of nation-states. There was indeed, amidst the catastrophe of war, an even greater sense of urgency that such men and women should emerge, and an even greater conviction that the old forms of life were irremediably rotten. It is not, therefore, surprising that Lawrence should, in *Women in Love*, concentrate upon those few who, he believed, might escape from the present shipwreck of civilization and found – at a later date – a new world.

In the first chapters of *Women in Love*, Lawrence gives us a panoramic view of England – of the industrial England of Gerald Crich, of the intellectual England of Hermione Roddice, of the *avant garde*, bohemian England of Rupert Birkin and of the *habitués* of the Café Pompadour – but quickly the focus of the novel shifts to Ursula who, even as she is drawn into the worlds of Shortlands and of Breadalby, maintains a distinct aloofness and distance. Indeed, in the major scenes in which the characters reveal themselves through actions or words, Ursula is present, providing resistance to and judgement upon the worlds into which she has been drawn: Birkin and Hermione in the schoolroom, Gerald bathing in the lake, the weekend at Breadalby, Gerald on his horse at the railway crossing, Birkin repairing his damaged punt near the Mill House, and finally, the water-party at Shortlands. Her aloofness, however, is not simply a formal device to provide a perspective from within the novel, for her strength and steadfastness serve the larger purpose of suggesting that there are individuals able to live through and counteract the present sickness. Ursula, on account of her self-realization in *The Rainbow*, is free from the drift and decadence of her contemporaries. She is, we see immediately, one of those fitted to be a constructor of the future.

Necessarily, the critical distance which Ursula maintains to the worlds into which she is drawn qualifies the reader's response to Rupert Birkin. When Birkin expounds his philosophy to her, after they have met while he is repairing the punt, Ursula dismisses as self-important exaggeration his fanatical desire to save mankind. For all his 'desirable life-rapidity', there was, she felt, 'this ridiculous mean effacement into a Salvator Mundi and a Sunday-school teacher, a prig of the stiffest type' (p. 122).[6] Significantly, Ursula refuses to accept Birkin's desire to encompass all mankind in the curative process of destruction, and her refusal is doubly important. Firstly, Ursula throws doubt upon Birkin's imagery of apocalypse, suggesting that apocalypse is not the inevitable fate of mankind, but the nightmarish imagining of those who had lost contact with the mystery of life and had fallen into a deathly, catastrophic view of the future; secondly, she refuses altogether Birkin's view that all mankind must be saved. She herself knew, Lawrence writes, suggesting that Birkin did not, 'the actuality of humanity, its hideous actuality' (p. 120). It is enough for Ursula that men and women – the few, exceptional men and women who recognize the spiritual crisis of the present – should save themselves, and it is to this task that she dedicates herself, seeking, after a serious relationship with Birkin begins during the fateful water-party at Shortlands, to extricate herself and the strange, remarkable, but seemingly doomed man she now loves, from the disaster which she knows will engulf the world in which they live. Mankind as a whole had gone too far, too irretrievably, into hideousness.

After the drowning which interrupts the water-party at Shortlands, Ursula and Birkin (who leaves for France) take stock of their lives, for the fact of death compels them to review their hopes and purposes. At first, Ursula feels that 'her life . . . was nearly concluded' (p. 183), but her mood of depression is a temporary one, for she recognizes that her frustration, and her helplessness, are common experiences and come from the corrupt values and oppressive realities of the world of the nation-state in which she is condemned to live: ' "A life of barren routine, without inner meaning, without any real significance," she felt. "How sordid life was, how it was a terrible shame to the soul, to live now!" ' (p. 185). Those who controlled the political and economic life of the nation-states had turned the sea:

into a murderous alley and a soiled road of commerce, disputed like the dirty land of a city every inch of it. The air they claimed too, shared it up, parcelled it out to certain owners, they trespassed in the air to fight for it. Everything was gone, walled in, with spikes on top of the walls, and one must ignominiously creep between the spiky walls through a labyrinth of life. (p. 185).

Ursula traces her sense of nullification to the mode of existence demanded of her within the world of nation-states, and, for the first time, contemplates abandoning altogether the country in which she has been brought up. It seems impossible for the individual – not least one who has achieved the kind of realization and insights Ursula has achieved – to remain permanently oppressed within this soiled and soiling world. When she meets Birkin again, he asks her if she had done anything important while he had been away. Her reply is direct and startling: 'I looked at England, and thought I'd done with it' (p. 241). Although she denies that this scrutiny is important, it is – in the trajectory of the novel – profoundly so, for Ursula realizes now that the only way to save herself, and to save Birkin, is to leave England – England as a nation-state, as one part of a system of nation-states. He is less certain: ' "It isn't a question of nations," he asserts, "France is far worse" ' (p. 241). Birkin makes such a qualification because he hopes, on account of his personal ties with Hermione Roddice and with Gerald Crich, to reverse England's 'race-exhaustion' and to call England back again to new life. For Ursula, however, this remains a false and grossly misguided belief: all ties with England, with Hermione and Gerald, had to be broken.

It is while visiting the jumble-market in Nottingham to buy furniture for Birkin's house that the underlying differences which separate them become manifest. As Birkin looks at the wares on sale, he comes across an 'arm-chair of simple wood, probably birch, but of such fine delicacy of grace, standing there on the sordid stones, it almost brought tears to the eyes' (p. 347). Birkin buys the chair because it seemed to express, in its line and strength, the spirit of England, but Birkin's sentimental nostalgia angers Ursula: 'I wish it had been smashed up when its day was over, not left to preach the beloved past to us. I'm sick of the beloved past' (p. 348). Ursula insists that they give the chair to a young couple whom she had seen at the market, 'so secretive and active and anxious the young woman seemed, so reluctant, slinking, the young man' (p. 346). He was, she realized, going to marry the young woman because she was pregnant. Birkin, however, remains uncomprehending, thinking that Ursula wants to divest herself of possessions, of a fixed habitation; but her motive is infinitely more complex. She was, we are told, attracted to the young man, who was.

a still, mindless creature, hardly a man at all, a creature that the towns have produced, strangely pure-bred and fine in one sense, furtive, quick, subtle. His lashes were dark and long and fine over his eyes, that had no mind in them, only a dreadful kind of subject, inward consciousness, glazed and dark. (p. 350).

The only outlet for his vitality, she thought, as he settled down to marriage, to a position within the nation-state, was furtive and subterranean, with 'the stillness and silkiness of a dark-eyed, silent rat' (p. 350). Yet there was, for all his furtive rat-like vitality, an element of meekness, of defeat about him, for he had made a compact with the society which had produced him. It was a society, Ursula realized, in which the individual could not live, in which individuality was completely crushed. By giving away the chair, Ursula symbolically rejected her own engulfment within such a society, the society of the nation-state. As they journey home on the tram, Birkin himself suddenly but decisively understood her motives. '"I want," he agreed, "to be disinherited"' (p. 354).

Birkin and Ursula marry, their marriage taking place on the understanding that they will leave England afterwards. As they journey across Belgium, Ursula sees a man with a lantern coming out of a farm-building. A familiar sight in her childhood, it reminds her of Marsh Farm, of the old intimate farm life at Cossethay. Its strange context, however, informs her of how far she had been projected from her childhood. As they arrive in the Tyrol, she accepts that she had now no 'anterior connections':

She was with Birkin, she had just come into life, here in the high snow, against the stars. What had she to do with parents and antecedents? She knew herself new and unbegotten, she had no father, no mother, no anterior connections, she was herself, pure and silvery, she belonged only to the oneness with Birkin, a oneness that struck deeper notes, sounding into the heart of the universe, the heart of reality, where she had never existed before. (pp. 399–400).

She had finally achieved that desire she had formulated at the end of *The Rainbow*, that refusal of an *allocated* place in the world of things, and although her decision to leave England cannot be separated from her rejection, in the name of individualism, of mass, democratic society, it is a decision, within the perspective of *The Rainbow* and of *Women in Love*, which is not negative but positive, not destructive but creative. She had finally managed to struggle free of the destructive forces of nationality and of nationalism; she had shed that special brand of Englishness from which neither Birkin nor Gerald could, without great – and in Gerald's case – fatal efforts, free themselves. At the end of the novel – in the saga of Birkin's contradictory but powerful love for Gerald, of Gerald's death upon the mountain-side – it is clear that Birkin could not make the easy break with the past which Ursula had made, but he had come to appreciate that Gerald could not have found his way to the positive renewal which he, under Ursula's guidance, had tentatively made. We are left in no doubt that Ursula's way to self-realization, to true individuality, by leaving England is the only way; nor are we left in any doubt that it is a way which involves the complete rejection of 'English' identity for something more real, more universal and ultimately more constructive.

There is much in Lawrence's novel, if this reading is correct, which is unsatisfactory, but before evaluation can begin, we need to be sure that we have managed, as fully as possible, to describe the kind of fiction Lawrence actually wrote, or the kind of perspectives he actually put forward, or the kind of rhetoric he actually used. When we consider that *Women in Love* was written in 1916, during a period of extraordinary political and military crisis, we might find his work, with its stress upon the survival of the exceptional individual amidst the collapse of modern civilization, a profoundly inadequate, even a contemptible response. Certainly, F. R. Leavis, otherwise the most stalwart defender of Lawrence, felt himself profoundly perplexed by the conclusion of *Women in Love*. Yet we need to reserve such censure until we have weighed fully the significance of Ursula's triumphant break from 'anterior connections'. When we see this break in the light of *Jean-Christophe*, it might seem to be a positive and radical gesture, for the quest for individual freedom is seen to be the one sure means of undermining the power of the modern nation-state. What is at issue, of course, is no longer simply a literary question, but an historical, a cultural, a political one as well. Would *The Rainbow* and *Women in Love* provide support for war-resistance, for conscientious objection, for a refusal of the State? Or do we find in them the last, desperate assertion of Individualism at the very moment when the conditions of Liberalism had been finally eclipsed? Or do the novels mystify the actuality of State power and State oppression by rendering it simply in terms of a disorder of the spirit? Individual judgements and individual answers will, of course, differ, according to the historical, or cultural, or political viewpoints of individual questioners, but whatever judgements and answers such questioners reach – if they are to be convincing – will need to be based upon the multiplicity of historical and literary evidence which contextual readings produce.

II

In the first part of this essay, I have suggested that, if we are to understand D. H. Lawrence's *The Rainbow* and *Women in Love* accurately, we need to place them in the context not only of English but of European literature, and specifically, of French literature; and in the context, not of the fiction of the nineteenth century but of the fiction of the early twentieth century. It is an assertion which almost inescapably involves the following questions. If this is the case, why has a quite contrary interpretation of Lawrence, dating from F. R. Leavis's *D. H. Lawrence: Novelist* (1955) been established and accepted within the English critical tradition, even by recent critics, such as Raymond Williams and Terry Eagleton, who rebut the form, if not the content, of Leavis's reading of Lawrence?[7] By what process of critical revision has the individualist and anti-nationalist perspective which I have described been transformed into the epic, quintessentially English one of F. R. Leavis's study?

Again, the contextual method, conscious that criticism, like literature, and reading, like writing, has to be placed in its cultural, social and political context, helps us to find an answer. For Leavis, as he makes his case for Lawrence, does so by rejecting the specific charges made against Lawrence in the most influential literary journalism of the 1920s and the 1930s. Against Wyndham Lewis, who had argued in *Paleface* (1929) that Lawrence advocated capitulation to mindless instinct, Leavis argued that Lawrence made plain that 'without proper use of intelligence there can be no solution of the problems of mental, emotional and spiritual health' (p. 310). Against John Middleton Murry, who had suggested in *Son of Woman* (1931) that Lawrence's fiction was the record of his sexual failure and of his deep hatred of women, Leavis asserted its health and normality. In *The Rainbow*, the pieties of life at

Marsh Farm, Leavis suggested, were clearly feminine and matriarchal: Lawrence celebrated throughout the novel the moral and creative vitality of women. Against Murry's assertion that Lawrence used his fiction after *The Rainbow* as a vehicle for his 'thought-adventures', Leavis defended the artistry of *Women in Love*. Against T. S. Eliot, who had suggested in *After Strange Gods* (1934) that Lawrence was an ignoramus who had come from an intellectual and spiritual tradition in decay, Leavis argued that Lawrence's nonconformist background was one of rich and sustaining intellectual life. He alerted Eliot to the 'extraordinarily active intellectual life enjoyed by that group of young people of which Lawrence was the centre' (p. 306). It was just such a rich and central tradition which Lawrence celebrated in *The Rainbow*, and as he did so, he celebrated an essential strand of English history. For the Congregationalism of Lawrence's youth had played an important part in English civilization as Eliot would see if he read Élie Halévy. The English nonconformist tradition was one from which the major works of nineteenth-century English fiction, from George Eliot to Thomas Hardy, had come. This tradition, and the fiction which it inspired, was not, as Eliot suggested, eccentric, but stood at the heart of English cultural, political and moral life.

Yet, in asserting Lawrence's normality, his love for and rootedness within English values and traditions, Leavis was engaged in defending Lawrence against a persistent and unusually grave charge, which underlies the criticism of Lewis, Murry and Eliot, that Lawrence had been no less than a traitor to his country during the First World War, and had continued to be so after the War with his support for Bolshevism. The allegation was seriously stated, and its truth widely accepted. It is a measure of Leavis's success in cultural rehabilitation that this central aspect of the immediate critical reception of Lawrence had been forgotten.

In the first two years of the First World War, Lawrence's public opposition to the War brought charges of treachery and of lack of patriotism, and the publication of *The Rainbow* in 1915, with its criticism of the nation-state, seemed to confirm them. Certainly, the banning of *The Rainbow* on the grounds of obscenity was widely, and correctly, thought to be a political act.[8] The morbid sexual content of *The Rainbow*, J. C. Squire argued in the *New Statesman*, revealing the prevailing association of Lawrence with the German cause, was suspiciously Hunnish. The book 'broods gloomily over the physical reactions of sex in a way so persistent that one wonders whether the author is under the spell of German psychologists.'[9] It was, however, with *Women in Love* in 1921 that the full case against Lawrence was made explicit. His most influential accuser was John Middleton Murry. 'It is part of our creed,' Murry wrote in the *Nation and Athenaeum*, 'that the writer must be responsible; but it is part of [Lawrence's] creed that he is not.'[10] His lofty and semi-official tone, passing considered judgement in the public interest, came from his recent, war-time role as censor at the War Office, but it came also from the new function which he, the most noted editor of the period, assumed for English criticism after the War. The English writer and critic should now, he believed, speak in the name of and in the defence of the special wisdom of the English race, which had been achieved through its Christian and its Protestant history. That should be his creed, for the English writer and critic was heir to a strain of heretical individualism, an instinct for freedom. This was English culture's unique contribution, politically and culturally, to world society. Even so, the impulse to freedom should never be anarchic; the individual should come freely to accept the loyalties and the allegiances which bound him, as an Englishman, to his people and to its unique heritage.

From this perspective, Lawrence, whose passionate individualism made him the 'most interesting figure' in English letters, had to be censured. 'We stand by the consciousness and the civilization of which the literature we know is the finest flower,' Murry insisted, but Lawrence was in rebellion against both:

If we try him before our court he contemptuously rejects the jurisdiction. The things we prize are the things he would destroy; what is triumph to him is catastrophe to us. He is the outlaw of modern English literature; and he is the most interesting figure in it. But he must be shown no mercy.

Murry's forensic language was not accidental. Lawrence, who had left England for America in 1918 *via* the Pacific route, was being tried *in absentia*. He, 'the outlaw of modern English literature', had repudiated his ties with and his allegiances to England and to English culture. His rejection of the decencies of English life, his opposition to the Allied cause in the War – which alone could explain his relish in portraying the collapse of English society in *Women in Love* and his own abandonment of England for foreign lands – these formed the implicit basis of Murry's public indictment.

Lawrence, Murry insisted, wanted above all to destroy that level of consciousness upon which European civilization was founded. Through Birkin, who had 'a negroid as well as an Egyptian avatar', Lawrence advocated, Murry wrote, quoting *Women in Love*, 'sensual mindless mysteries to be achieved through an awful African process.' This process was, for Murry, a literal degradation, a falling back to the 'sub-human and bestial, a thing that our forefathers had rejected when they began to rise from the slime'. Lawrence, quite simply, delighted in imagining the overthrow of England by the forces of darkness and of barbarism. The qualities of Lawrence's genius 'no longer delight us', Murry had announced at the beginning of his review: 'They have been pressed into the service of another power, they walk in bondage and in livery.' Murry's language is vague and shrill, but its import would be clear to a contemporary audience. Lawrence had rejoiced during the War to think of England defeated by the Prussians whom he served, just as he rejoiced after the War, to think of his native country overthrown by his new masters, the Bolshevists.

When Murry returned to Lawrence in his major study of Lawrence's novels, *Son of Woman* (1931), he made use of the new languages of psychoanalysis and of sociology, but his charge of treachery against Lawrence remained the same. Lawrence was, Murry argued, a dangerous demagogue, for the novel had become a vehicle for his 'thought-adventures', his aim as a writer 'to discover authority, not to create art' (p. 173).[11] He had gone to America as a second Moses, as a Law-giver who 'should bring its soul to consciousness'. If the Mahatma Gandhi could convulse and revivify a whole Empire, he suggested, 'there was no reason why Lawrence should not give laws to a people' (pp. 169–70). Lawrence's intention in America had been to bring about, through the disintegration of traditional, white consciousness, the end of Western civilization. By comparing Lawrence's teaching with that of Gandhi, by suggesting their common revolt against the West, Murry indicated the revolutionary threat Lawrence's teachings were thought to pose.

But why should Lawrence do this? Murry found a ready psychological and sociological explanation in Lawrence's upbringing. Although born into the working class, with its warmth of human contact, Lawrence had been dominated in childhood by his mother. Having aspirations to middle-class gentility, she caused Lawrence to repress his sexual vitality as gross and vulgar. Accordingly, he grew up a guilt-ridden sexual weakling, 'a sex-crucified man' (p. 21), and remained 'a child of the woman' (p. 73), with deep resentment at his inadequacy and limitations. In his dreams, he was 'a wild, untamed, dominant male' (p. 73), yet he wanted also to be a child, with the happiness and oblivion of childhood.

Sons and Lovers, Murry suggested, had been an assertive fantasy of social and sexual independence. *The Rainbow*, which concentrated throughout on unsatisfactory relationships, first of Anna and Will, then of Ursula and Anton, reflected the failure of his marriage to Frieda. It was 'radically, the history of Lawrence's final sexual failure' (p. 88). Thereafter, he took his revenge upon the social order itself, which the mother and wife enshrined, in fantasies of destruction and of extravagant sexual assertion. *Women in Love*, in which Birkin-Lawrence demanded of Ursula a kind of sexual or sensual homage, was the first of a series of aggressive fantasies in which the female, insatiably demanding satisfaction, was annihilated by the man who could not satisfy her (p. 118). The woman was humiliated, and the man formed, in the place of marriage, emotional alliances with other men. Love was turned into hate, loyalty into betrayal and the quest for life became the unconscious veneration of chaos and of death. In *Women in Love*, Lawrence envisaged a whole culture within a death-miasma in order to 'feed his sense of doom and death and corruption; to fulfil his own injunction that "we must disintegrate while we live"' (p. 330). In his American writings, Lawrence exulted in the destruction of England and of Europe, and hoped for his own, vengeful resurrection by absorbing the dark blood-consciousness of America's primitive races. Yet for Murry, these writings, with their fantasies of leadership, with their celebration of primitive communism, merely expressed Lawrence's power-fantasies and his craving for death (p. 333). It was clear that the Bolshevist Lawrence, embittered by his sexual perversity and by his proletarian origins, wished, in the spirit of revenge, to destroy the normal and wholesome world of culture, refinement and adult relationship, from which he had been excluded.

Murry was not the only critic to find in Lawrence's work the example of a resentful or treacherous Bolshevist temperament. Wyndham Lewis, whose writings of the 1920s and 1930s were concerned to identify those writers who, in his opinion, were working towards the overthrow of the West by what he termed 'Oriental Bolshevism', found Lawrence to be the most prominent and the most dangerous foe of the West: 'In contrast to the White Overlord of this world in which we live, Mr Lawrence shows us a more primitive type of "consciousness", which has been physically defeated by the White "consciousness," and assures us that the defeated "consciousness" is the better of the two' (*Paleface*, 1929, p. 193).[12] Lawrence was, Lewis suggested, 'a natural communist' because he was unmanly, preferring the mindless and feminine merging of Oriental Bolshevism to the masculine separateness of the Greco-Christian West:

With *Sons and Lovers* ... he was at once hot-foot upon the fashionable trail of incest; the book is an eloquent wallowing mass of Mother-love and Sex-idolatry. His *Women in Love* is again the same thick, sentimental, luscious stew. The 'Homo'-motive, how could that be absent from such a compendium, as is the nature of Mr Lawrence, of all that has passed for 'revolutionary,' reposing mainly for its popular effectiveness upon the meaty, succulent levers of sex and supersex, to bait those politically-innocent, romantic, anglo-saxon simpletons, dreaming their 'anglo-saxon dreams,' whether in America or the native country of Mr Lawrence? (pp. 180–1).

Lewis suggested that Lawrence advocated Communism and homosexuality in order to encourage young Anglo-Saxons to repudiate the masculine dreams of Empire which had inspired their fathers, in favour of the feminine and homosexual fantasy of subjugation beneath an Oriental Bolshevist despotism. Lawrence was the most sinister and the most subtle propagandist against the West.

T. S. Eliot, similarly, saw Lawrence's ideas and writing to be the principal challenge to traditional values and ideals in England and America. What made the task of maintaining these values and ideals in the modern period particularly difficult, Eliot stated in *After Strange Gods* (1934), was the undermining of intellectual and religious orthodoxy by pro- testant heresies. The chief clue to the immense influence of Lawrence's work was to be found in the decay of Protestantism in England and America, and in the rise of a semi-educated public unable to grasp the intellectual definitions by which orthodoxy in thought and in religion had been maintained. In Eliot's view, D. H. Lawrence was the foremost example of heresy in modern Anglo-Saxon literature. Influenced by the degenerate Protestantism of his infancy, with its 'vague, hymn- singing pieties' (p. 39), educated on a fare of English literature notable, in Eliot's judgement, only for its eccentric and individualist morality, Lawrence lacked 'the critical faculties which education should give' (p. 58).[13] Lawrence started life 'wholly free from any restriction of tradition or institution'. He had 'no guidance except the Inner Light, the most untrust- worthy and deceitful guide that ever offered itself to wandering humanity' (p. 59). It is hardly surprising, therefore, that Lawrence should come to see himself as a second Messiah, or that he should win a large following among 'the sick and debile and confused', appealing not 'to what remains of health in them, but to their sickness' (p. 61). It was, nevertheless, the influence of Lawrence's supposedly ill-educated and perverse ideas upon the young with which Eliot concerned himself, for, following Murry and Lewis, he saw Lawrence as the instru- ment of sinister and demonic forces, which threatened to destroy the Christian West. 'His acute sensibility, his violent prejudices and passions and lack of social and intellectual training,' Eliot argued, made Lawrence 'admirably fitted to be an instrument for forces of good or of evil' (p. 59). It seems, for a moment, that Eliot will withhold final judgement, but his censure is all the more effectively made by being delayed. Not trained, he continued, as had been the mind of James Joyce, Lawrence's mind was not 'always aware of the master it is serving' (p. 59).

A review of Lawrence's early critical reception reveals how

much Leavis's championship of Lawrence involved an essentially liberal recovery of his work from the often hysterical and inflexibly reactionary misreadings to which it had been subject. Yet the cost of such a rehabilitation, as we have seen, was considerable, for as Leavis tried to counter the effect of previous readings, to cancel what he considered to be a distortion of Lawrence, he not only removed Lawrence from the literary and historical context in which he had written, but also made his work acceptable by ignoring its original political intentions. If we wish to read and understand *The Rainbow* and *Women in Love* accurately, we have, I believe, to restore them to their original contexts. This essay is an attempt to sketch one way out of many in which this can be done, and to show how much the past criticism of Lawrence's *The Rainbow* and *Women in Love* has proceeded by falsifying or repressing those original contexts. Of course, to readers long instructed in the contextual method, my account of it may seem to refer to the prehistory of modern criticism, and is, therefore, the procedure of an archeologist rather than that of an innovator. Even so, the archeologist can usefully remind his or her readers of the difficulty of reconstructing the past accurately and warn them that our tools of excavation, if too crudely used, can obliterate altogether the object under examination.

NOTES

1 F. R. Leavis, *D. H. Lawrence: Novelist* (London: Chatto & Windus, 1955).
2 D. H. Lawrence, *The Rainbow* (London: Heinemann, 1963).
3 See Helen Corke, *D. H. Lawrence: The Croydon Years* (Austin: University of Texas Press, 1965), p. 29. 'In this way we read ... among other things, the ten volumes of Romain Rolland's recently published *Jean-Christophe* ....'
4 Romain Rolland, *Jean-Christophe*, 4 vols. trans. Gilbert Cannan (London: Heinemann, 1928). All subsequent references are to this translation.
5 See letter to Martin Secker, 16 January 1920, quoted in Colin Clarke (ed.) *The Rainbow* and *Women in Love* (London: Macmillan, 1969), p. 31.
6 D. H. Lawrence, *Women in Love* (London: Heinemann, 1966).
7 See Raymond Williams, *The English Novel from Dickens to Lawrence* (London: Chatto & Windus, 1970), pp. 177–9; Terry Eagleton, *Exiles*

and Emigres (London: Chatto & Windus, 1970), pp. 202–4; Terry Eagleton, *Criticism and Ideology* (London: New Left Books, 1976), p. 157–61.

8   See Emile Devalenay, *D. H. Lawrence: The Man and His Work. The Formative Years, 1885–1919* (London: Heinemann, 1972), pp. 235–48.

9   See R. P. Draper, *D. H. Lawrence: The Critical Heritage* (London: Routledge & Kegan Paul, 1970), p. 106.

10 See Colin Clarke (ed.), *D. H. Lawrence, op. cit.*, pp. 67–72.

11 John Middleton Murry, *Son of Woman* (London: Cape, 1931).

12 Wyndham Lewis: *Paleface* (London: Chatto & Windus, 1929).

13 T. S. Eliot: *After Strange Gods: A Primer of Modern Heresy* (London: Faber & Faber, 1934).

7 Making and Breaking the Novel Tradition

Stuart Laing

I

It seems self-evident that an indispensable task, perhaps the principal task, of literary study is to discover which works are to be valued most. The process is necessarily one of comparison, of relative placing – the key questions being, in Leavis's words:

> What, on testing and re-testing and wider experience, turn out to be my more constant preferences, what the relative permanencies in my response, and what structure begins to assert itself in the field of poetry with which I am familiar? What map or chart of English poetry as a whole represents my most utmost consistency and most inclusive coherence of response?[1]

This is how the individual critic operates to serve 'the common pursuit of true judgement', the phrase of Eliot's which Leavis endorsed as 'how the critic should see his business'.[2] Judging is intimately related to mapping or charting, to seeing works in relation to each other and to the establishment of a literary history or sense of tradition within which valuations of individual works can be more fully understood. Eliot's conception of tradition is central here:

> No poet, no artist of any art, has his complete meaning alone. His significance, his appreciation is the appreciation of his relation to the dead poets and artists. You cannot value him alone; you must set him, for contrast and comparison, among the dead. I mean this as a principle of aesthetic, not merely historical criticism.[3]

Leavis, in purporting to sum up Eliot's view of 'tradition', further embellishes it with some emphases of his own:

> The individual writer is to be aware that his work is of the Literature to which

it belongs and not merely added externally to it. A literature, that is, must be thought of as essentially something more than an accumulation of separate works: it has an organic form, or constitutes on organic order, in relation to which the individual writer has his significance and his being.[4]

'Literature' or 'tradition' as an organism or order within which individual works are positioned, both descriptively and qualitatively – this has been and remains the fundamental principle underlying the organization of most English syllabuses in higher education. Genre courses, period courses and studies of individual authors (most notably Shakespeare) all derive from this principle – and the result is characteristically an overall course structure which seeks to harmonize historical and evaluative approaches to literary study. A more recent attempt to formulate the implications of this in an explicit way is George Watson's *The Study of Literature*, the two central claims of which are that 'the study of literature is itself a historical study' and that: 'the fact of literary excellence, in the last resort is what the study of literature seeks to examine'.[5]

On the face of it there is here the possibility of a conflict between an historical emphasis and critical/evaluative search for excellence. This is avoided by stressing the necessarily interpretative work of any historian:

The literary historian too tries to tell what happened in literature. And when he commits himself, by comment, selection, or silence, to the view that some literary events are more important than others, he is behaving as other kinds of historians behave.[6]

For Watson, the writing of literary history and the judgement of individual works are integrated procedures, each indispensable to the other. Together they constitute the aims of literary study.

One important consequence of this, in syllabuses and in critical practice, is the effective separation of written texts into two categories – which are named variously as the serious and the trival, the universal and the emphemeral, or the 'high' and the popular. Frequently a degree of interchange between the terms of these oppositions takes place so that, for instance, the serious and the popular come to be necessarily opposed. This kind of thinking may reveal itself implicitly, as in the introduction of separate 'popular literature' options within a literature syllabus (the implication being that the accepted canon – the necessary core – is or was unpopular); or the surprise readers are assumed to feel when being informed that Shakespeare, Bunyan or Dickens were in touch with 'popular culture' (the fallback position here being that this was an *authentic* popular culture, unlike the debased one of today).[7]

The more general position here is that some central critical process of separation and gradation is necessary to maintain cultural standards or even to maintain culture itself. This is stated openly in the title and argument of Leavis's pamphlet *Mass Civilisation and Minority Culture*, in Eliot's plea for the retention of cultural stratification,[8] and, again looking to a more recent work, in Malcolm Bradbury's *The Social Context of Modern English Literature*, which argues that:

An essential aspect of culture is precisely that it embodies systems of preference and selectivity that enable us, or have enabled us, to think of certain activities as *more* cultured or *less* cultured. In short they have enabled us to think of a hierarchy of culture and a factor of criticism and discrimination at the heart of its functioning.[9]

The emphasis through all these arguments is upon the selection of the few (texts, activities, people) from among the many – to ensure continuity of a certain set of values in the face of the threat of 'mass civilisation' (Leavis), 'equalitarianism' (Eliot) and 'the louts in the back row' or 'proletariat groups who manifest not culture but cultural discontent' (Bradbury).[10]

It is not the purpose of this essay to suggest that the need to evaluate should (or could) be dispensed with, either in literature or in the culture as a whole. What needs to be recognized, however, are the conditions under which any such process of evaluation takes place. At the immediate level it is a question of which (and whose) values are being endorsed, for what purpose and on the basis of what aesthetic and political assumptions ('political' being used in the sense of Orwell's formulation that 'the opinion that art should have nothing to do with politics is itself a political attitude'[11]). Above all, the source of value must be seen as the valuer and not as residing in innate properties of the object valued. The valuer must accept full responsibility for his or her judgements and for the premises on which they are based. Leavis certainly recognized this responsibility, although his formulations concerning the task of the critic indicate that he found some of the implications troubling:

His first concern is to enter into possession of the given poem (let us say) in its concrete fulness, and his constant concern is never to lose his fulness of possession, but rather to increase it. In making value-judgements (and judgements as to significance), implicitly or explicitly, he does so out of that completeness of possession and with that fulness of response. He doesn't ask, 'How does this accord with these specifications of goodness in poetry?'; he aims to make fully conscious and articulate the immediate sense of value that 'places' the poem.[12]

The intricacy and delicacy of this operation are implied in the phrase 'out of'; value, in some way, emerges out of the poem with the critic's responsibility being the attainment of that 'full', 'complete' possession from which, by an indirect route, evaluation will happen. Emphasis is laid on the critic's self-effacement and on total identity between his response and the poem's innate qualities ('concrete fulness'); it is precisely the repetitions of 'fulness', 'completeness' and 'fully', that argue for not even a small space of 'abstract' aesthetic formulations. The critic does not so much possess the poem, as the poem the critic; he is indeed 'a man possessed'.

Eliot's discussion of this area is more relaxed, although some of the implications are the same:

No generation is interested in Art in quite the same way as any other; each generation, like each individual, brings to the contemplation of art its own categories of appreciation, makes its own demands upon art, and has its own uses for art. 'Pure' artistic appreciation is to my thinking only an ideal, when not merely a figment, and must be so long as the appreciation of art is an affair of limited and transient human beings existing in space and time. Both artist and audience are limited.[13]

Here is a clear recognition of an unavoidable relativism in the process of valuing, although it is significant that it is a source of mild regret and an indication of our 'limited' human condition rather than an active affirmation of the human construction of value. The implication is that somewhere a 'correct order' does exist even if all we can do is merely approximate to it.[14]

Eliot's admission of human weakness and Leavis's ingenious formulations are, however, brushed aside by George Watson in his attempts to substantiate his claim that what is to be studied is 'the fact of literary excellence'. He admits little possibility of genuine disagreement concerning the nature of this 'excellence'.

Excellence is self-validating, and those who cannot see this are not capable of recognising excellence for what it is. Only a man without a literary sense, or one in whom a passing mood of depression had usurped the place of judgement, would ask whether literature is worth studying.[15]

The resort to tautology (excellence can only be recognized by those who can recognize excellence – only those with a literary sense can recognize the value of studying literature) indicates the attempt to divorce the whole process of valuing from the activity and the choices of the valuer. The implications of this position are very baldly stated:

If anyone were to deny the judgement that the *Iliad* is a great poem we should all know what to think of the freedom of his opinions.

The question whether Shakespeare was or was not a great dramatist is scarcely open to debate at all.[16]

Behind these desperate attempts to invoke a common-sense consensus lies, of course, the Arnoldian fears of the consequences of letting everyone do what they like – the collapse of present cultural standards which would then follow. It is perhaps tempting to ask precisely who 'we' are, so secure in 'our' knowledge and opinion of epic Greek poetry. However the comment of Shakespeare is perfectly correct. To ask such a question would constitute a scandal which could scarcely be coped with, given the amount of cultural and economic capital invested in the 'fact' of Shakespeare's greatness. Equally, to ask such a question would also be to raise issues concerning the process of valuing, the institutional pressures operating within it, and the purposes for which such valuing is carried through.

A rather less alarming way of raising this issue was proposed twenty years ago by Raymond Williams in *The Long Revolution* with the idea of the 'selective tradition'. The radical elements of this argument stressed that the components of a tradition were not necessarily selected on a basis of general human values. A tradition might equally reflect 'many kinds of special interest, including class interests'.[17] This point, in itself, is not necessarily all that different from Eliot's stress on the fallibility of 'limited' human capacity, and indeed there are moments when Williams also seems to suggest that the ideal situation would be to correct the local fluctuations of partial selection. However, the main thrust of the argument is very different in its stress on accepting openly our own responsibility for such selection: 'To put on to Time, the abstraction, the responsibility for our own active choices is to suppress a central part of our experience.'[18]

A great deal of Williams's work can be seen as the result of taking up this challenge and responsibility – in particular the opening up of new areas for cultural studies (in *Communications, Television, Technology and Cultural Form* and Part Two of *The Long Revolution* itself) and in his most innovatory work on written texts – *The Country and the City*. On the other hand, however, his book on the development of the English Novel (*The English Novel from Dickens to Lawrence*) is essentially an Eliot-like enterprise in re-adjusting the tradition and an exercise in offering new kinds of explanations for why whose writers and texts who have conventionally been thought excellent are indeed the best.

In this latter activity Williams can be placed firmly alongside such diverse Marxist critics as Arnold Kettle, Lucien Goldmann and Terry Eagleton. All of these share the view that the great works as already established are indeed great – but crucially not for those reasons of autonomous literary value advanced by bourgeois criticism. The value of great literature is rather that it offers a privileged, sometimes unique insight into the ideological configurations of some historical moment. Arnold Kettle gives a humanist version of this when he argues that Shakespeare's positive values are those of 'humanity' – this being defined historically as: 'man in his fullest aspirations realizable in the concrete situation of England of the sixteenth and seventeenth centuries.'[19]

Goldmann places more emphasis on the ideological level. His 'reflectionist' position is at its most complex and convincing in the account of Racine and the Jansenists in *The Hidden*

God. Williams's own position is more difficult to place although, as he has indicated, his own idea of art-works as carriers of historical specific 'structures of feeling' has something in common with Goldmann's emphasis on great art as the embodiment of 'world-visions'; differences between them relate to Goldmann's concern with categories of *thought* as opposed Williams's emphasis on lived *experience*.

Among the boldest claims made, however, are those in Eagleton's *Criticism and Ideology*. First he establishes the general argument that literature can provide a special form of historical evidence:

Literature, one might argue, is the most revealing mode of experiential access to ideology that we possess. It is in literature, above all, that we observe in a peculiarly complex, coherent, intensive and immediate fashion the workings of ideology in the textures of lived experience of class-societies.[20]

It is then argued that some texts do this better than others (by virtue of a particular author's mode of insertion into an ideological field). One example given concerns a comparison of Trollope with the great novelists of the nineteenth and early twentieth centuries:

The ideological matrix of Trollope's fiction (as with all writing) includes an ideology of the aesthetic – in Trollope's case, an anaemic, naively representational 'realism' which is merely a reflex of commonplace bourgeois empiricism. For Eliot, Hardy, Joyce and Lawrence, by contrast, the ideological question is implicit in the aesthetic *problem* of how to write; the 'aesthetic' – textual production – becomes a crucial, overdetermined instance of the question of those real and imaginary relations of men to their social conditions which we name ideology.[21]

In practice this means (as is implied here, in those authors selected for discussion in Chapter Four of *Criticism and Ideology* and in *Myths of Power*) that a prime purpose becomes the provision of new explanations of why the great are great:

The literary texts selected for examination by Marxist criticism will inevitably overlap with those works which literary idealism has consecrated as 'great'; it is a question of challenging the inability of such idealism to render more than subjectivist accounts of the criteria of value.[22]

Eagleton is, in fact, only slightly less annoyed than George Watson at the thought of attempts to challenge the accepted scale of literary judgements, although in place of people with no 'literary sense' there is here reference to 'literary ultra-leftism'. Eagleton is equally defensive about the position of Shakespeare. He condemns 'neo-proletkult' thinking which:

aims an unintended insult at – to choose merely one example – those Lancashire mill-girls of early Victorian England who rose an hour before work to read Shakespeare together. It would be a curious kind of materialist critic who would now wish to inform those women, in wise historical retrospect, that they were wasting their time over a reactionary hack.[23]

There is clearly a lot at stake here. The need for a consensus of accepted literary values, and the desire to maintain the existing one (with Shakespeare as its centre) are deeply rooted among a range of critics across the critical/political spectrum. A bizarre united front can, on this issue, close ranks to protect the 'tradition' against threat, whether from men with no literary sense or louts in the back row, neo-proletkult advocates or discontented proletariat groups, literary ultra-leftists or temporary depressives – a frightening mob of barbarians without.

In practice much textual literary criticism is concerned with the recognition, explanation and adjustment of this tradition. In effect, particularly if the process of syllabus-making and teaching are included as well, it is also a case of the tradition's being actively made and reinforced – as Williams has noted of any hegemonic process, 'it has continually to be renewed, recreated, defended and modified'.[24] This activity, in the case of the literary tradition, faces some of its most difficult tasks in dealing with contemporary works (meaning here, at any given time, anything written within about the last 15–20 years). There is no consensus of judgements to appeal to, or even to revalue. There is only, on one side, a set of loosely defined principles to apply and, on the other, a continual arrival of a heterogeneous mass of new material, vast in bulk and range and often difficult to classify (particularly since the advent of cinema, radio and TV). The primary need is to perform certain central tasks of discrimination as soon as possible – not so much those of deciding who are the best authors, as of deciding how to separate the serious and the permanent from the trivial and ephemeral, of how to begin to keep the continuities of tradition and literary history alive.

For earlier periods consensus has largely been established on these distinctions. In nineteenth-century studies there may be debates about the relative merits of Dickens and Thackeray, but G. W. Reynolds is not worthy of consideration. At the turn of the century Hardy and Conrad may be compared, but Marie Corelli (or even Olive Schreiner) are already placed elsewhere (or rather nowhere). In moving nearer the present, however, the distinctions become harder to maintain and the more texts there are which hover between the categories – apparently waiting for 'time' to decide their fate. It is, of course, the human activity of valuing which takes the decisions and it is in an examination of the ways in which literary criticism finally positions such texts that the mechanisms of constructing the literary canon, the tradition (and hence the educational syllabus) become apparent.

One group of such texts (i.e. texts which do not present themselves clearly as either serious/permanent or popular/ ephemeral) appeared around the late 1950s and early 1960s – the early novels of the 'provincial realists', John Braine, Alan Sillitoe, David Storey and Stan Barstow. The second section of this essay examines some of the ways in which literary criticism has attempted to place these writers – particularly that kind of criticism which takes as its task the need to map the direction and development of that crucial sub-area of the general literary tradition, the 'English novel'.

II

When John Braine's first novel, *Room at the Top*, was published in March 1957 it received unusually extensive coverage in the literary and weekly press. It was serialized in the *Daily Express* and went on to sell 35,000 copies (all hardback) in its first year of publication. A major reason for this was the way in which the author, and even more the novel's hero, were assimilated into the category of 'Angry Young Man'; John Wain (on the periphery of the group as labelled) has pointed out that:

> '*Room at the Top*, for example, was an instantaneous success because it
> appealed to a set of expectations which has been aroused, but not fully
> satisfied by its predecessors.[25]

During 1957 and 1958 articles in general political and
cultural journals stated the case for the novel's contemporary
relevance in more detail. Geoffrey Gorer, in *New Statesman*,
argued that the plot structure of Braine's novel (together with
those of Amis's *Lucky Jim* and Osborne's *Look Back in Anger*)
reflected problems of class mobility and allegiance which had
grown out of the 1944 Education Act. Even more directly, in
Encounter, Frank Hilton claimed that the heroes of the three
works were representatives of a 'new class' which had arisen in
the twentieth century and, more particularly, since the Second
World War. The germs of these arguments can be found in
many early reviews of Braine's novels, as well as in reviews,
articles and books (particularly *Declaration*) discussing Wain,
Amis, Osborne and the 'Angry School' from 1954 on (although
the 'Angry Young Man' label did not appear until 1956).[26]

It is in the context of this that the unusually swift notice
taken on Braine's novel in an academic journal of literary
criticism should be viewed. The title of the article – 'Tank in
the Stalls' (*Hudson Review*, Autumn 1957) – by its reference to
a Sassoon poem, indicates one of its main aims – an emphasis
on considering this new 'school' of writers in a wider literary
historical context. In the article John Holloway admitted that
Amis, Osborne and Braine 'reflect contemporary social
pressures and tensions', but went on to ask what this amounted
to:

> The essence of the matter is that these novels merely illustrate, in varied
> detail, local or transient forms of permanent social stress in English life up
> and down the country; and that to do so has been a recurrent feature of the
> English novel. If the heroes have something new in common, they have
> something old in common too.[27]

Reference is made to ancestors of the 'new hero' in Kipps,
Mr Polly, Jude Fawley and Bob Sawyer. The argument moves
from the defensive position of warding off sociologists in

search of data towards a more positive, specifically 'literary', interpretation. The texts are set in the context of an English reaction against European and American avant-garde influences: 'English writing, for good or ill, is reverting to some of its indigenous traditions.'[28]

Braine and Amis are now re-situated in terms of *literary* history (the 'traditions' of 'English writing') and brought within the bounds of academic literary critical concerns:

In the novel we are reverting to our well-established nineteenth century preoccupations: the detail of our provincial and local life; our elaborate and multiple gradations of money, influence or power; and what has perhaps always been intimately linked with these, our processes of sexual selection.[29]

The use of the generic phrase 'the novel' indicates the way in which the critical process was to continue. While plays (*A Taste of Honey*, the Wesker trilogy), films (of novels by Braine, Sillitoe, Barstow and Storey), novels, television (*Coronation Street* began in 1960) and many kinds of reportage (from Hoggart's *The Uses of Literacy* to Sigal's *Weekend in Dinlock*) testified to a general cultural preoccupation with the contrast between traditional (usually Northern) working-class culture and the new affluence, in the early and mid-Sixties the first book-length studies (as well as a number of articles) mapping the 'post-war English novel' were beginning to appear. All, in one form or another, used the accepted idea of the existence of 'the novel' as a tradition or some general organism into which individual texts became absorbed. The 'post-war novel' was a sub-division of this – an area to be internally mapped and then to be related to the history of the English novel as a whole (or possibly 'the novel' as a whole as an international cultural form).

In the Sixties neither of these critical tasks proved to be easy. The received history of the English novel up to the mid-twentieth century had three phases. First, there was the eighteenth-century novel ('the rise of the novel'), a time of experiment, trial and error. This was followed by the period of assured triumph – the nineteenth-century social realists from Jane Austen through Dickens and Eliot to Hardy. Finally came a crisis in the form, the arrival of modernism in various guises – Conrad, Lawrence, Joyce, Woolf. The logic of this developmental model was that the mid-twentieth-century novelist should either be unable to write at all ('death of the novel') or should continue the modernist experiment. The lack of either of these in the Thirties could be explained away (particularly when seen from the Fifties) by the imbalance of the normal relations between contemporary social problems and literature in the 'red' decade. The 1940s were, generally, forgotten entirely—the war years being either a cultural desert or a special case, and 1945 on being a slow run-up to the Fifties. This state of the tradition in limbo could not, however, be maintained; the Fifties had to make sense and Holloway's formulations (this is not at all to suggest that he was the first to make them) provided the way forward.

James Gindin's *Post-War British Fiction* (1962) developed one aspect of this – noting that 'many young writers have been attempting to return to a traditional nineteenth-century theme' (man and society, conduct and class).[30] This provides one theme of his book. His more original contibution was to suggest that post-war novelists had, in general, married this to a more contemporary 'existential attitude'. This formula allowed Gindin to construct a map in which Braine was acknowledged but given a low valuation ('caught in endless repetitions of maudlin self-pity'), while according a major status to Sillitoe. Sillitoe appeared alongside Iris Murdoch and Angus Wilson as the most impressive of the new writers manifesting the existential attitude; they are contrasted to the three 'most over-rate writers', Snow, Durrell and Colin Wilson. Overall the book has a clear strategy in its arguments for cohesion. Gindin established links with the earlier English novel, but was also able to argue for a unity of mood among post-1945 fiction through the existential attitude which steered a course between 'Marxist determinism', 'Nazi bestiality' and subservience to modern government. Equally, by emphasizing general underlying philosophy, Gindin avoided questions of aesthetic form. Golding, Iris Murdoch, Doris Lessing and Sillitoe could all be grouped together without any qualms.

This generally optimistic view of the state of the English novel was not shared by Gilbert Phelps in his essay 'The Novel Today' (1964). The essay begins by arguing that a 'decline' has taken place:

The trend of the English novel since the war has, on the whole, been analogous to that of the poetry of the period – a turning aside from the mainstream of English literature, and a tendency to retreat into parochialism.[31]

Post-war novelist are then divided into four groups (even though one of these turns out to consist of 'those younger writers who belong to no particular category') – among these are the so-called 'Angry Young Men'. Here Braine and Sillitoe are given a position and again Sillitoe is preferred. His hero is more 'fully realized' and the book gives 'a more profound picture'. However the group as a whole are negatively valued in line with the general argument for a decline:

These novelists fail... to live up to the standards represented by the great writers of the past... not in their subject-matter... but in their lapses in artistic detachment and control.[32]

Reference is further made to 'marked decline in the quality of writing' and 'lack of craftsmanship'. As opposed to this, the article goes on to argue that Angus Wilson is one of the few post-war writers to have made a contribution to the 'great tradition of English fiction'.

The whole article is a model of its kind. Historical placing and evaluation go hand in hand. The direction of the 'tradition' is mapped and the strategies of excluding and protecting are in play; Barstow and Storey are excluded, Braine peripheral, and Sillitoe acceptable with reservations. And if a developmental notion of 'the novel' is hard to sustain then at least a kind of holding operation can be carried through. The article concludes:

While therefore it remains true that the achievement since the war does not equal that of the earlier years of the century, there is at least evidence that the English novel is by no means a spent force.[33]

Among the most negative of Sixties' mapping operations was that of Rubin Rabinovitz's *The Reaction Against Experiment in the English Novel 1950–60* (1967). The argument was not new:

Most of the post-war writers conscientiously rejected experimental techniques in their fiction as well as in their critical writings, and turned instead to older novelists for inspiration.[34]

The originality of the book lay in its emphasis on the deliberateness of this reaction and the degree of documentation advanced to support this claim. The discussion concentrates mainly on Amis, Snow and Angus Wilson, with Sillitoe and Braine as supporting examples, and Storey and Barstow as minor figures.

The major work of mapping and evaluating occurs in the final chapter. Golding, Iris Murdoch, Muriel Spark, Durrell and Nigel Dennis are cited as 'exceptions to the general rule of anti-experimentalism' and as 'among the finest writers of their time'. The negative valuation is explicit. The decade 'has not been a very fruitful one for the novel':

The novelists of the 1950s have not produced fiction which approaches the quality of the novels of the writers whom they have imitated. Nor, for that matter, is their work as good as the fiction of the writers whom they have rejected....[35]

The evaluation of the texts is part of the process of establishing their relationship to 'the novel' as a whole. Their failure to fit the required models might normally by reasons for exclusion as unworthy of critical attention; however, in the absence of enough texts which do fit, they may be included as failures and regressions.

To move from the Sixties to the Seventies in this kind of critical work is to enter a period dominated by three critics – David Lodge, Malcolm Bradbury and Bernard Bergonzi. Lodge has, in fact, been writing on the subject since the early Sixties and his book *The Language of Fiction* (1966) contains an exemplary instance of the kind of Sixties critical map already discussed. In the context of an elaboration of Spender's distinction between the 'contemporary' and 'the modern' there is a set-piece comparison between passages from Joyce's *Portrait of the Artist as a Young Man* and *Room at the Top*.

The evaluation here is never in doubt, elevating the 'modern' over the 'contemporary' (which, Lodge notes, today dominates 'the English novel'). The comparison is developed through a set of oppositions – 'elaborate linguistic craft' against 'ordinary prose discourse', 'poetic devices' against 'the dead metaphors of cliché'. Braine's passage is 'looser and thinner in texture'; he fails in 'the fundamental literary task of realization in language'.[36] A clear process of exclusion is here carried through by the reference of Braine's novel to a set of principles embodied in the 'modern' tradition. *Room at the Top* is virtually declared not 'literary', not least because of its use of explicit contemporary social reference.

In the shift from Sixties to Seventies novel criticism, Malcolm Bradbury's essay on 'The Novel' from 1945–65 constitutes something of a transitional account. The scope of the essay is international, but the main concern is with English writing and a general map is proposed:

The post-war English novel has had at least two main streams. One is social documentary, which seemed dominant in the 1950s.... The other is, however, a marked visionary or philosophical strain, concerned with an alternative reality not defined primarily in social terms.... This tendency seems to have become even more marked in the 1960s....[37]

Braine, Sillitoe and Storey (and belatedly Barstow) are acknowledged as in the first group, although with the 'mythic' *Radcliffe*, Storey is seen as having a foot in the other camp also. *Room at the Top*, however, lacks 'moral density', while *Saturday Night and Sunday Morning* has 'thin... moral centre'.

In attempting to draw all the threads together, Bradbury opts for a kind of modified Gindinism:

Behind the exploration of modern society there runs a deep sense of personal crisis, of value deprivation, of social uncertainty and aimlessness, and that the sense of cultural uncertainty which touches a good deal of postwar English writing has found a variety of modes for its expression.[38]

The degree of generalization here suggests both a need to try and establish some unifying principle or theme, and the extreme difficulty of doing so. The essay closes with a foretaste of future directions in the English novel (and so, concomitantly, in its criticism), by citing *The Golden Notebook* and *The Magus* as examples of 'the revival of aesthetic debate in the novel'.

Bernard Bergonzi's *The Situation of the Novel* (1970) is in part a response to (and contribution to) such a revival. It gives itself a wider brief than most of the accounts already discussed, both in not tying itself to post-war texts, and in discussing European and American fiction alongside British. The general aim is to go beyond:

the customary academic notion of the novel as a complex but essentially self-contained form, cut off from the untidiness and discontinuities of the world outside.[39]

There is however no break with the idea of 'the novel' as a collective organism. The book is concerned with 'the contemporary novel as the product of a particular phase of history' and 'the cultural attitudes implicit in the recent English novel'.[40] The book's title itself is the clearest example of how critical issues throughout are centred on or returned to the health, significance and possibilities of development of 'the novel' in general.

The standard developmental model (discussed above) of the history of the novel is endorsed and a recognition made of a current situation (post–1930) in which a range of styles are equally available and applicable. In this situation, differences between English and American novels are examined as exemplars of national cultural characteristics (the assumption of common unified national cultures is quite striking). Generally there is a defence of the relative parochialism and stress on common-sense realism of the English novel as reflective both of important English values (liberalism), and of some innate strengths of the novel form itself, connected with a central interest in narrative and character – 'the novel form still remains intractable to radical transformation'.[41] The defence is, however, not total; there is some stress on the need for 'balance' between English timid common-sense and both European post-modernism and American fabulation.

Bergonzi's perspective leads to favourable critical judgements for a mixed group of post-war English writers. On the one hand, there are those who seem almost self-consciously to have attended to the task which Bergonzi's claims his own book is addressing – 'to attempt to define what it means to be English at the present time'. Nigel Dennis, Evelyn Waugh,

Anthony Powell, Angus Wilson and Andrew Sinclair are all seen in this way. A different group (although there are some overlaps) are those who have taken on board some of the self-consciously aesthetic concerns discussed in the book – John Fowles (briefly noted), Anthony Burgess, Flann O'Brien, Doris Lessing (in *The Golden Notebook*) and, less enthusiastically, B. S. Johnson.

In many ways Bergonzi's book is the most wide-ranging and thoughtful book on 'the novel' to have emerged since 1945. This makes all the more important the exclusions it operates. Braine and Barstow do not appear at all, while Sillitoe and Storey have respectively one or two minor references each. The effect of the book, in its sweeping and generalizing cultural mapping, is to exclude more thoroughly than any previous account the untheoretical 'regional' novels of the late Fifties and early Sixties. In retrospect the intention of the whole book appears as an attempt to upgrade the novel as a contemporary form both by claiming for it a value as a national cultural barometer, and a revived status as a legitimate arena for serious aesthetic endeavour. Neither of these roles could be usefully filled by (for example) *Saturday Night and Sunday Morning* or *This Sporting Life*.

David Lodge's essay 'The Novelist at the Cross-roads' (first published in *Critical Quarterly* in 1969) had in fact already prefigured a number of the arguments of Bergonzi's book. The essay promises 'an overview of the nature and development of 'the novel' and has two kinds of emphasis. First there is (in the conclusion) 'a modest affirmation of faith in the future of realistic fiction' and a making of the same ideological links as Bergonzi – 'if the case for realism has any ideological content it is that of liberalism'.[42] Equally, however, this affirmation is made in the face of an awareness of a wave of new developments in the writing of novels (documentary, fabulation, 'problematic novel'). It is these other possible 'roads' which pose difficulties. The metaphor of the crossroads is central to the way the essay makes sense of its material. The novelist is 'a man standing at a cross-roads':

The road on which he stands (I am thinking primarily of the English novelist) is the realistic novel, the compromise between fictional and empirical modes.[43]

The effect of this image is similar to the more familiar one of the 'stream' used by both Phelps and Bradbury (see above). 'The novel' appears as a route of inexorable development along which all novelists inevitably travel (or fall by the way-side, get trapped in a back-water, etc.). Within the particular argument of Lodge's essay, this leads to an imperative: 'The novelist who has any kind of self-awareness must at least hesitate at the cross-roads....[44]

This is an important formulation for Seventies' novel criticism – both as a measure for judging texts and as a programme for cultural production (of novels and of 'the tradition'). It remains the dominant theme in the final attempt at mapping the contemporary novel to be discussed here – the 1979 collection of essays on 'The Contemporary English Novel' in the Stratford-upon-Avon Studies series.

The editors' aims are, in relation to their subject, to 'draw a map of general significances', 'to suggest a broader canon... and above all a more serious status'.[45] The book is a summation of Seventies' criticism – the English novel seen as the site of a contest and reconciliation between traditional 'realistic' virtues and aesthetic/modernist principles. The majority of essays take up an aspect of this opposition and corral a series of texts and writers within it (themes include fiction and history, the anti-novel, realism and experiment, fiction and documentary, parody and self-consciousness, character and abstraction). In a number of essays John Fowles's *The French Lieutenant's Woman* emerges as *the* representative text. The editors term it 'an exemplary book of the 1960s'; other contributors see it as 'a typically English experimental game', 'a brilliant novel of deserved fame', 'a book that concentrates many of the problems of the contemporary English novel'.[46] Its attraction is its combination of a liberal concept of character, a self-consciousness and celebration of the nineteenth-century English novel and an apparent coming to terms with experimental fiction – it displays just the right amount of 'hesitation' and sense of itself as a novel. It perfectly articulates what emerges as the underlying question to put to individual texts – where do they stand on questions of realism, fictionality and 'style', above all how do they position themselves in relation to 'the novel'.

The editorial preface indicates openly that 'the bias away from the fiction of the 1950s, covered in other studies, has been deliberate'. Throughout the whole book Braine and Sillitoe are each mentioned once (in the same sentence), Storey three times and Barstow not at all. This particular aspect of the critical map has probably now become established – although it is likely that Storey may be allowed to re-appear at some stage. Braine, Sillitoe and Barstow are, however, clearly excluded as 'the novel' tradition is re-made with those texts which are amenable (and often deliberately place themselves as such) to the idea of 'the novel' as a continuous, developmental, self-referential and, often, national enterprise.

III

It should be clear that the implications of the above comments are in no way to suggest that Braine or Sillitoe should be reinstated as important writers of the post-war English novel. Indeed, given the premises of most of the critics, their exclusion is justified. What is important is not the fate of particular authors, but rather the way that emphasis on 'the novel' as the point of reference imposes a very particular and narrow set of questions as the concerns of literary study. In the case of post-war English fiction, texts have been measured against one or more of three yardsticks – the nineteenth-century tradition, the early twentieth-century modernists and, more latterly, contemporary developments in forms of fiction in Europe and America. Works which are found acceptable are then pulled together into a series of categories which themselves constitute the direction of the contemporary English novel and affirm continuities with the past achievements and masterpieces of the novel tradition.

What is missed, through the pressure to select and homogenize all texts into a unified tradition and single scale of achievement is the possibility of recognizing the existence of a variety of kinds of writing produced under divergent conditions and serving a range of needs. To imagine this would be to suggest a different attitude towards literary values.

The present idea of the literary tradition places impossible demands upon written texts by implying, or stating, that they are the most valuable products of the whole culture – either by virtue of their moral exemplifications or their embodiment of historical/ideological experience. Now it is probably true that all academic disciplines will tend to develop and sustain theories about themselves which explain why their particular enterprise is especially important, but this is not everywhere so detrimental to the area under study as it is in the case of literature. The emphasis on discovering, confirming and transmitting the literary tradition prevents any detailed attention to the diversity of kinds of cultural activities and functions being performed in and around the areas of writing and reading. In the case of the field of criticism discussed above, emphasis on the state of 'the novel' leaves little place for discussions of structures of publication and authorship, the role of educational institutions in constructing readers and being a primary market for certain kinds of contemporary work, the impact of film, radio and telivision on outlets for, and styles of, writing and even the role of literary criticism itself as a determinant of the production of texts.

As regards the question of value itself: it is important to recognize it as a matter of human construction and political choice, not of the intrinsic properties of a text. The questions of what literature should be for and which books (or other kinds of work) should be read – and written – are important and necessary, although they are not the same questions as those concerning the position writing and reading have had in the past and have today. Both sets of questions are needed, but they cannot simply be run into each other, particularly when this produces a situation where judgements of value masquerade as historical truths, and literary history becomes a catalogue of examples of 'excellence'. It is time to call again for the death of the novel, not in the spirit of Steineresque apocalypse, but to liberate writing. The novel is dead – long live novels, writers, readers and students of literature[47], as long as they begin by asking all those questions which for the guardians of the tradition are 'scarcely open to debate at all'.

NOTES

1   F. R. Leavis, 'Literary Criticism and Philosophy' in *The Common Pursuit* (Harmondsworth: Penguin, 1972), p. 214.
2   From the Preface to *The Common Pursuit*, p. v.
3   T. S. Eliot, 'Tradition and the Individual Talent', *Selected Essays* (London: Faber & Faber 1951), p. 17.
4   F. R. Leavis, 'Literature and Society', *The Common Pursuit*, p. 184.
5   G. Watson, *The Study of Literature* (London: Allen Lane, 1969), p. 22.
6   *Ibid.*, p. 23.
7   For examples of this see Leavis, 'Literature and Society', G. H. Bantock, 'The Social and Intellectual Background' *The Modern Age* ed. B. Ford, (Harmondsworth, Penguin, 1964), and R. Williams, *The English Novel from Dickens to Lawrence* (London, Chatto & Windus, 1970).
8   F. R. Leavis, *Mass Civilisation and Minority Culture* (Cambridge: Minority Press, 1930). T. S. Eliot, *Notes Towards the Definition of Culture*, (London: Faber & Faber, 1948).
9   M. Bradbury, *The Social Context of Modern English Literature* (Oxford: Blackwell, 1971), p. 237–8.
10   *Ibid.*, p. 240.
11   G. Orwell, 'Why I Write', *Collected Essays, Journalism and Letters, Volume One* (London: Secker & Warburg, 1968), p. 4.
12   Leavis, 'Literary Criticism and Philosophy', p. 213.
13   T. S. Eliot, *The Use of Poetry and the Use of Criticism* (London: Faber & Faber, 1933), p. 105.
14   In the same paragraph as the passage quoted Eliot notes that – 'the longer the sequence of critics we have, the greater amount of correction is possible.'
15   Watson, *op.cit.*, p. 22.
16   *Ibid.*, p. 27.
17   R. Williams, *The Long Revolution* (Harmondsworth: Penguin, 1965), p. 68.
18   *Ibid.*, p. 70.
19   A. Kettle, 'The Progressive Tradition in Bourgeois Culture', *Radical Perspectives in the Arts* (Harmondsworth: Penguin, 1972), p. 165.
20   T. Eagleton, *Criticism and Ideology* (London: New Left Books, 1976), p. 101.
21   *Ibid.*, p. 181.
22   *Ibid.*, p. 162.
23   *Ibid.*, p. 166.
24   R. Williams, *Marxism and Literature* (Oxford: Oxford University Press, 1977), p. 112.
25   J. Wain, *Sprightly Running* (London: Macmillan, 1962), p. 201.
26   G. Gorer, 'The Perils of Hypergamy', *New Statesman*, 4 May 1957, and F. Hilton, 'Britain's New Class', *Encounter*, February 1958.
27   J. Holloway, 'Tank Among the Stalls', *Hudson Review*, Autumn 1957, p. 142.
28   *Ibid.*, p. 144.

29 *Ibid.*, p. 144.
30 J. Gindin, *Post-War British Fiction* (London: Cambridge University Press, 1962), p. 4.
31 G. Phelps, 'The Novel Today', in B. Ford (ed.), *The Modern Age* (Harmondsworth: Penguin, 1964), p. 475.
32 *Ibid.*, p. 489.
33 *Ibid.*, p. 495.
34 R. Rabinovitz, *The Reaction Against Experiment in the English Novel 1950–1960* (New York and London: Columbia University Press, 1967), p. 2.
35 *Ibid.*, p. 168.
36 D. Lodge, *The Language of Fiction* (London: Routledge & Kegan Paul, 1966).
37 M. Bradbury, 'The Novel' in C. B. Cox and A. E. Dyson (ed.), *The Twentieth Century Mind 3: 1945–1965* (London: Oxford University Press, 1972), p. 331.
38 *Ibid.*, p. 346.
39 B. Bergonzi, *The Situation of the Novel* (London: Macmillan, 1970), p. 7.
40 *Ibid.*, p. 7.
41 *Ibid.*, p. 29.
42 D. Lodge, 'The Novelist at the Cross-roads', *Critical Quarterly*, 1969, p. 131.
43 *Ibid.*, p. 118.
44 *Ibid.*, p. 121.
45 M. Bradbury and D. Palmer (eds), *The Contemporary English Novel*, Stratford-Upon-Avon-Studies 18 (London: Edward Arnold, 1979) pp. 11 & 15.
46 *Ibid.*, p. 13, p. 28 (A. S. Byatt), p. 54 (B. Bergonzi), p. 152 (R. Burden).
47 The concept of 'literature' itself requires further investigation of the kind already carried out by R. Williams, *op. cit.*, Part One Chapter Three, Tony Bennett, *Formalism and Marxism* (London: Methuen, 1979) and Tony Davies, 'Education, Ideology and Literature', *Red Letters*, No. 7.

Index

Achebe, Chinna 103–4
Althusser, Louis 106–8, 109–12
Andrewes, Lancelot 16–20
Arnold, Mathew 53–4

Bakhtin, Mikhail xv, 88, ch. 4
    passim
Barthes, Roland 9, 13, 14, 16, 49,
    83, 94, 104
Baudelaire, Charles 89
Benjamin, Walter 5, 11, 20
Bergonzi, Bernard 236, 238–9
Blackmur, R. P. 65–8
Bloom, Harold 21–2, 48, 70,
    72–4, 126–7
Booth, Wayne 74–6
Borges, Jorge Luis 20–2, 23
Bradbury, Malcolm 225, 237
Braine, John 231–2, 234, 235,
    237
Brooks, Cleanth 68–70

Céline, Louis Ferdinand 108–9,
    112–13
characterization 94–5, 104–5,
    115, 117, 118–19, 155–6
Crane, Hart 67–8
Culler, Jonathan xvi, 7, 11, 78–9

Deconstruction ch. 1 *passim*,
    70–4, 78–89, ch. 4 *passim*
de Man, Paul 9, 11, 70, 71
Derrida, Jacques 4, 6, 9–12, 16,
    19, 23, 49, 70, 71, 74, 80–8,
    100, 113–14, 127, 137–40
Donoghue, Denis 7–8

Eagleton, Terry 102, 112, 214,
    228, 229–30
Eliot, T. S. 11, 16, 17, 53, 55,

    103, 163, 215, 220, 223, 225,
    226
Empson, William 60

Ferguson, Charles 143–4
Fish, Stanley 8, 70, 79–80
Forster, E. M. 120, 175, 182
Foucault, Michel 1, 41, 98, 119
Fowler, Roger 126
Fowles, John 237, 240
Freud, Sigmund 22, 46, 47, 56–7,
    107, 118, 170, 180
Fry, Roger 158–63, 164, 166,
    167, 169, 175, 176, 179

Gindin, James 234
Goldmann, Lucien 228

Halliday, Michael 125–6
Harvey, W. J. 94–5
history 8, 12, 13, 47–9, 52–6, 73,
    82–4, 85–6, 93–5, 105
history/ideology ch. 3 *passim*

Iser, Wolfgang 76–8, 129

Johnson, Dr Samuel xvii, 14–16
Joyce, James xv, xvii, 5, 23,
    25–48
    Dubliners 26
    Stephen Hero 25–6
    A Portrait of the Artist as a
      Young Man 26–8, 31–3
    Ulysses 29–30, 31, 33–6,
      132–3, 135, 180
    Finnegans Wake 23, 25, 29, 30,
      37–48, 132
    Selected Letters 36

Kermode, Frank 9, 22

Knights, L. C. 60
Kristeva, Julia 9, 132

Lacan, Jacques 22, 23, 33, 82, 107
Lawrence, D. H. 35, 97, ch. 6 *passim*
Leavis, F. R. 57–8, 94, 97, 99, 100–1, 102–3, 199–201, 213, 214–5, 221, 223, 225, 226
Leitch, Vincent 10, 23, 49
Lévi-Strauss, Claude 83, 86, 141
Lewis, Wyndham 214, 219–20
literature (as academic/critical institution) 2–3, 99, ch. 7 *passim*
Lodge, David 8, 9, 23, 48, 236–7, 239–40
Lowry, Malcolm
    Under The Volcano 133–5
Lukács, Georg 94, 105

MacCabe, Colin 113–14
Macherey, Pierre 100, 101, 105, 107–8, 111
Mansfield, Katherine 181
Mauron, Charles 160–3, 164, 167, 170, 176, 179
McTaggart, J. 100–2, 170
Miller, J. Hillis xvi, 5–7, 9, 13–14
Mitterand, Henri 108–9, 112–13
Moore, G. E. 160–2, 170, 179
Mulhern, Francis 102
Murry, John Middleton 214–19, 220

Naipaul, V. S. 95
    A House for Mr Biswas 114–19
Nationalist criticism 99–100, 104–6
New Criticism xii–xv, ch. 2 *passim*, 101–3
Nietzsche, Friedrich 73

Ortega y Gasser, José 147–59

Post-structuralism xvi, ch. 1 *passim*, ch. 4 *passim*
Pound, Ezra xi–xii

Pynchon, Thomas
    The Crying of Lot 49 135
    Gravity's Rainbow 135–6
    V 135

Quiller-Couch, Sir Arthur ix–xi

Ramchand, Kenneth 100–1, 102, 103
Ransom, John Crowe 63–5
realism ch. 3 *passim*
Richards, I. A. xi–xii, 57, 58–9, 61–3
Richardson, Dorothy 180, 183
Rolland, Romain
    Jean-Christophe 202–4, 207–8

Said, Edward 46, 93, 96, 114
Sarraute, Nathalie 178
Saussure, Ferdinand de xvi–xvii, 2–5, 8–9, 12–13, 22–3, 83, 138–9, 140–1
Searle, John 139
Sillitoe, Alan xv, 234, 235
Stevens, Wallace 65–6
Structuralism ch. 1 *passim*, 86, ch. 4 *passim* vide (supra) Althusser, Bakhtin, Barthes, Macherey, Saussure.

Traversi, Derek 60–1
Trilling, Lionel 55–7

Watson, George 224, 227
Weinreich, Uriel 128, 130, 142
Williams, Raymond 227–8, 229
Woolf, Virginia 159–96
    Jacob's Room 164, 172, 184, 185
    Mrs Dalloway 163, 165, 173, 181, 182, 191, 193, 195
    To the Lighthouse 165–7, 175, 181, 182–3, 186, 188, 192, 195
    The Waves 184, 187, 189, 192, 195–6
    The Years 174, 186, 193–4
    Between the Acts 174, 191

: